IMAGES
of America

MT. HEALTHY

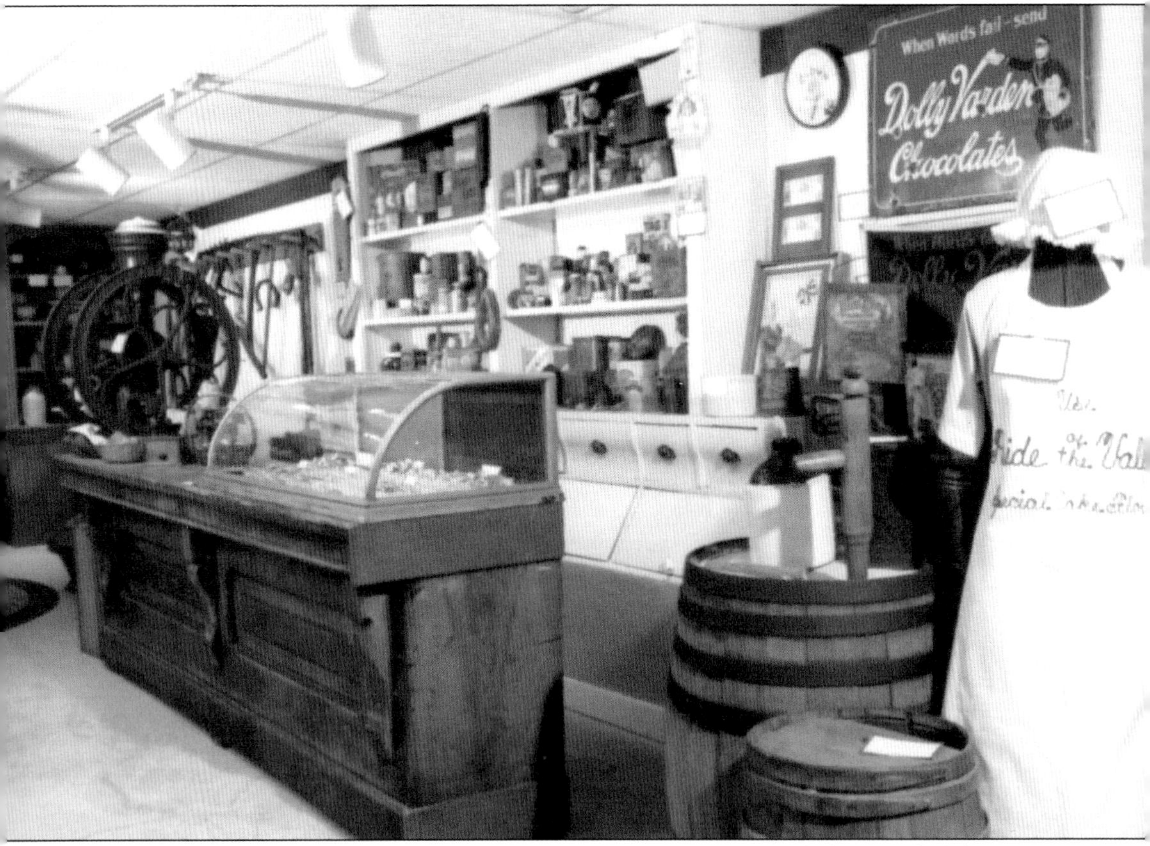

This book is dedicated to the Mt. Healthy Historical Society and the wonderful community of Mt. Healthy. It is a great place. This is a general store recreated on the ground floor of the Mt. Healthy Historical Society Museum. Here one can find authentic displays of local artifacts.

On the cover: The forest of Mt. Healthy held beautiful trees and plants, including mature white oaks. These giant oaks provided the perfect wood for one of Mt. Healthy's first industries, making barrels, or coopering, as it was called. To get a feel for what the early forest looked like, visit nearby Winton Woods, a Hamilton County Park. (Courtesy of Mt. Healthy Historical Society.)

IMAGES
of America

MT. HEALTHY

Sue Korn Wilson and
Kathleen Mulloy Tamarkin

ARCADIA
PUBLISHING

ISBN 978-0-7385-6156-1

Published by Arcadia Publishing
Charleston, South Carolina

Printed in the United States of America

Library of Congress Catalog Card Number: 2008923915

For all general information contact Arcadia Publishing at:
Telephone 843-853-2070
Fax 843-853-0044
E-mail sales@arcadiapublishing.com
For customer service and orders:
Toll-Free 1-888-313-2665

Visit us on the Internet at www.arcadiapublishing.com

Contents

ACKNOWLEDGMENTS

Writing the history of a community takes more than just the work of the authors. Without the shared knowledge of those who love Mt. Healthy, this book would not have been possible. The Mt. Healthy Historical Society greeted us with open arms. It allowed us to use any and all of the materials and photographs in its archives. Our fondest memories were our Thursday-morning chats with the historical society gang and their wonderful stories of friends, family, and neighbors. They brought the history of Mt. Healthy alive to us in a way far more valuable than books and papers ever could. The regulars included Dave Huser, Vierling Blum, and Ron Packer.

Marian Blum, the historical society's curator, was a fountain of information. Her enthusiasm for Mt. Healthy history was contagious, and her extensive knowledge was very helpful.

Other community members who shared their photographs and stories included Thelma King Arnold, Cheryl Bauer, Ken Carpenter, Robert Curley, Clayton Coleman, Carol Sunderhaus Deyhle, Rev. Michael Doerr, Bill Effler, Carol Sue Ehrhardt Ferguson, Bonnie Hardwick Fitzharris, Jeanne Gettle Gourley, Kevin Grace, Lucille Brinkman Green, Mary Grote, D. J. Hamm, Shirley Haus, Gene Hessler, Penny Stout Huber, Suzanne Weickel Hull, Robert Hunter, Phyllis Hauer King, Bill Korn, Verna Korn, Chris Lane, Hilda and Leroy Meier, Arlette Merritt, Greg and Audrey Korn Miller, Joy Cumbow Packer, Carol Rutz, Ray Rissel, Fred Schumacher, Nancy Stricker, Lori Summe, Jerry Sunderhaus, Carmen Ehrhardt Trisler, Chuck Wilson, Gregory Wilson, and Fr. Gil Wolher

To all, we offer our grateful thanks.

Additional thanks go to senior acquisitions editor Melissa Basilone and Midwest publisher John Pearson of Arcadia Publishing, who were always able to answer our questions and give us direction.

All photographs in this book have come from the Mt. Healthy Historical Society unless otherwise indicated. Proceeds from the sale of this book will be contributed to this wonderful organization. The Mt. Healthy Historical Museum at 1546 McMakin Avenue is open every Tuesday, Thursday, and Saturday from 9:00 a.m. to 11:00 a.m. The telephone number is 513-552-3939. If you are lucky, the gang will be gathered around the fireplace sharing stories.

INTRODUCTION

On September 30, 1794, Pres. George Washington issued a deed to John Cleves Symmes for 311,682 acres of land situated in the Northwest Territory. The area Cleves chose was north of the Ohio River between the Little Miami River on the east and the Great Miami River on the west. The tract included Hamilton County and approximately half of what is now Butler and Warren Counties. The land was named the Miami Purchase and became very attractive to Revolutionary War veterans seeking a new life for themselves and their families.

Roads, or traces, were forged between major junctions connecting settlements within the Miami Purchase. Areas along those routes grew into communities that served the settlers as well as travelers. The major route between Losantiville (Cincinnati) and Fort Hamilton was called Hamilton Turnpike. It was along this route, approximately eight miles north of Losantiville, where Mount Pleasant was created. Hamilton Turnpike was the main street of the settlement.

In October 1817, settlers John LaBoiteaux and Samuel Hill laid out the village around the existing north-south trace and called it Mount Pleasant. They named the east-west streets with numbers, and the north-south streets had names such as Main Street. Around 1921, the streets were renamed, mostly after popular pioneers. As farmers sold their land for development, they often gave one of the streets their own name, such as Hastings Avenue and Seward Avenue. For convenience and clarity, throughout this book the current names are used.

Mount Pleasant's location along the turnpike allowed for the establishment of a variety of businesses. The village quickly became one of the earliest thriving villages in Springfield Township. Surrounding communities could find whatever they needed in the various shops and stores that lined Main Street. Two comfortable hotels catered to the needs of the traveler. Liveries cared for horses and buggies. And because of the abundance of hardwood in the area, coopering (barrel making) flourished. Today the business district continues to serve Mt. Healthy and the surrounding communities.

The rolling hills, rich soil, and abundant water attracted families from many diverse backgrounds. Settlers coming from Pennsylvania and New Jersey met families from Connecticut, Virginia, and Massachusetts, some of which included former slaves. All banded together to create a community.

National and world affairs also played their part in forming Mount Pleasant. Fleeing the turmoil in Europe, German immigrants found the hills of Ohio a perfect substitute for their homeland. It is known that between 1841 and 1847, twelve families moved together from the Wuhl and Oberhausen areas of Germany to Mount Pleasant. German-speaking churches and schools grew, and many customs were integrated into the fabric of the village. Irish, French,

Welsh, and Swiss immigrants also found their way to Mount Pleasant, and they too have left their mark.

With such a diverse population, it is understandable that in the mid-1800s the antislavery movement was on the minds of many citizens. Such early pioneers as the LaBoiteauxs, the Carys, the Scotts, and the Aikens were actively involved in protecting slaves fleeing from the south. Some families converted their barns and basements into sanctuaries. Other families prepared food, and local doctors cared for the sick and injured. The turmoil caused a few local churches to close their doors until the issue was resolved.

In 1828, when Mount Pleasant applied to the state for its own post office, it was discovered that a Jefferson County village had the same name. To avoid confusion, Mount Pleasant changed its name to Mt. Healthy.

Following the Civil War there was a lot of relocation. Many families moved west where land was cheaper and opportunities were great. For example, members of the Lane family moved to Elkhart, Indiana, and other families moved west into southern Indiana to cities such as Brookville.

Although the early settlers came to the area to farm the land, cottage industries flourished. As the years progressed, tailor shops were established that met the needs of large clothing manufacturers in nearby Cincinnati. It was estimated that at the peak of operations, 20 tailor shops were in business in Mt. Healthy at one time. Often the entire family worked in the tailor shop. Children played outside, and babies slept among the cut fabric. Frequently the shop was attached to the house so as to have easy access between business and home. But improvement in transportation and the trend toward centralized manufacturing ended the tailoring business as it was known.

Gathering together to worship has been a strong element in Mt. Healthy. Since its settlement in the early 1800s, faith groups have prospered. Respect for each person's right to believe as he or she wishes has always been a cornerstone of the community. In 1825, residents built the Mount Pleasant Union Meeting House for the use of all denominations and the exclusion of none. Presbyterians, Universalists, Restorationists, Old School Baptists, and Mormons all used the building. Today the choice of faith-based groups is larger than ever before.

Residents have enjoyed the benefits of a strong education and later success in life. Over the years, these educated people became entrepreneurs and small-business owners. They have also contributed to the financial world as bankers and in related fields. Many educators are former graduates who passed along their love for education to the next generation.

As a community, Mt. Healthy has met the challenge of change. Old customs seamlessly blend with modern life, giving the community a sense of stability and permanence. This community continues to be a good place to live.

Mt. Healthy has been the home of many poets. Alice and Phoebe Cary are well known; others are not. It is a Mt. Healthy tradition to include poems in most public ceremonies. The following is Aldena Runyan's poem "Our Heritage," as it sums up the feelings of many about Mt. Healthy. The poem was included in a 1968 publication. "I wonder what the 'folks' would say, / That walked these streets so proud and gay, / I wonder if they know, / I wonder if they care / How proud we are of the great heritage we share? / I hope they know we like the trees, / The streets, the sidewalks, all of these. / I hope they know we're glad they came / To carve the place and give it a name, / I hope they know we're proud to be a part of them."

One

Naming the Village

In 1793, John Ludlow selected the name Mount Pleasant for the village he planned along Hamilton Turnpike. However, fear of Native Americans discouraged settlers. In October 1817, John LaBoiteaux and Samuel Hill laid out a village at the same location. Due to its fresh air and stunning, wooded setting, they also selected Mount Pleasant as the name of the village. The Native Americans were gone, and this village thrived.

In 1828, when Mount Pleasant applied for a local U.S. post office, it was discovered that another Mount Pleasant had already laid claim to the name. The Mount Pleasant along Hamilton Turnpike was required to find a new name.

When compared to other Ohio communities, the residents of Mount Pleasant seemed to be healthier and to live longer lives. In the autumn of 1832, the Cincinnati region experienced a cholera epidemic, the most dreaded 19th-century disease. Although stagecoach villages were vulnerable to the contagious disease, Mount Pleasant experienced little effect. In 1850, another devastating cholera epidemic killed one in eight Cincinnati residents but few in Mount Pleasant. Folks began referring to the village as "Mt. Healthy."

Although unknown at the time, cholera was being spread through contaminated water. At an elevation of 837 feet above sea level, Mount Pleasant is set on high, rolling ground that drains naturally, allowing little chance to breed disease bacteria.

Residents lived to an advanced age due to eating hearty foods and benefited from the availability of doctor care. It is said that in 1900, Mt. Healthy had more aged population than anywhere else in Ohio. An 80 year old was looked upon as comparatively young.

By 1884, the post office and local residents used the name Mt. Healthy exclusively, and the village was incorporated as such in 1893. By 1900, this village was the only known Mt. Healthy in the United States, and Mayor Alexis Brown claimed, "There is no healthier spot in the world."

For purposes of clarity and to follow the pattern of early settlers, through 1849 the authors have referred to the village as Mount Pleasant. After 1850 Mt. Healthy has been used.

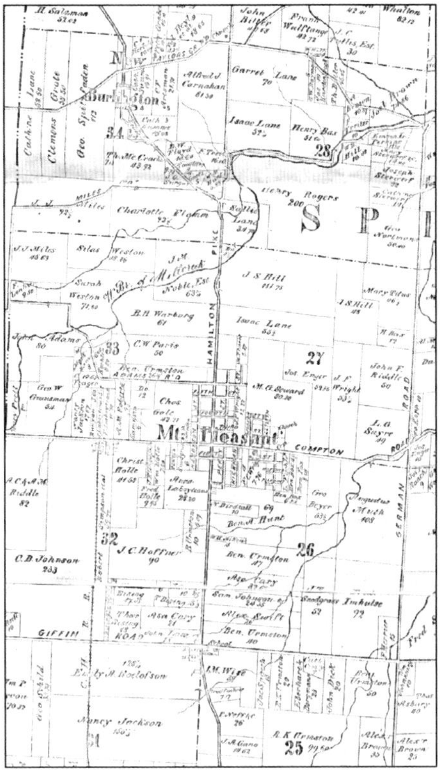

Sections 26, 27, 32, and 33 of the Symmes Purchase were surveyed by Israel Ludlow. In 1793, Ludlow's brother John placed an advertisement in the first Cincinnati newspaper, the *Centinel of Northwest Territory*, seeking settlers. At that time, potential settlers had no interest in his Mount Pleasant, mainly due to their fear of the Native Americans. Ludlow abandoned his plans. Ten years later, settlers began to arrive and the village grew rapidly.

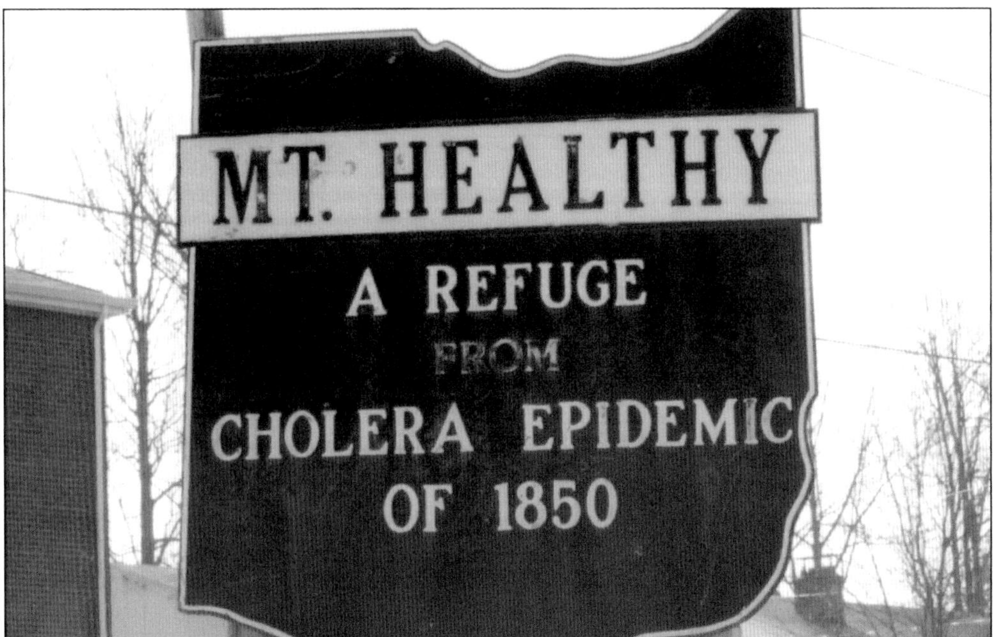

Mount Pleasant was referred to as Mt. Healthy because of the good health experienced by its residents. During the cholera epidemics of 1832 and 1850, there were fewer illnesses and deaths than in the crowded, larger city of Cincinnati, mostly due to fresh air and clean water. (Author's collection.)

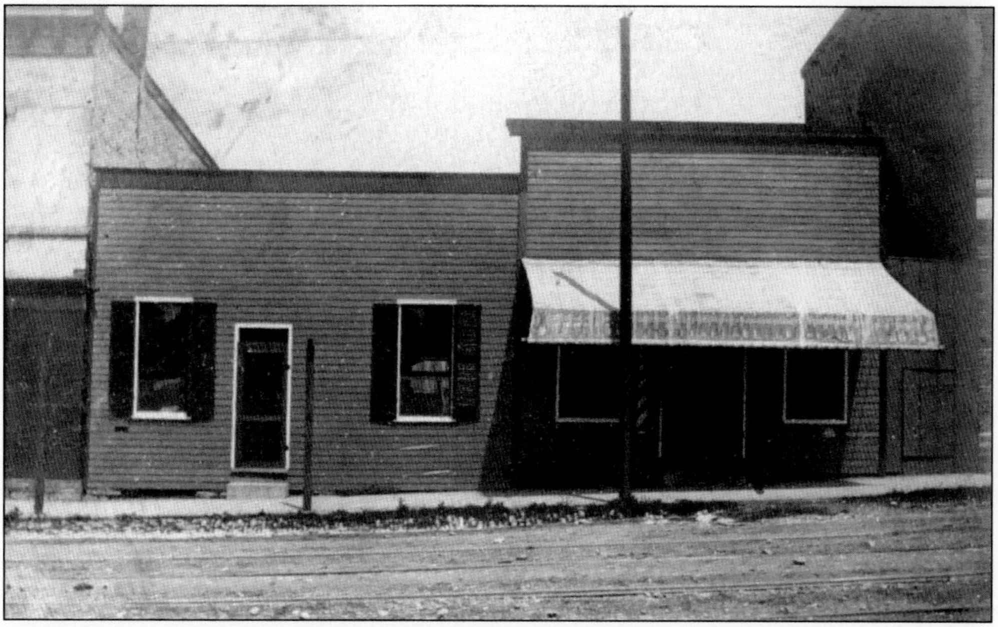

In 1828, Mount Pleasant had grown in population, so it was natural to apply for a U.S. post office. Since another Mount Pleasant existed in Jefferson County, the post office system required the selection of a new name. Having avoided the 1832 cholera epidemic, many already referred to their village as "Mt. Healthy." Thus the name became a reasonable choice. The first post office is on the left.

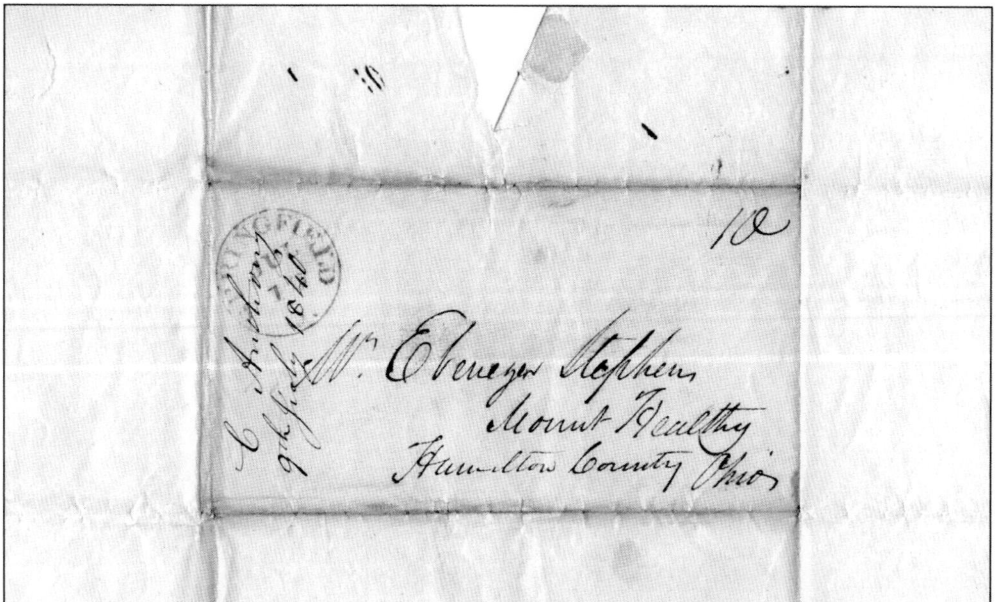

Ebenezer Stephens's letter from a Springfield, Massachusetts, contact was written in 1840. It was common to fold the paper to form an envelope and then seal it with a dot of wax. The sender's name and date of mailing are shown under the stamp. During this time, residents referred to their village as Mount Pleasant but used Mt. Healthy as their postal address. After 1884, Mt. Healthy was used for all matters.

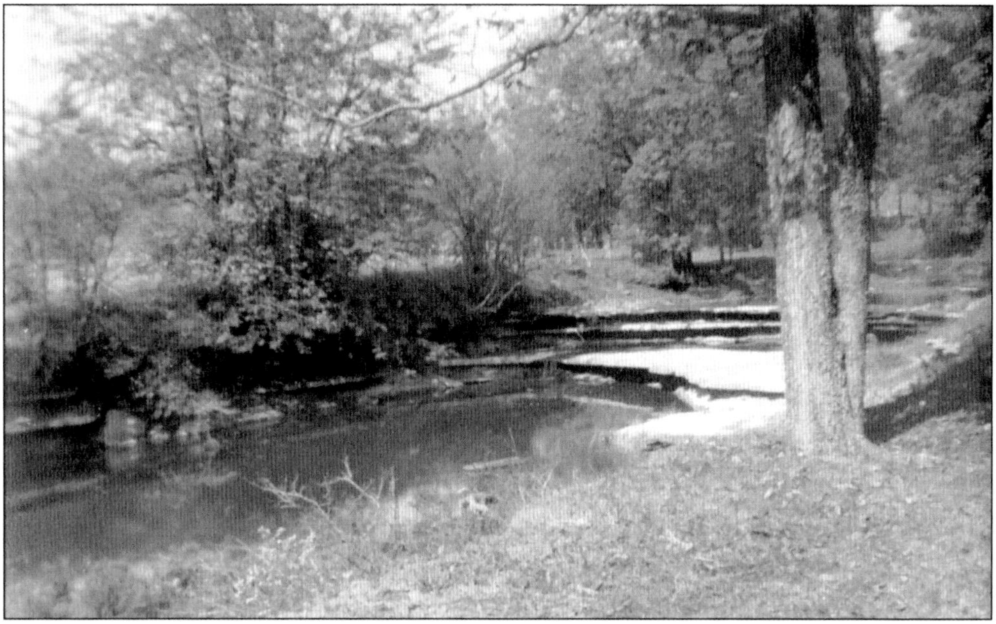

There were many reasons for the healthy environment of Mt. Healthy. Located about 837 feet above sea level and situated on rolling woods that provide natural drainage, contaminated water is unlikely. There was always splendid and abundant well water. In fact, it was not until 1908 that the residents voted to install a city waterworks system.

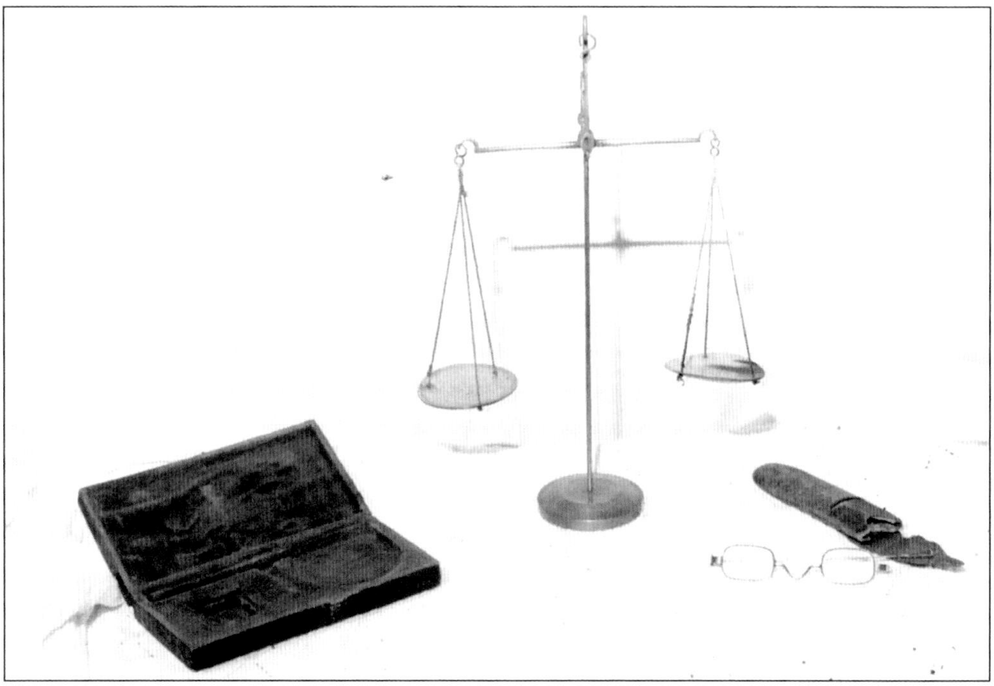

Mt. Healthy was fortunate to have local doctors and dentists from its earliest days. The doctors who helped keep settlers healthy included William McGill, Alexander B. Luse, Dr. McCullough, and John Wright. Luse carried this medical scale in his saddlebags so that he could weigh powders for medicines.

GOETTA

1 lb. pork sausage
1 quart water
1 1/4 cup pinhead oatmeal
2 bay leaves
1 small onion, finely chopped
Salt and pepper to taste

Combine sausage and water in medium size pot with a lid. Stir together. Stir in oatmeal, add bay leaves and chopped onion. Bring to a boil, then reduce heat so mixture simmers gently. Cook uncovered, stirring every 15 minutes so that the mixture does not stick. Cook for 2 hours, then add salt and pepper as needed. Cook 15 minutes longer. Spoon off fat if you see any accumulating on the surface of the mixture. Pour into 5x9 loaf pan. Cover and refrigerate.

Cut into 1/3 inch slices and fry in a hot (non-stick) skillet about 3 minutes each side or until Goetta is crisp and well browned.

Eating energy-rich foods provided good nourishment for the hardworking settlers. The German tradition of eating hearty Goetta was popular. Goetta was flavorful and was made of ingredients that were readily available. (Author's collection.)

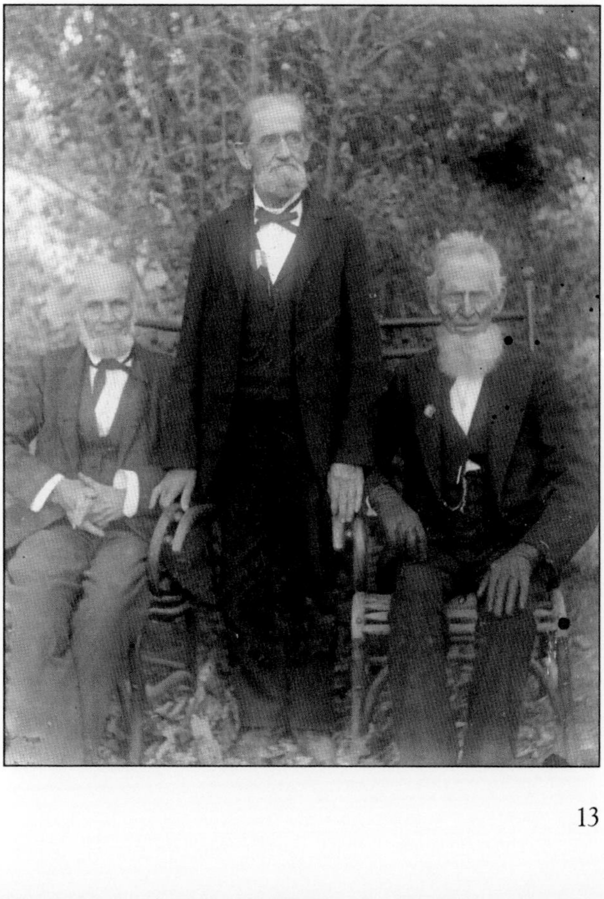

Aware that many residents had long lives, Oliver Goggin (center) originated the idea for a gathering of the Springfield Township Pioneer Association. Goggin, Philip Dom (left), and Francis Carr Wright planned the first meeting for September 8, 1894, at Johnson's Grove. Elected officers were Aaron V. Lane, president; Wright, vice president; and Goggin, secretary. Annual picnics were held on the first Saturday in September until 1916.

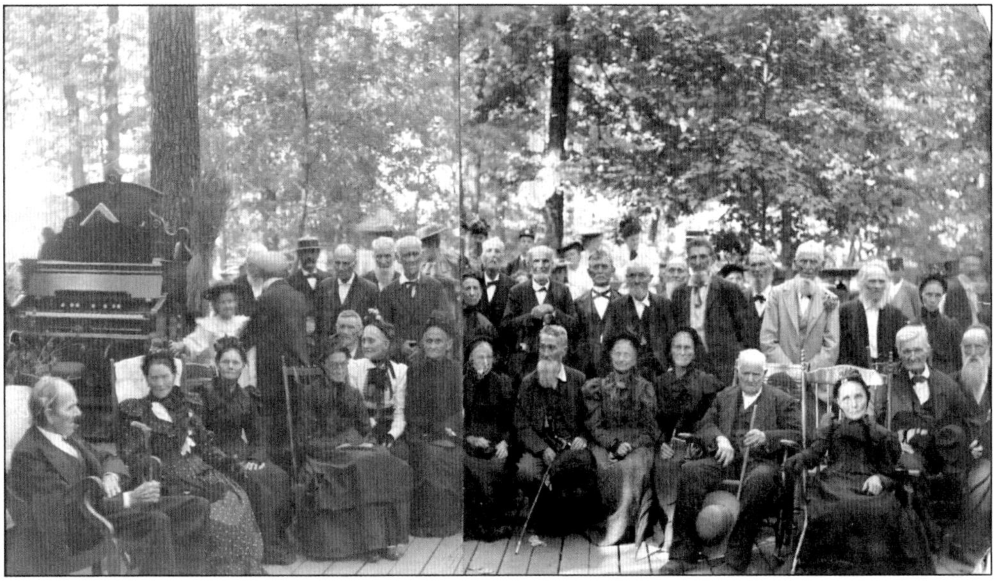

The first meeting of the Springfield Township Pioneer Association was held in 1894, with most attendees being between 40 and 90 years old. Those between 70 to 90 years of age gathered on a large platform complete with rocking chairs. Those present included Louis Hoel, age 90, the oldest native-born resident of Springfield Township, and Julia Wright, age 76, the oldest native-born Mt. Healthian still living in Mt. Healthy.

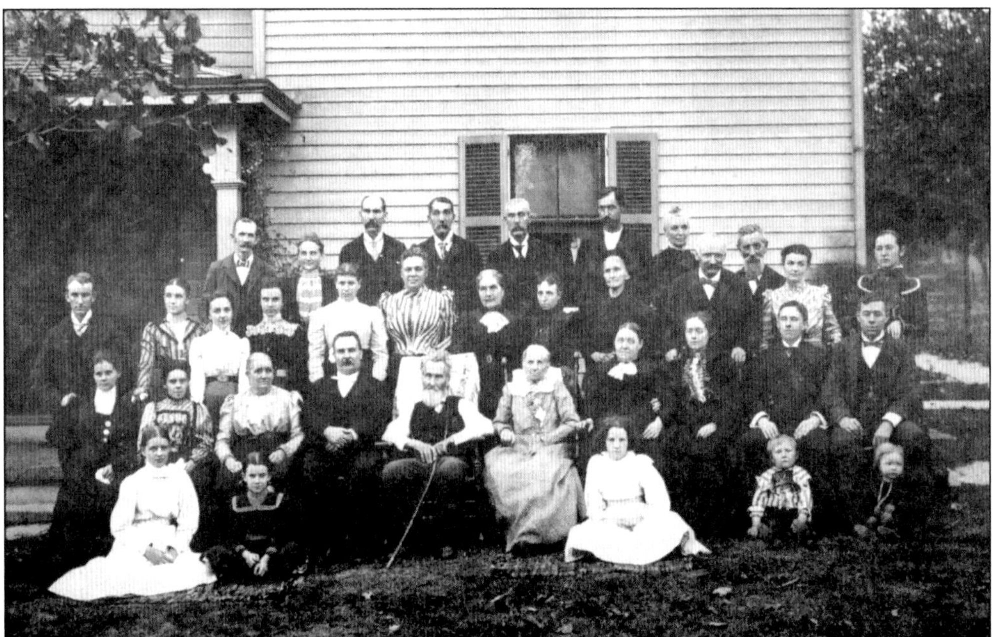

Joel (age 91) and Ann (age 92) Wright Brown (seated, front center) celebrated their 70th wedding anniversary on October 14, 1899. They lived with their daughter Emma Perrine and her family. The party took place at the Perrine residence and included family and friends from far and wide. Many were members of the following pioneer families: LaBoiteaux, Wright, Hurd, and Morse.

Two

ATTENDING TO SPIRITUAL LIFE

Religious and political freedom was important in the lives of early settlers. Many had strong religious convictions. German immigrants sought freedom from religious persecution and their country's political turmoil. The Lutheran, Methodist, and Catholic churches conducted services in German, a practice that continued until the World War I era, when everything German became unpopular.

The Mount Pleasant Union Meeting House was created in 1826 for "the use of all denominations and the exclusion of none." The first congregations that used the meetinghouse were the Presbyterians, United Brethren, and Lutherans. Small groups of worshipers gathered until they gained enough members to build their own churches. By 1853, most congregations had moved into their own church buildings. Mt. Healthy's skyline was full of church steeples. Only the Church of the Assumption congregation met in nearby Catholic churches until their local numbers were large enough for their own church.

Most of the churches that were organized at the meetinghouse exist today. However, several churches are gone, such as the African American church and the Presbyterian church. When the College Hill Presbyterian Church was established closer to where many Presbyterians lived, the Mount Pleasant Presbyterian Church lost membership and disbanded in 1874. Other groups that met in the meetinghouse were the Christian Connection, Swedenborgians, Restorationists, Unitarians, Universalists, Old School Baptists, Mormons, and Quakers. Most members of these groups moved on to other churches and other communities.

Many Mt. Healthy pioneers were buried in family plots on their own farms. Mt. Healthy has several cemeteries. The Hoffner Graveyard was once the yard of the United Brethren Church. The Steward Graveyard evolved into the Mount Pleasant Cemetery where graves are in three sections, including Protestant, African American, and the St. Mary Catholic section. The Arlington Memorial Gardens was opened in 1932 and is an active burial place for Mt. Healthy residents.

This chapter explores the earliest Mt. Healthy churches. However, there are other young churches that thrive in and around Mt. Healthy, confirming the continuing diversity of religious beliefs.

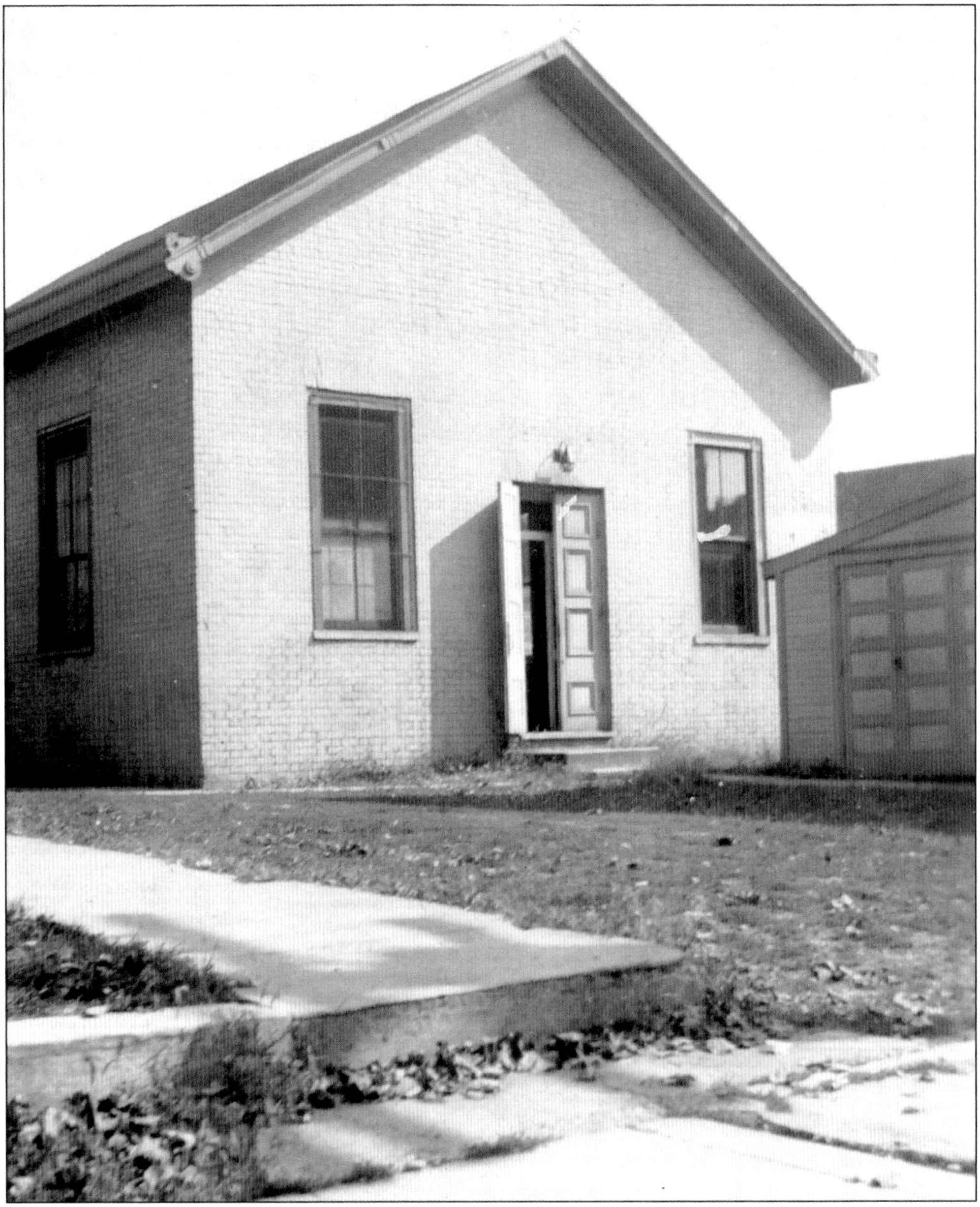

The Mount Pleasant Union Meeting House was built as a place of worship on land purchased from Samuel Hill, cofounder of Mount Pleasant, and his wife, Mary, for $25. The Free Meeting House, as it was called, was centrally located near the northeast corner of Compton Road and Perry Street. Gen. Samuel F. Cary reported that the Presbyterians and Universalists were the denominations that contributed most labor to the erection of the brick building. It became the gathering place for worship of all denominations from 1826 until 1948 and was the founding location of most Protestant churches of the village. Based on Hill's article of agreement, signed in 1825, should scheduling disputes arise over the use of the building, they were settled by casting lots. Five elected trustees oversaw scheduling and maintenance of the meetinghouse. The original board of trustees included Nathan Compton, Richard Conklin, Peter J. LaBoiteaux, William Lyet, and Isaac Jessup.

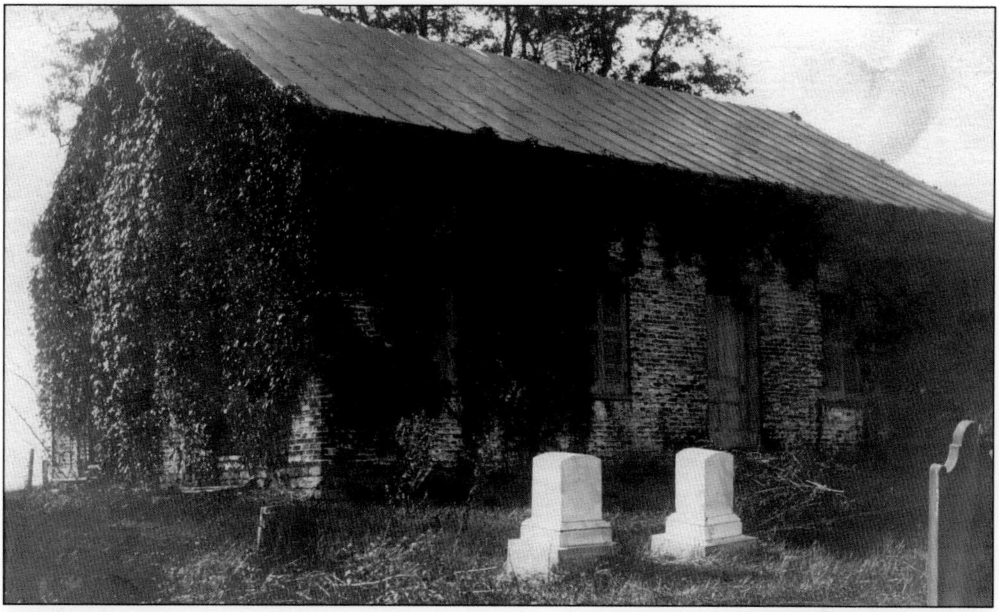

The west branch of the Mill Creek Baptist Church was established in 1910 on west Compton Road. In 1816, the congregation moved to north Springdale Road near Pippin Road where the old churchyard cemetery was located on a high hill. There existed 114 gravestones, recording the names of many pioneers. Earliest church members included the Comptons, Hills, Stouts, and Skillmans. The church building is no longer standing.

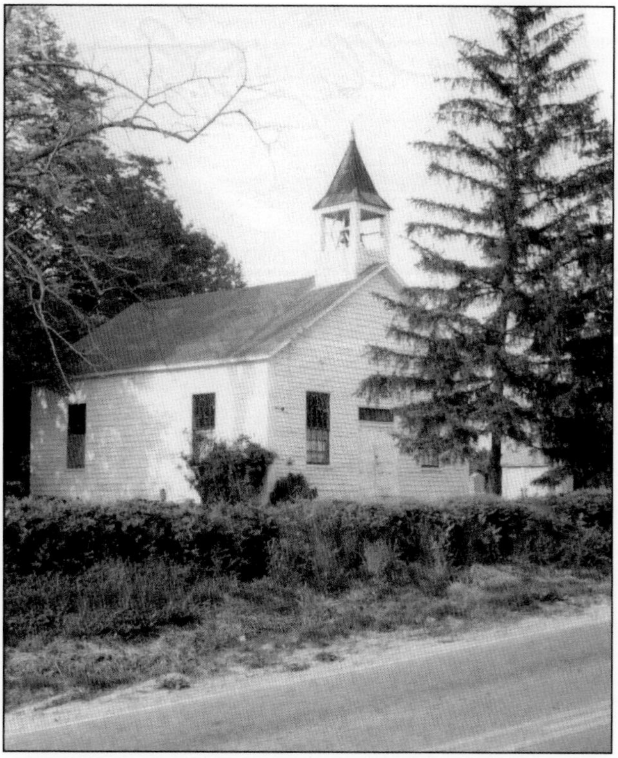

The Unity Church, rebuilt in 1910, stands near the burying grounds of New Burlington on land donated in 1816 by James Carnahan. As the earliest church in the region, it served diversified creeds and at one time held services in English in the morning and German in the afternoon. Early members were the Carnahans, Lanes, and Franciscos. The church is found on Springdale Road west of the New Burlington Cemetery.

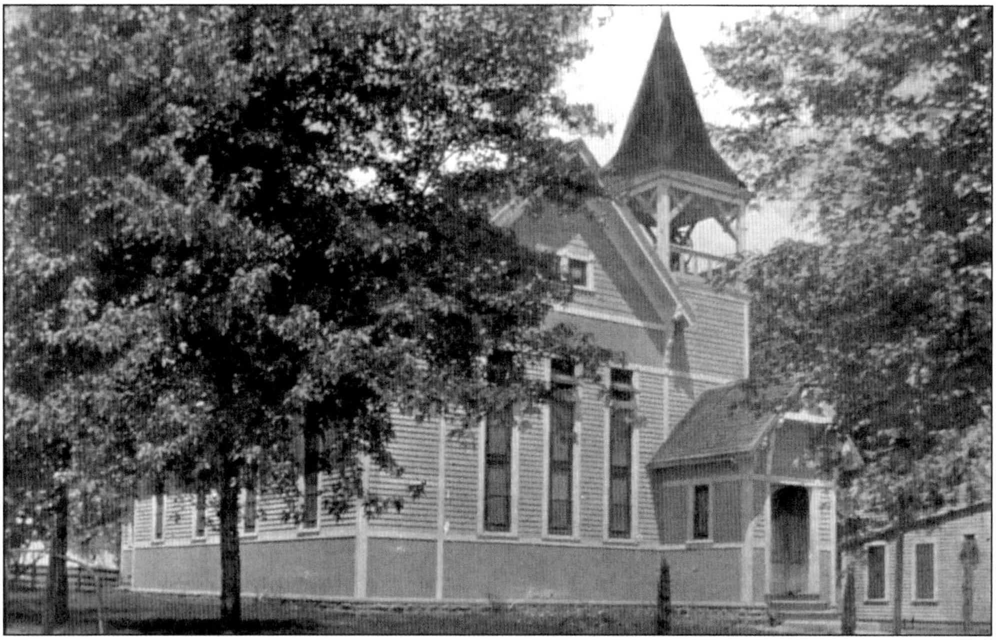

The Mount Pleasant Christian (Disciples of Christ) Church was organized in 1839 by followers of Alexander Campbell. Early members were Reuben Compton, Isaac Sparks, and Isaac Lane, with David Burnet as first pastor. The first church was completed in 1848; a second one was completed in 1885. This is the 1885 church, completed under guidance of Rev. Archibald McLean.

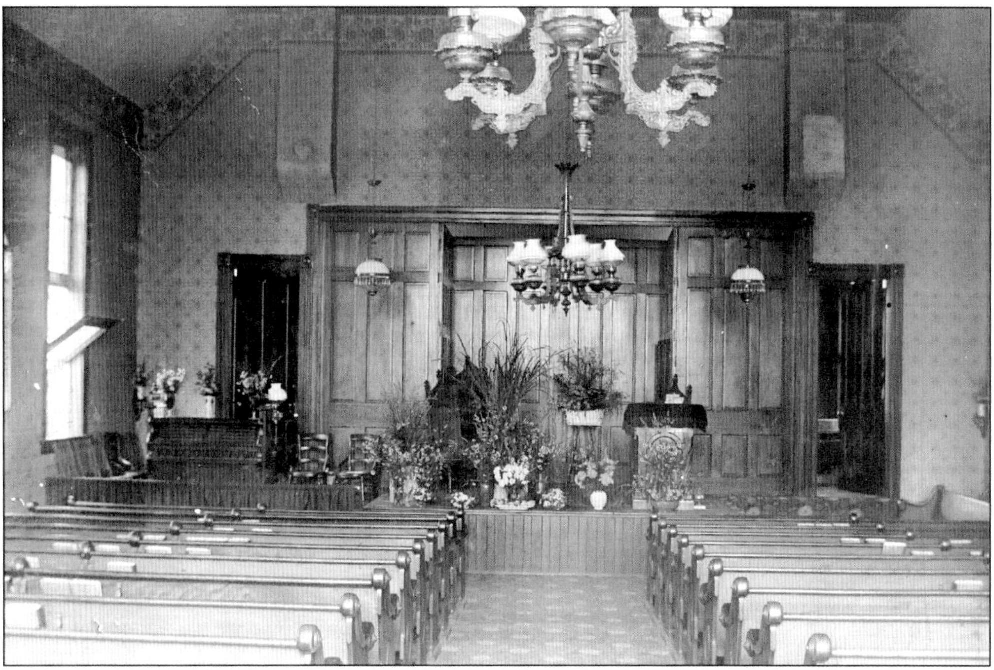

This shows the interior of the 1885 church as it looked in 1897 for a reception celebrating McLean's return from his world tour. Later McLean was secretary for 19 years and president for 20 years of the Christian Foreign Missionary Society and fourth president of Bethany College. This building was remodeled and enlarged in 1910 under Rev. C. O. Cossaboom.

"Aunt Sallie" LaBoiteaux, as she was known, was a lifelong member of the Mt. Healthy Christian Church. For over 50 years, she taught primary age boys in Sunday school. On her 86th birthday, her boys sent postcard greetings from around the world. She was the daughter of early pioneers Ben and Mary (Gogin) Runyan and the wife of Frederick LaBoiteaux, whose grandfather plotted Mount Pleasant in 1817.

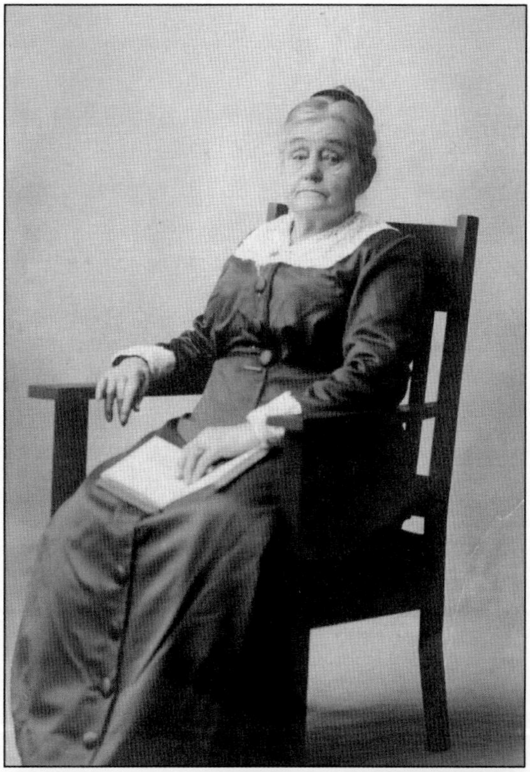

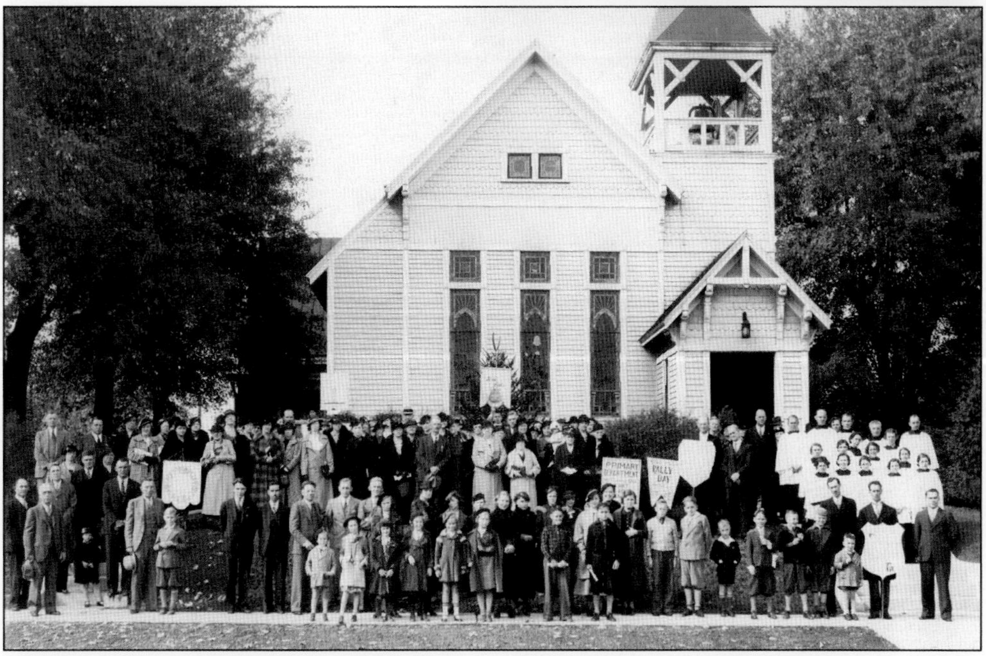

The large congregation of Mt. Healthy Christian Church gathered for Rally Day in 1936. Rally Day involved a parade where children were recruited for the primary Sunday school program. As the parade moved through town, children joined in and then ended at the church. The tall man in front of the church door is the much-loved Cossaboom, who served as reverend for 33 years.

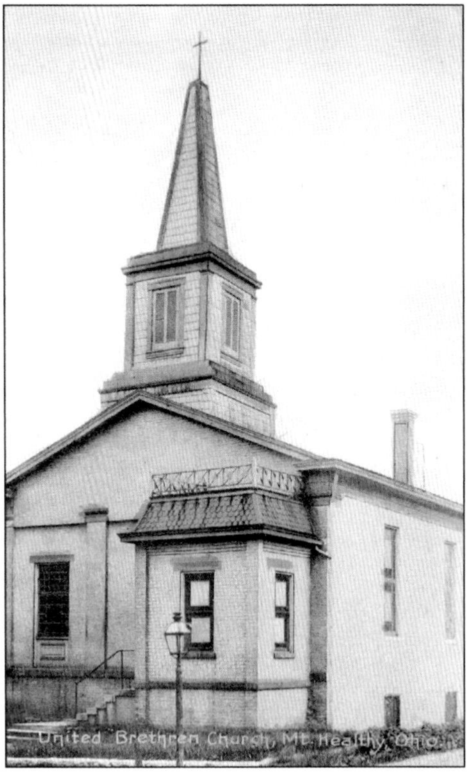

The first United Brethren in Christ Church was organized in 1833 on south Perry Street and has the oldest existing congregation. In 1850, the 61 members voted to build a new meetinghouse (pictured), facing Compton Road at Perry Street at a cost of between $3,000 and $4,000. This building served the needs of the congregation until 1922, when the church was repaired and a new wing added to the east side.

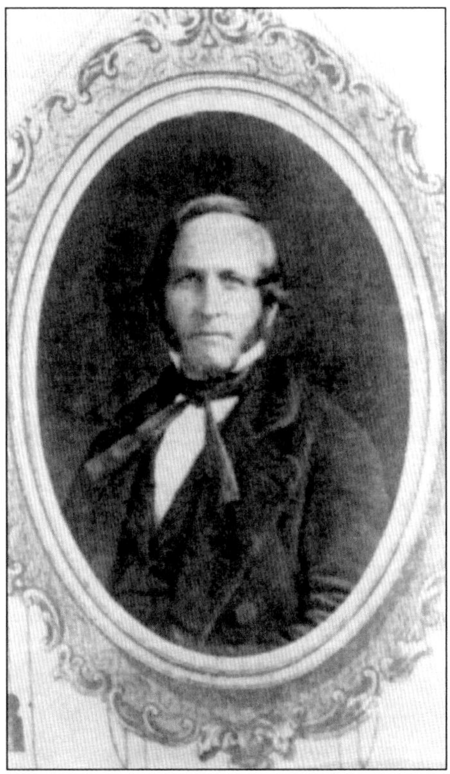

Thomas Hoffner came to Mount Pleasant in 1826 from Pennsylvania. The Hoffner family helped establish the local United Brethren Church. In order for services to be held every Sunday, Rev. Elias W. Hoffner (pictured), Thomas's son, served as part-time pastor beginning in 1848. He later served as class leader from 1854 to 1870. In 1905, to honor Elias and his family, the church became known as the Hoffner Memorial United Brethren Church.

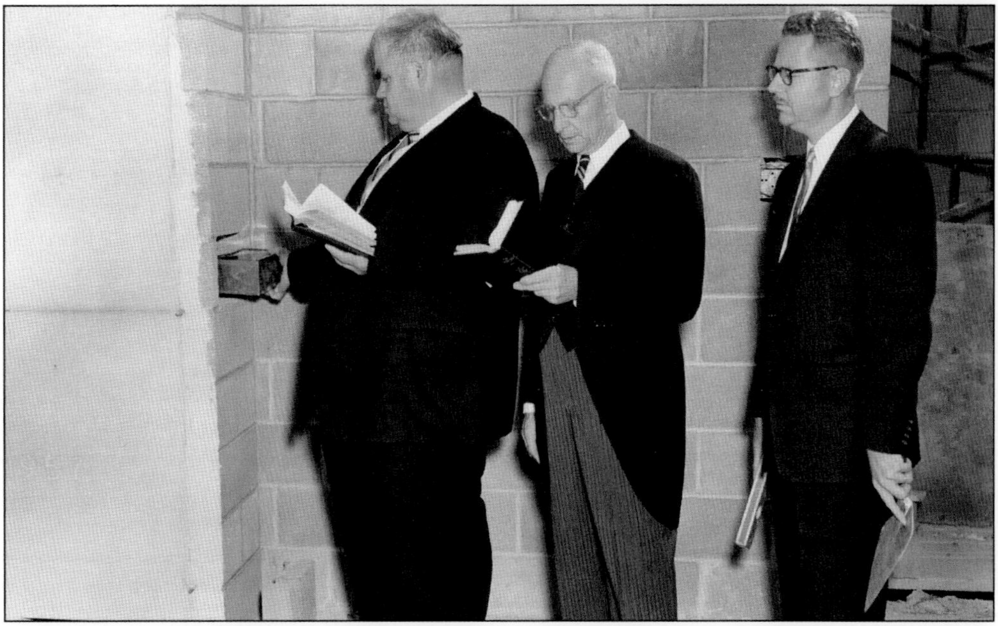

Participants in the October 6, 1957, cornerstone laying of the United Brethren Church were Dr. William K. Messmer (left), conference superintendent who officiated at the ceremony; Rev. Robert V. Pelton (center); and Robert Reuter, building committee member and mason. The old church was used as a Sunday school until 1966 when it was torn down for the 1967 completion of a new education building.

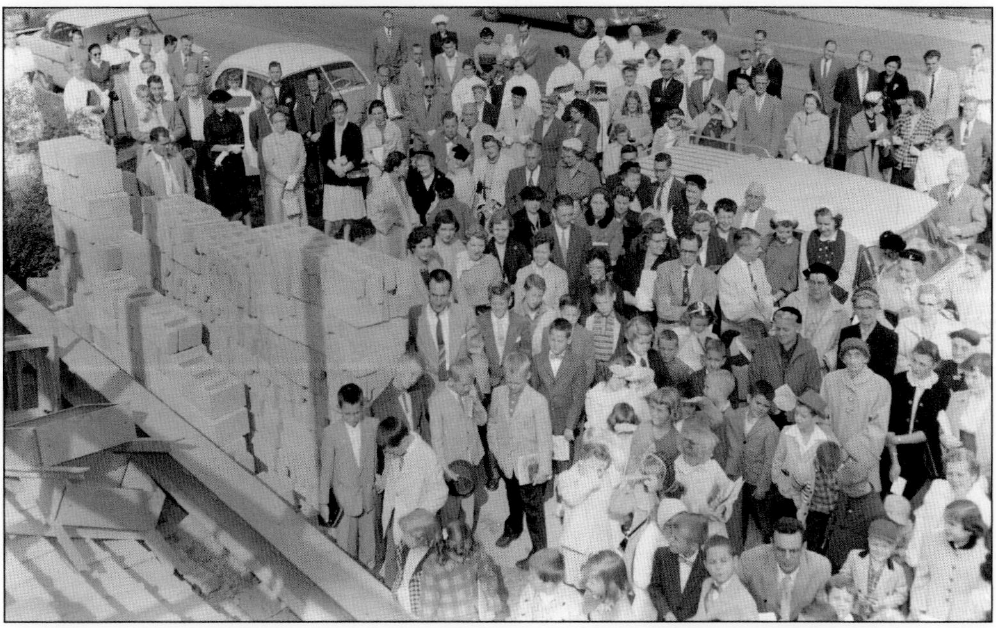

Members turned out for the cornerstone laying of the new United Brethren Church. The increase in membership was due to the influx of many new families coming to Mt. Healthy in the late 1940s and 1950s. On November 11, 2001, the Epworth United Methodist Church (north building) and Heritage United Methodist Church (south building) voted to merge into the Mt. Healthy United Methodist Church.

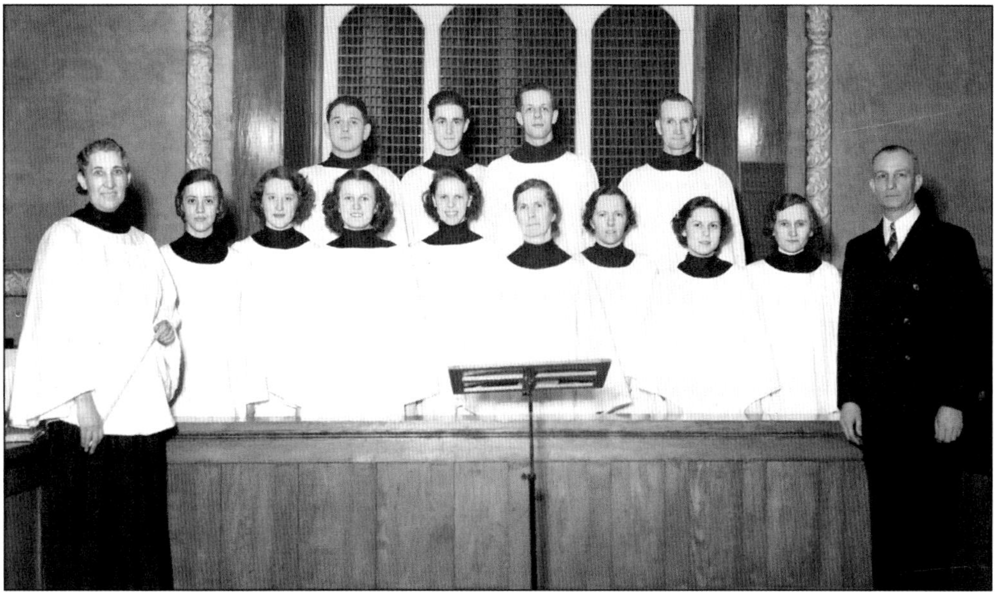

Mt. Healthy churches value their music and choirs. This is the 1938 United Brethren choir. Pictured from left to right are (first row) Stella Nott, Louisa Berndt Brooks, Thelma Wells, Elaine Koch Witschger, Myrtle Berndt Beck, Stella Noble, Nell Hoffner, Ruth Hoffner Zimmerman, organist Evelyn Jacoby, and Rev. Robert V. Pelton; (second row) unidentified, Jack Chambers, William Berndt, and Clifford Risk. Pelton served the longest pastorate in the church's history, from 1936 until 1959.

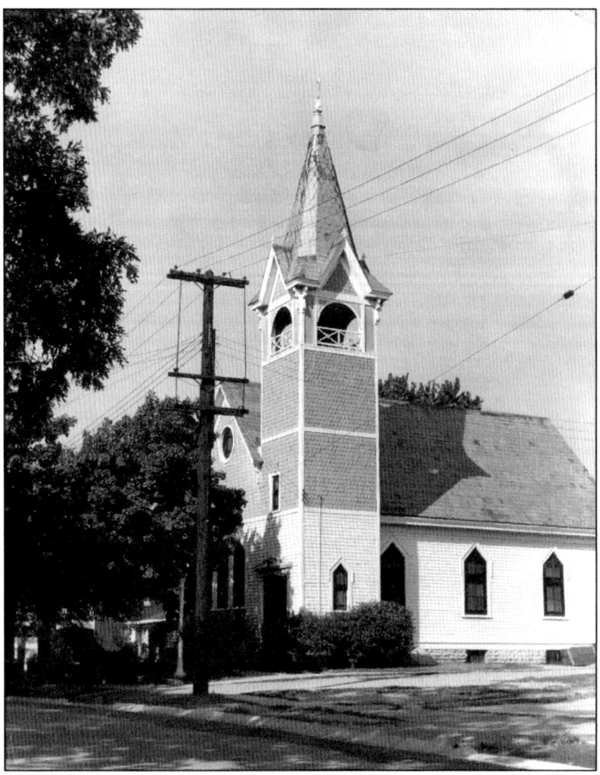

The small-frame German Methodist Church of 1850 was replaced with this building in 1891 at a cost of $3,700. Early services were conducted in German. In 1910, the church abandoned German-language services for English, with Rev. James P. Simmonds being the first pastor to preach in English. As the United States moved toward World War I, speaking German became unpopular.

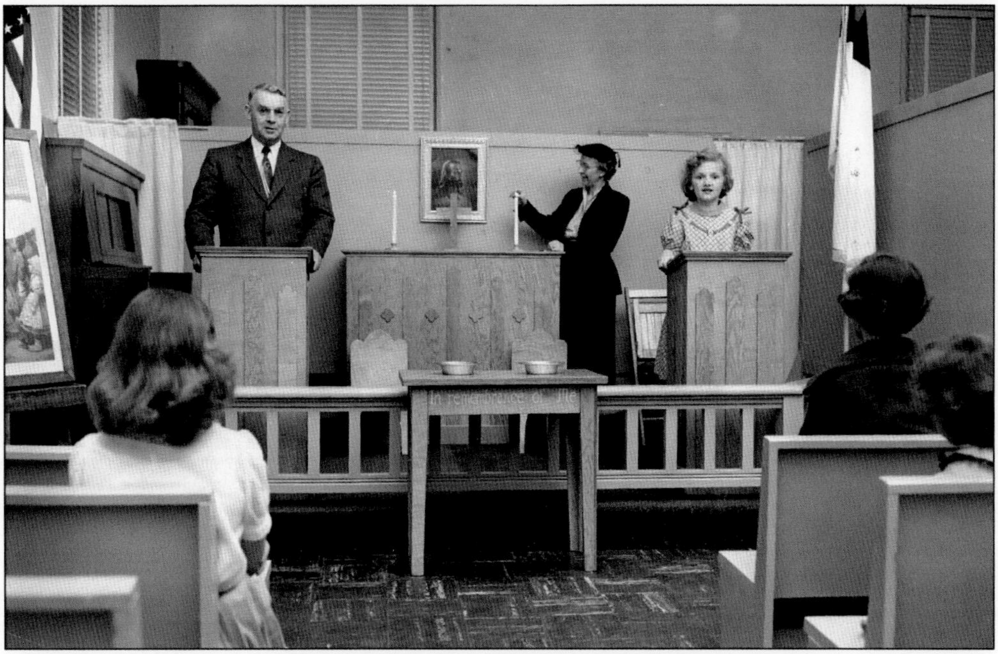

In 1949, planning began for a new sanctuary with fund-raising activities such as the Lord's Acre Pop Corn, grown by the Men's Club, and candy making that became a longtime tradition. Pictured in the sanctuary, from left to right, are Rev. Frank Clarke, unidentified, and Joyce Westendorf. On January 9, 1955, the last service was held in the old church.

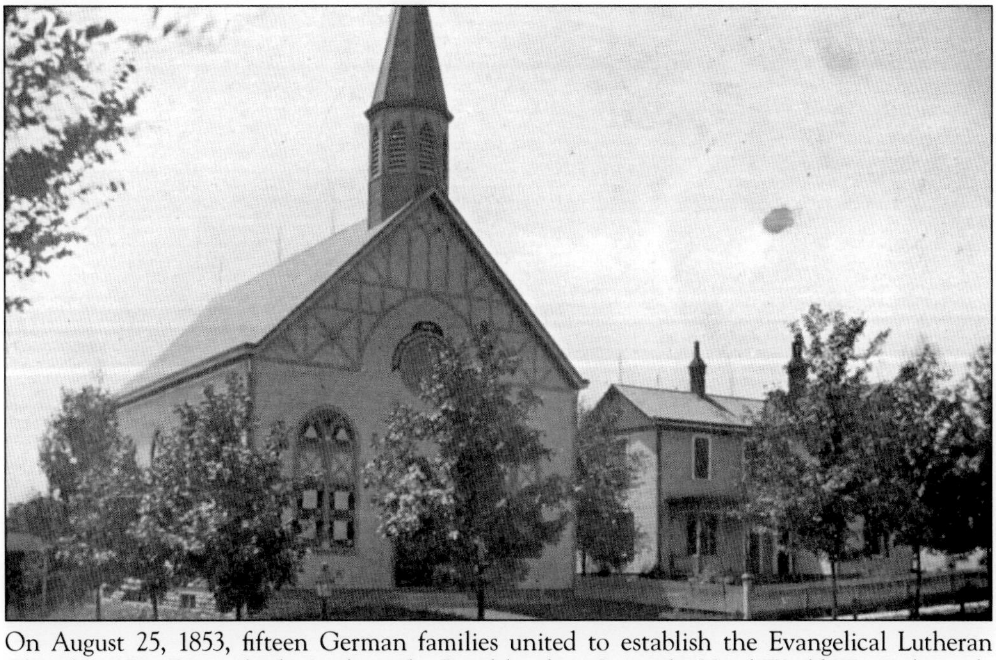

On August 25, 1853, fifteen German families united to establish the Evangelical Lutheran Church, or Die Evangelische Lutherische Dreifaltigskeit Gemeide. Until World War I, the early service was in German and the second in English. Rev. Paul Schmidt was known for his services in German between 1896 and 1910. Pictured here is the 1890 church. The 1853 church building was known as Trinity Hall and later became the education building.

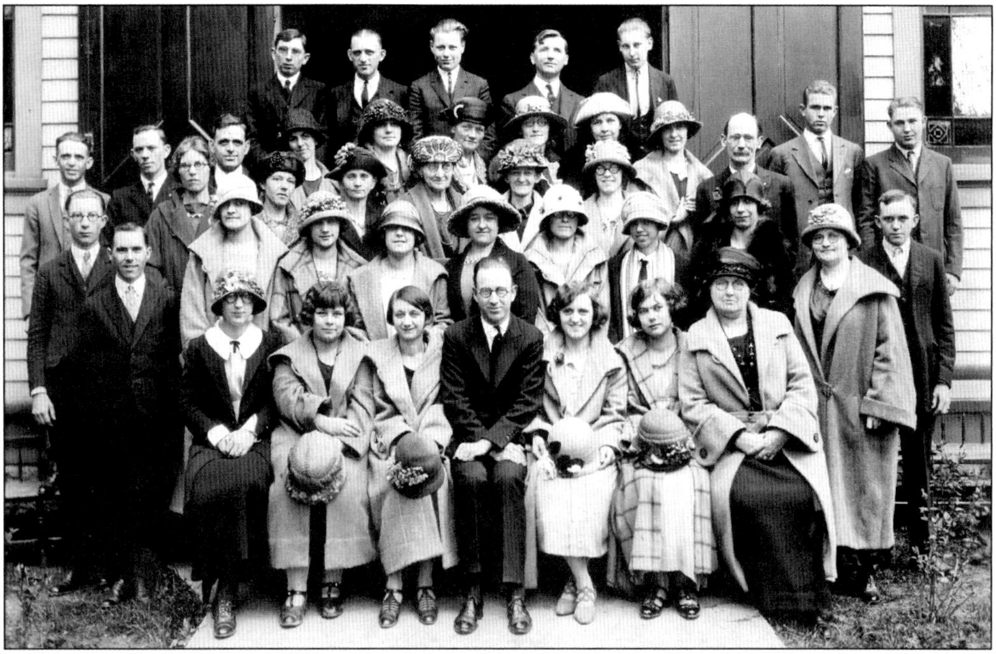

This photograph is believed to be of the last Bible class to meet in the old Evangelical Lutheran Church before it was razed in order to build a new church. Last services were held on a sunny Easter Sunday in 1927. Rev. Oscar Smith, pastor between 1922 and 1934, sits in the center of the front row.

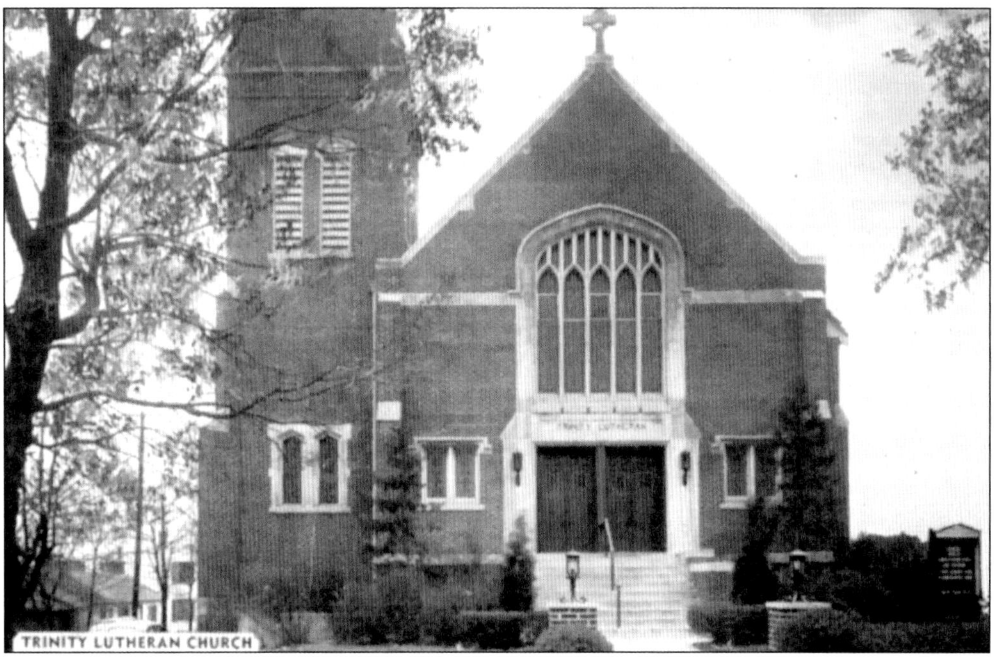

On February 5, 1928, the new Trinity Lutheran Church was dedicated. An important component in the steeple was the church bell named "Hope" (or Hoffnung), which called members to worship since 1891. It is still used and rings every day. In 1890, the Sunday school children paid $219.50, gathered penny by penny, for the 1,007.5-pound bell.

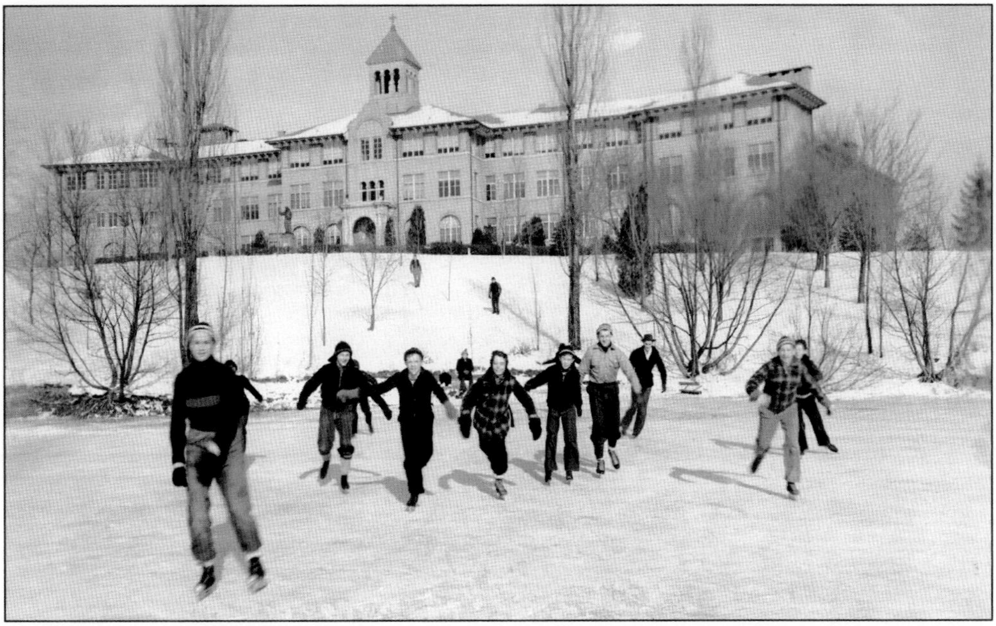

Priests were needed for the growing German Catholic population. In 1858, a classical four-year high school course for boys opened in downtown Cincinnati. In 1924, the St. Francis Seminary moved to 127 acres north of Mt. Healthy. Originally the grounds were bare, but over the years, pine trees were planted by the man-made lake. It became a beautiful campus. St. Francis closed in 1980. (Courtesy of Lucille Brinkman Green.)

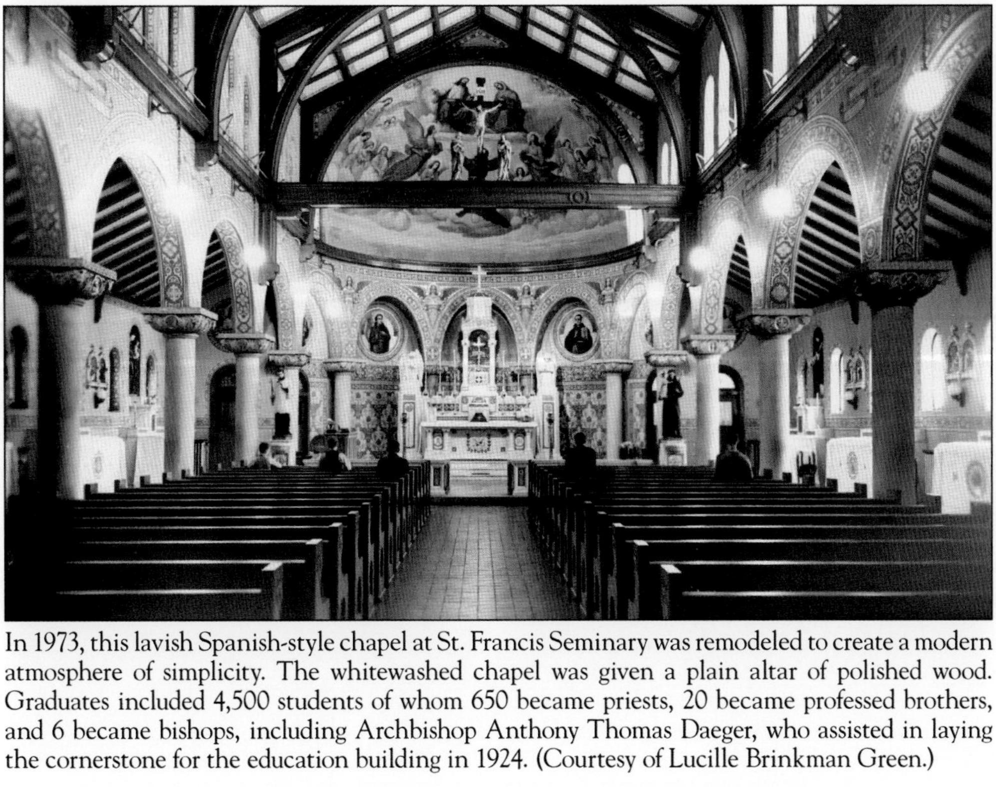

In 1973, this lavish Spanish-style chapel at St. Francis Seminary was remodeled to create a modern atmosphere of simplicity. The whitewashed chapel was given a plain altar of polished wood. Graduates included 4,500 students of whom 650 became priests, 20 became professed brothers, and 6 became bishops, including Archbishop Anthony Thomas Daeger, who assisted in laying the cornerstone for the education building in 1924. (Courtesy of Lucille Brinkman Green.)

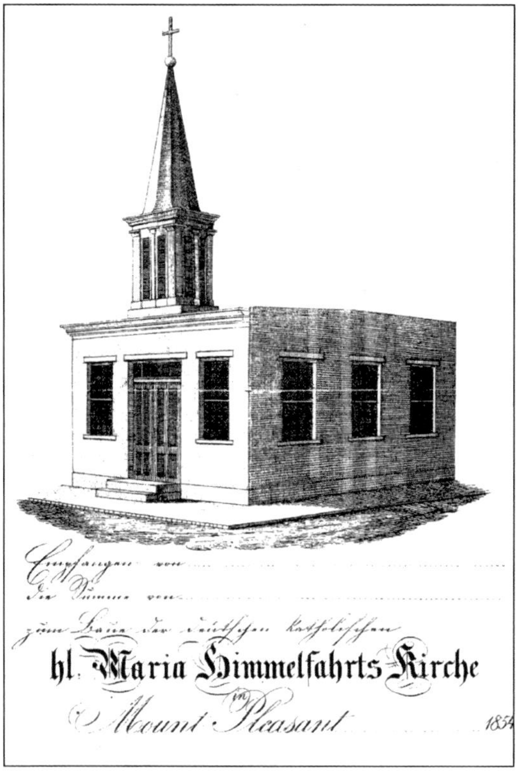

During the 1850 cholera epidemic, many German immigrants fled to Mount Pleasant. With no Catholic churches in the community, they traveled back to Cincinnati or to White Oak to attend services. By 1854, the Mount Pleasant Catholic population was large enough to support its own church. On August 5, 1855, the first Church of the Assumption of the Blessed Virgin Mary was dedicated.

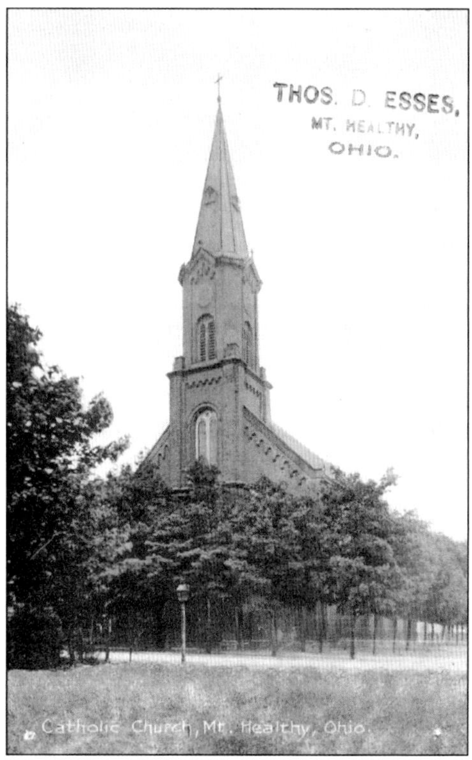

By 1869, the Church of the Assumption of the Blessed Virgin Mary had grown so large that the original building could no longer serve the parishioners' needs. In April of that year, Rev. Herman Jahanning called on parishioners to assist in the planning and building of a new church. To reduce cost, clay and the machinery to manufacture bricks were donated by parishioners. The church was dedicated on November 20, 1870.

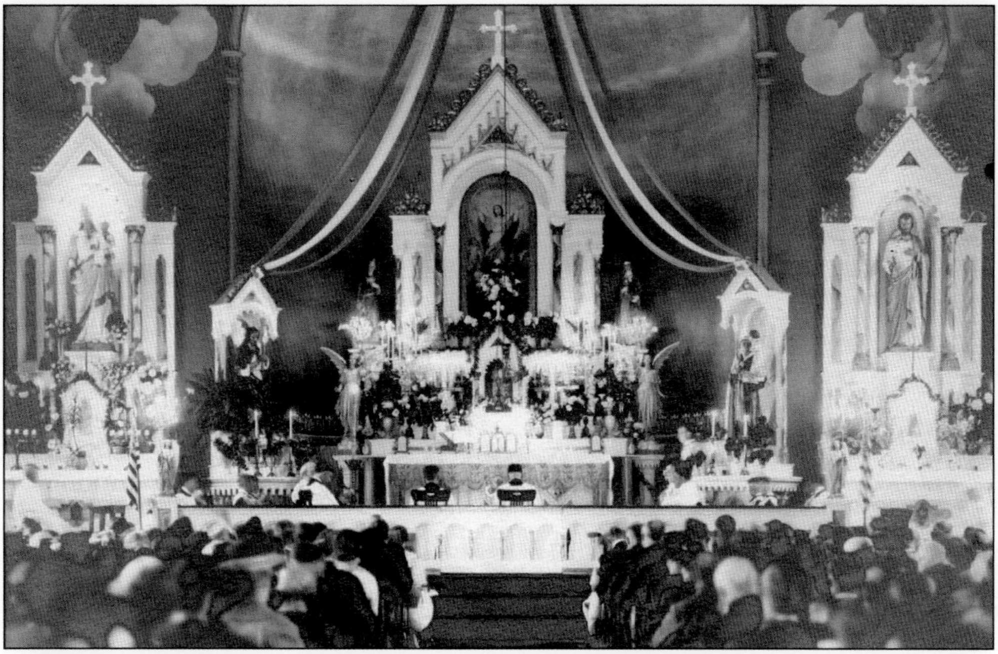

In 1893, the interior of the second Church of the Assumption underwent a major renovation. Under the watchful eye of Rev. Bernard Roesener, the main altar received new statues, stained-glass windows were added, and frescoes were painted on the ceiling. This photograph shows the church beautifully decorated for the first mass celebrated by Fr. Edward Summe, as he became pastor on March 21, 1921.

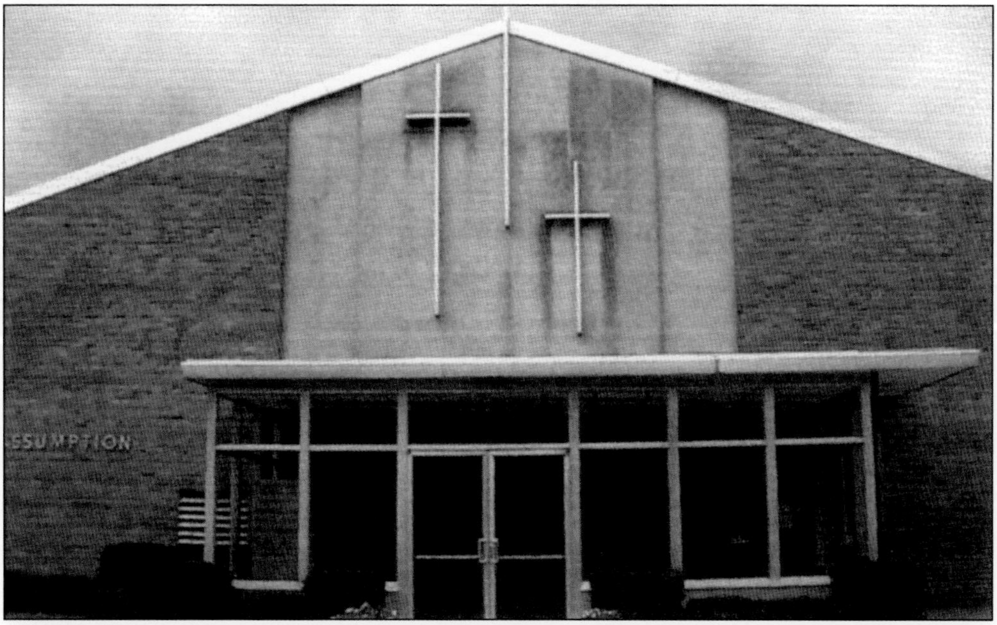

As the years passed, concerns about the safety of the second Church of the Assumption began to emerge. By 1954, it was determined that a new church must be constructed. The dedication of the new church and hall took place on December 8, 1957. This new building included eight additional classrooms for the grade school in the lower level with the church proper located above.

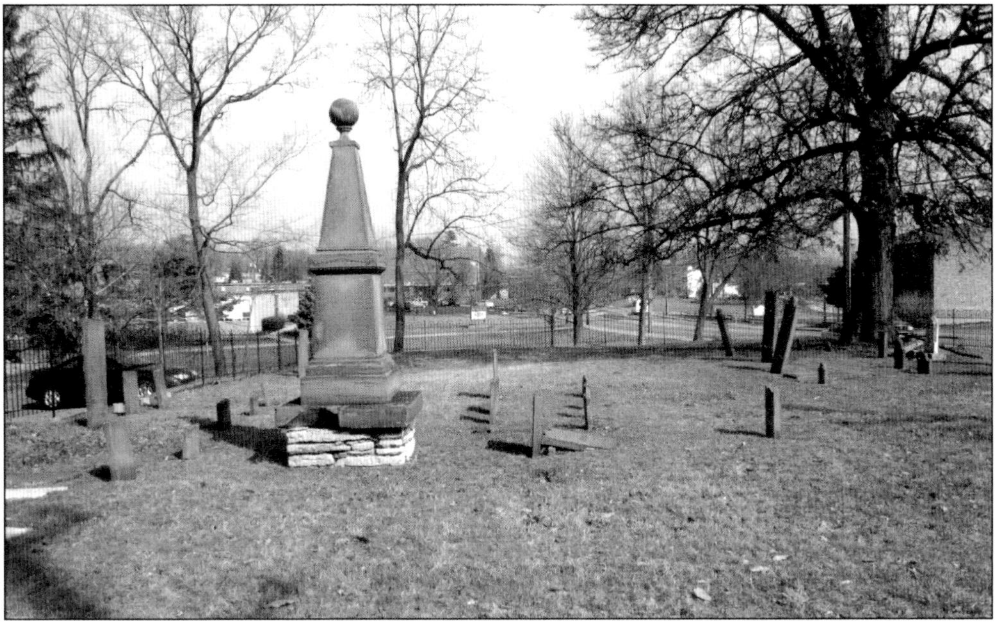

Peter LaBoiteaux, his wife, Keziah, and their children came to Springfield Township in 1804. Eighty-three acres of their land was sold to Benjah Cary, although one acre was reserved as a burial ground for the Cary and LaBoiteaux families. Located at the intersection of Galbraith Road and Hamilton Pike, this small plot became the cemetery for the community, most of whom were related to one another. (Author's collection.)

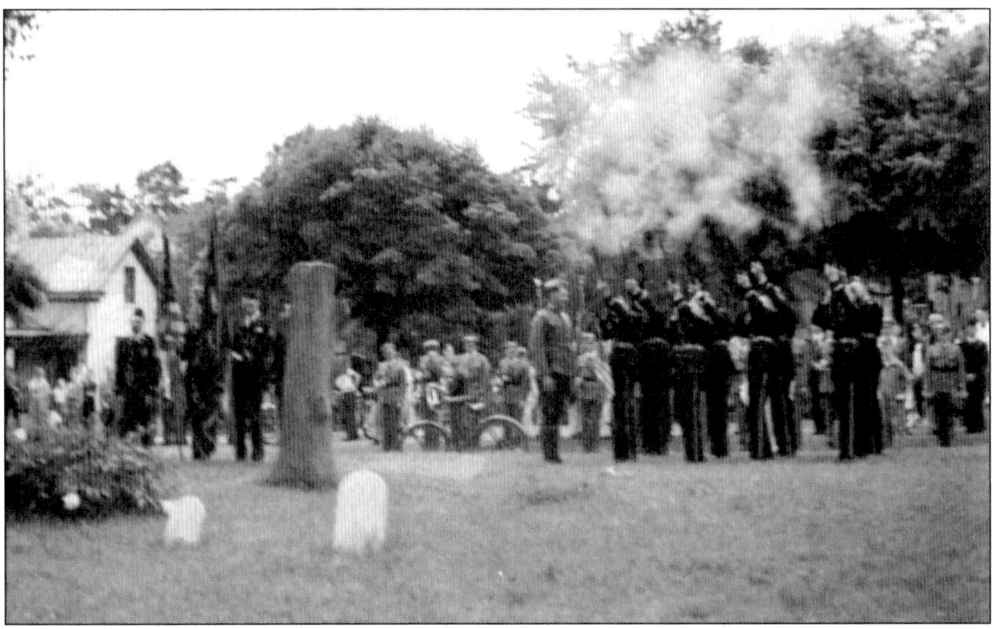

The first United Brethren Church was erected on south Perry Street in 1833, with Elias W. Hoffner, Solomon Hayes, and John Hickman elected as trustees. The church building is now gone. However, the churchyard, known as the Hoffner Cemetery, holds the graves of many of the early church founders, including Thomas Hoffner and his wife, Abigail. Shown is a Decoration Day tribute to veterans.

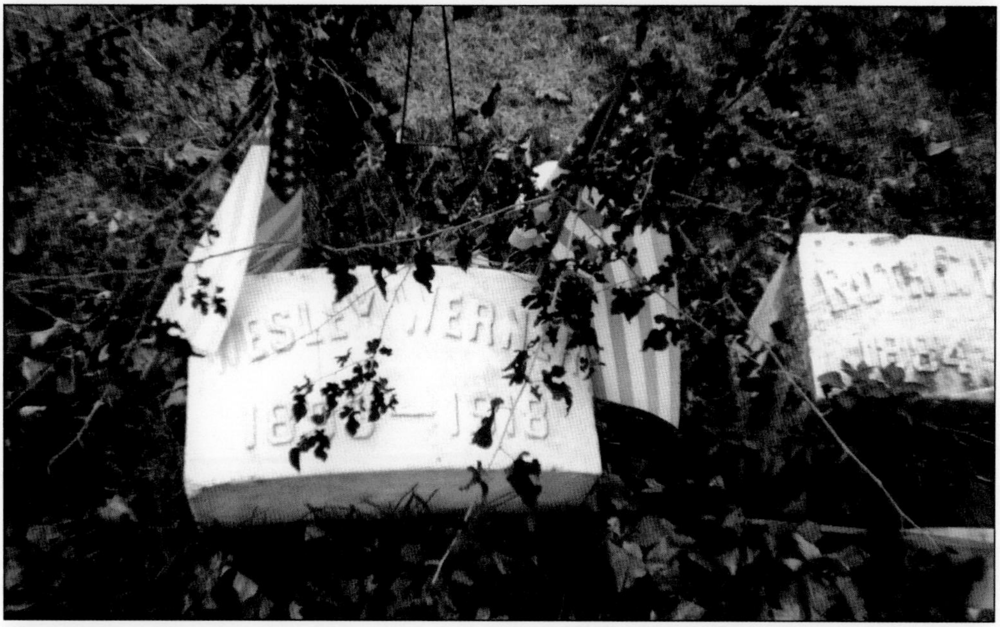

The Mount Pleasant Cemetery was opened in 1819. The Mount Pleasant Cemetery Association operated the property between 1865 and 1944. The graves include 35 Civil War, 2 Spanish-American War, and 8 World War I veterans. Wesley Werner was among them. The American Legion Wesley Werner Post No. 513 and Werner Avenue were named to honor Werner, the first Mt. Healthy man to lose his life in World War I. (Author's collection.)

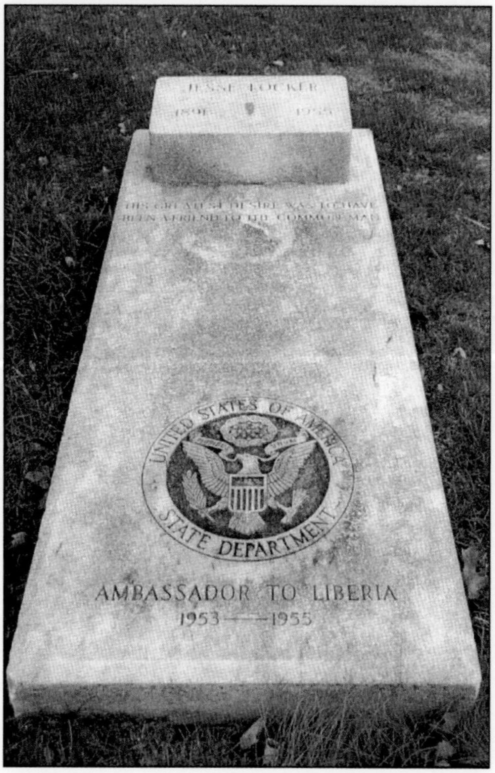

Protestants, African Americans, and German immigrants are buried in the old Mount Pleasant Cemetery, which is located at 1454 Compton Road. One of the largest funerals ever held was for African American Jesse Locker, who died in 1955, just two years into his appointment as ambassador to Liberia. His grave states, "His greatest desire was to have been a friend to the common man." (Courtesy of Gregory Wilson.)

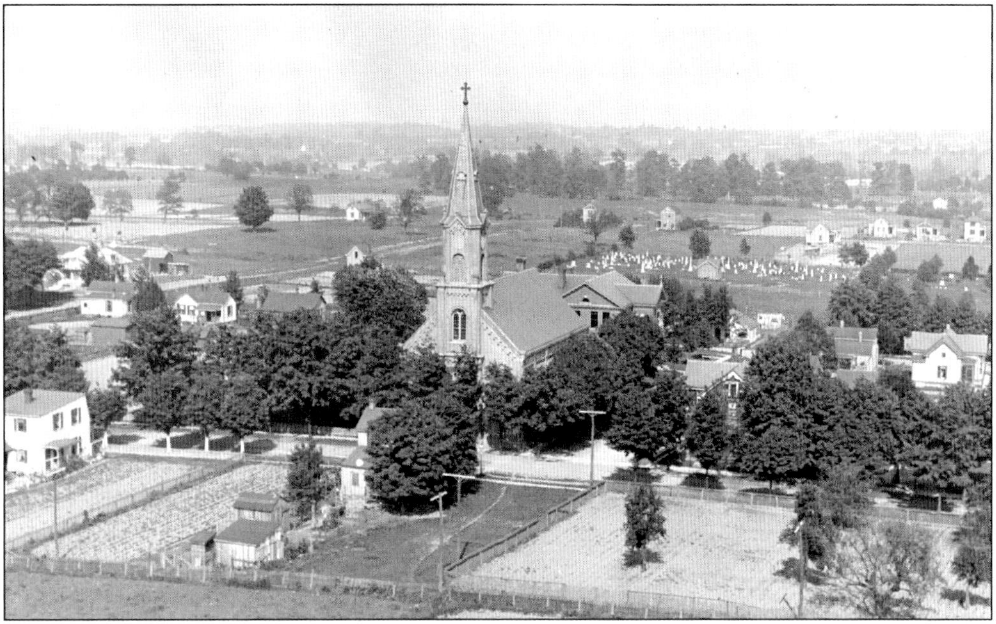

Early members of the Church of the Assumption of the Blessed Virgin Mary were German immigrants. To them, the church was called Heilige Maria Himmelfahrts Kirche. Because of this translation, the church was often referred to as St. Mary's. The parish cemetery, located adjacent to the church, continues to be called St. Mary's Cemetery. This photograph shows the second Church of the Assumption with the cemetery in the background.

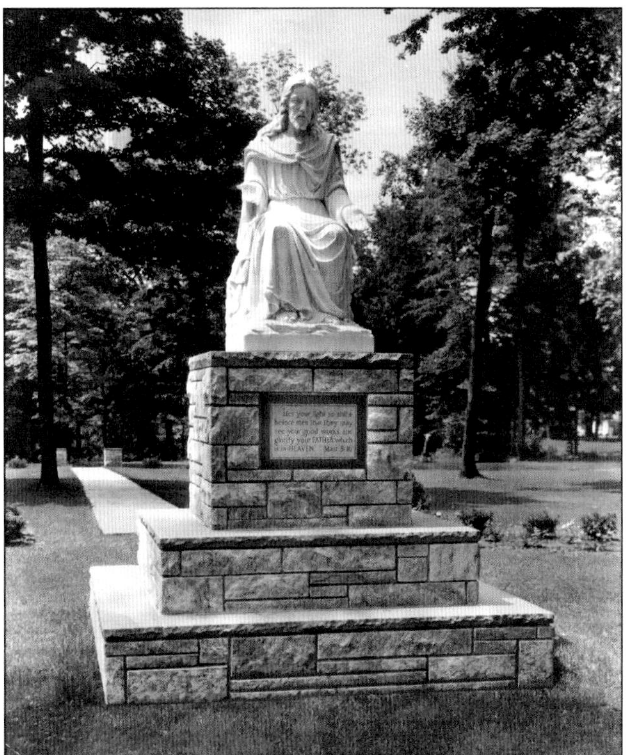

Arlington Memorial Gardens was established in 1934 on land that pioneer Abner Johnson originally owned. Today sculptures by artists Dominic Zappia and Aldo Buttini are admired throughout the cemetery. This sculpture in the Sermon on the Mount Garden reads, "Let your light so shine before men that they may see your good works and glorify your Father which is in Heaven. Matthew 5:16." (Courtesy of Arlington Memorial Gardens.)

Three

Structuring City Services

The community of Mount Pleasant grew from its original 1817 plat set by John LaBoiteaux and Samuel Hill. Settlers took pride in helping each other succeed.

On August 10, 1893, with the cholera epidemic behind them and the name changed to Mt. Healthy, residents celebrated the official designation as an Ohio village. Electing officers for the village council was the first order of business. On August 19, 1893, D. J. Smith became the first official mayor of Mt. Healthy. A police marshal was elected, and a system of laws was created to keep order. Police and volunteer fire departments were created, and a council of community leaders worked together to direct the village's growth. As expansion continued, an acting chief of the volunteer fire department was also appointed.

Because the village was growing so rapidly, the need to increase services became a priority. In 1894, the village council decided that services would be paid for through a tax, or mil, rate of 6.30. That rate soon increased to 9.0 and 10.0 mils. As the population stabilized, so did the tax rate.

To keep up with the modern amenities, in 1908, water was supplied to the village through a contract with the Village of College Hill. Water could now be delivered directly to a resident's home instead of pumped up from a well. In April 1910, Mt. Healthy received gas and electricity from the Union Gas and Electric Company. Telephone service soon followed, with the "party line" being the economically popular choice.

As the years rolled by, the community took pride in its efficient government and dependable city services. Its public servants were known by their first names and appreciated for their dedication and hard work. Mt. Healthy was a good place to live.

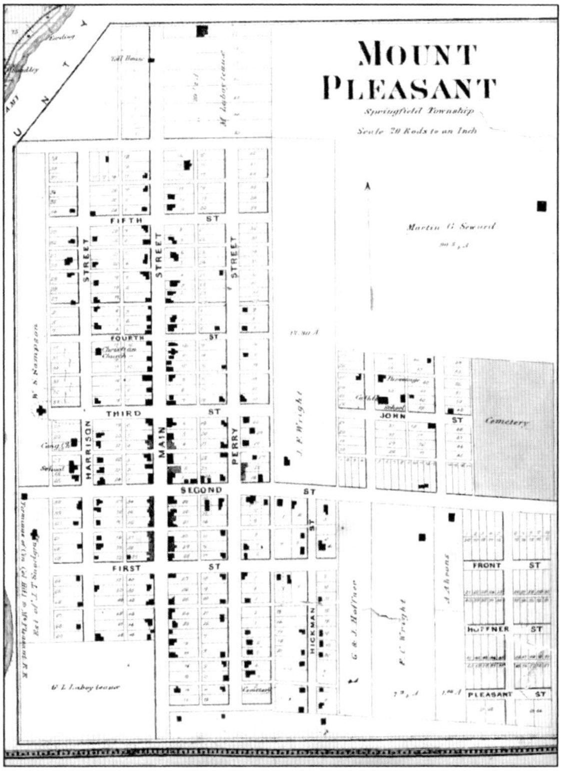

In 1817, early settlers John LaBoiteaux and Samuel Hill joined together to plat the original village of Mount Pleasant. They designed all streets to be 66 feet wide, with 20-foot-wide alleys running behind them. All were laid out north and south or east and west. To serve local residents as well as travelers, the center of commerce was purposely situated along Hamilton Turnpike.

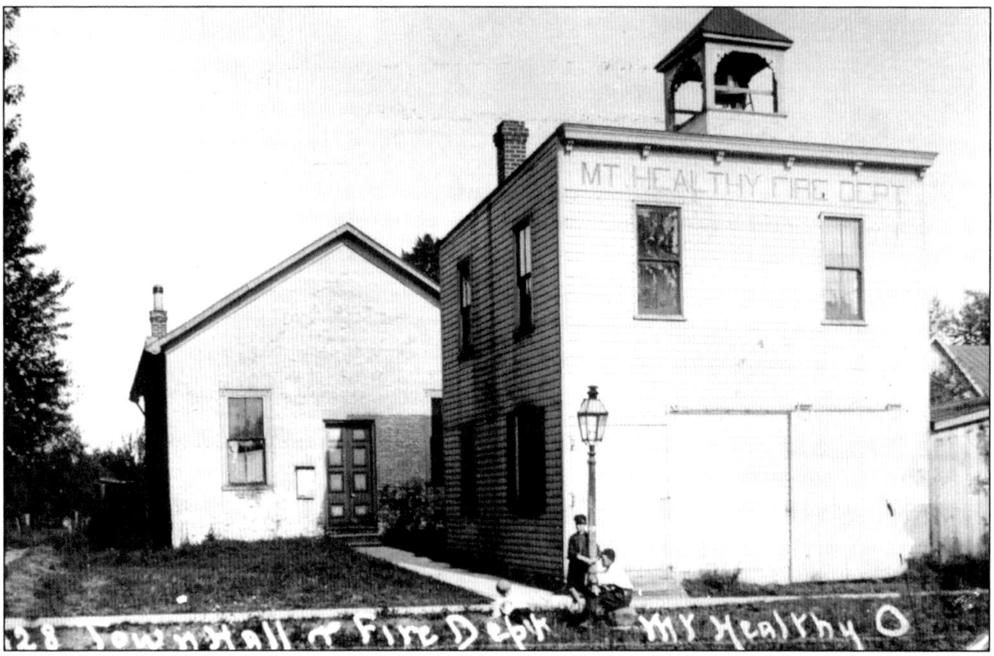

In 1910, the municipal center of Mt. Healthy was located near the northeast corner of Compton Road and Perry Street and consisted of a firehouse and town hall. Since 1855, the Mount Pleasant Union Meeting House served as town hall, with bars forming two jail cells in the front of the building. The firehouse was built in 1904 for $458 plus $30 for the second-floor meeting room.

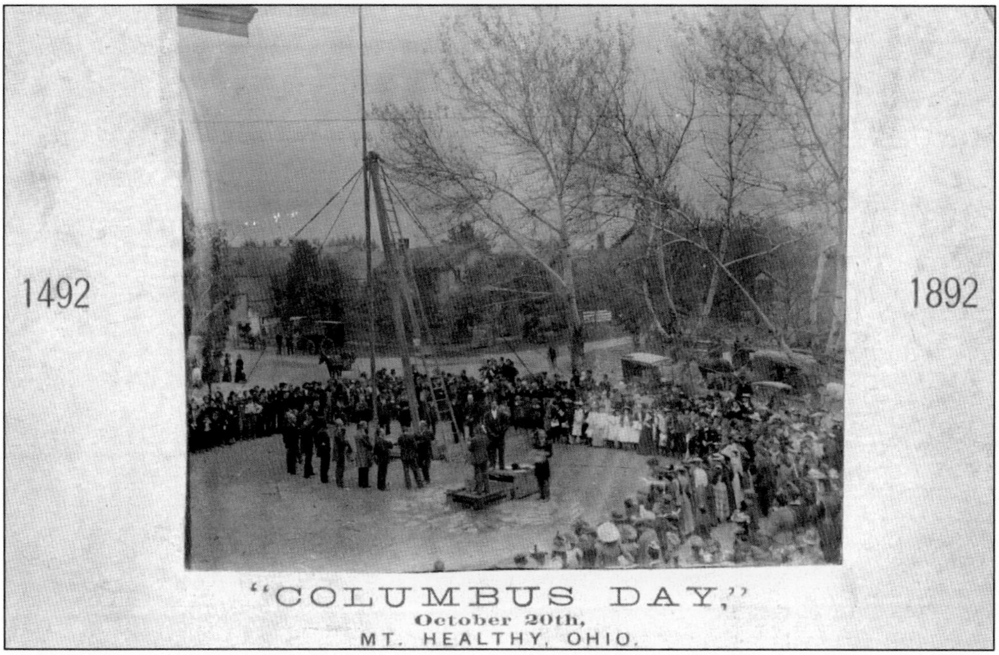

On October 20, 1892, Mt. Healthy commemorated the 400th anniversary of the first voyage of Christopher Columbus by raising the American flag in the school yard located at the northwestern corner of Harrison Avenue and Compton Road. With the town's rapid growth, residents were also looking forward to the official village designation that would come in August 1893.

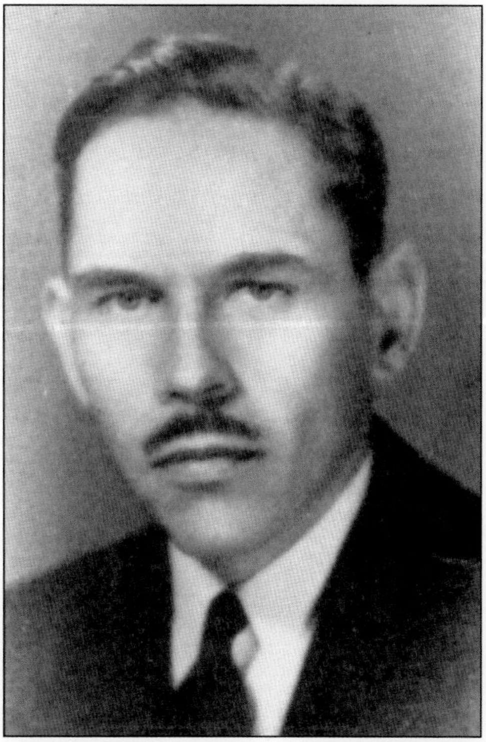

The first village council meeting was held on August 19, 1893. Election results for village officials were certified, and new officials were sworn in. Beginning with D. J. Smith as the first mayor continuing to Joe Roetting, current mayor, there have been 23 different mayors. Mayor Carson Hoy (pictured) served from 1928 to 1943, the longest service by any mayor.

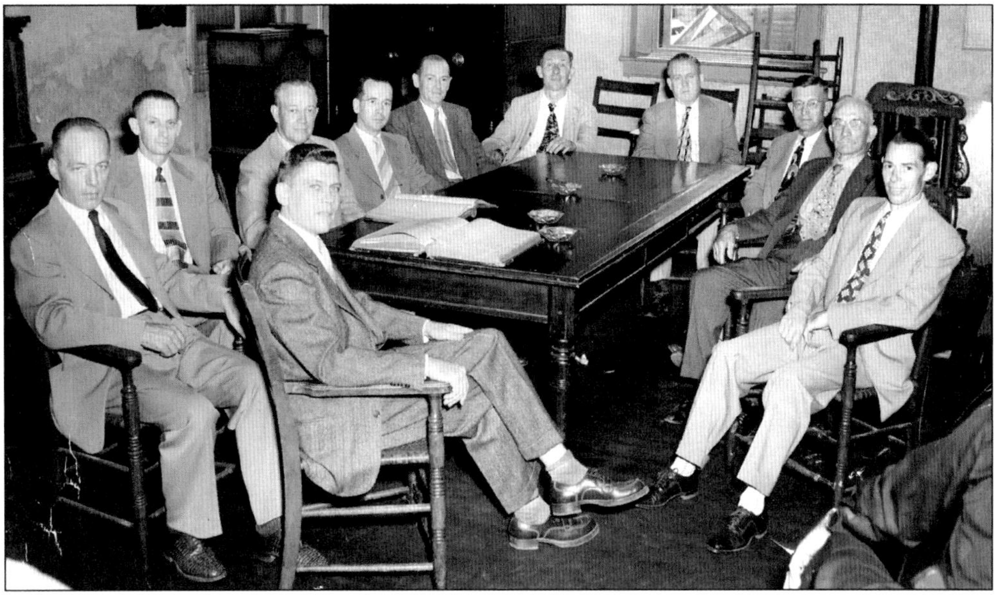

In September 1948, the 1948–1949 Mt. Healthy village officers gathered in the old free meeting house just before the cornerstone laying for the new Mt. Healthy Municipal Building. Walter Korn, mayor, is in the center, and from left to right are Herman Strassel, treasurer; Walter Main, engineer; Edward G. Ruoff, clerk; Carl Ware, councilman; Paris Smith, councilman; John Meyer, councilman; Thomas Graham, councilman; Philip Urban, councilman; Edward Jamison, building inspector; and Claude Wright, councilman. Vincent Stehlin, solicitor, was absent.

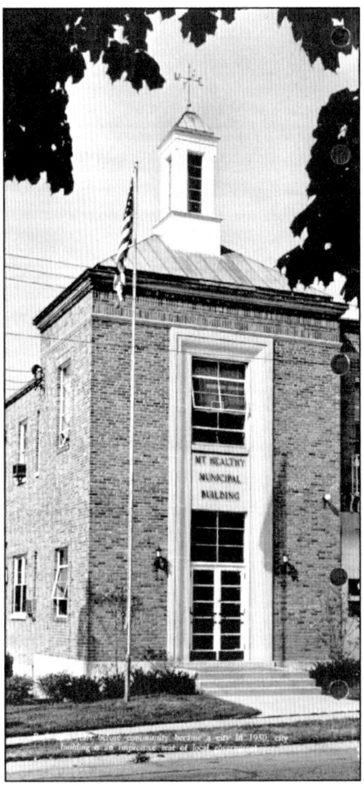

Mt. Healthy has had only two municipal buildings, the Mount Pleasant Union Meeting House that was used for 55 years and the building pictured at left. It was constructed in 1948 and housed all the city service departments. Centrally located at Perry and McMakin Streets, the municipal building is next to the veterans' memorial, the municipal park, and the swimming pool.

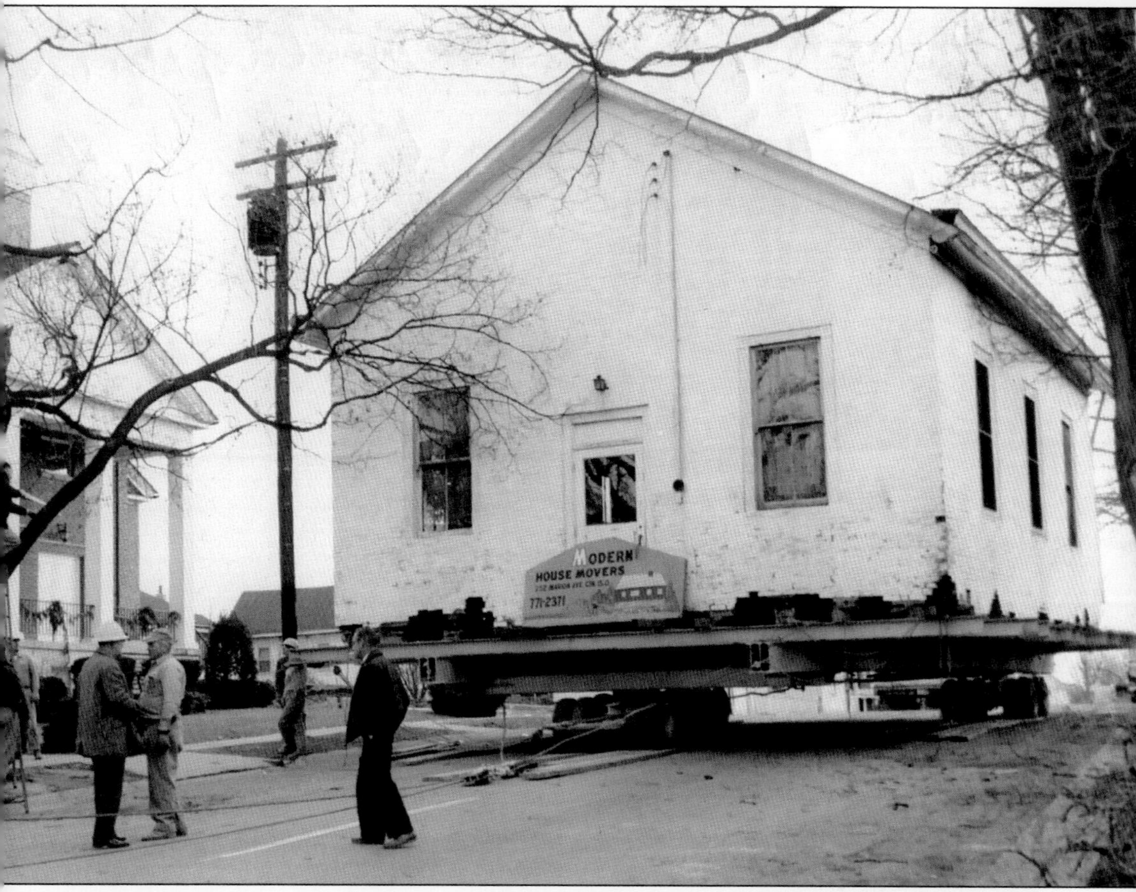

Due to the foresight and efforts of the Meeting House Preservation Committee, today the old meetinghouse is known as the Mt. Healthy Historical Society Museum and is operated by the Mt. Healthy Historical Society. On a cold December 27, 1965, the Mount Pleasant Union Meeting House was moved to its present location facing McMakin Street next to the municipal park. The first stages of the work of moving the estimated 150-ton brick building were completed in the morning. Several hours later, the meetinghouse was headed north on Perry Street. The move cost $6,000, with money contributed by many individuals, businesses, and civic and religious organizations. Preservation committee members included George E. Hunt, Carl Spitzfaden, Wilford Sizelove, Albert Klenk, Frank Stout, Earl W. Muskopf, and Mayor Albert Wolf, with support from many others.

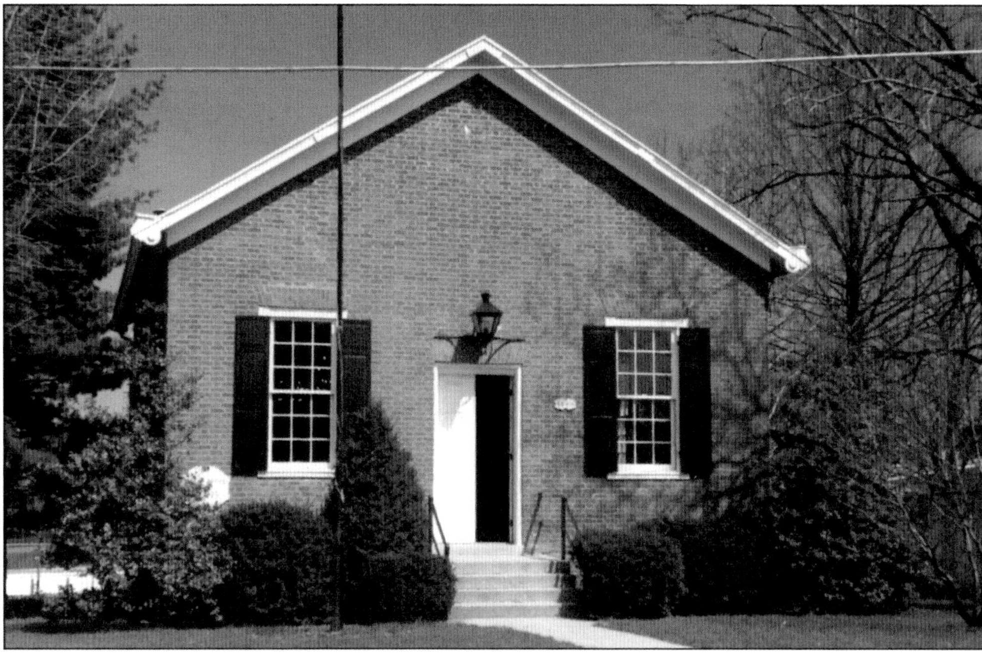

By 1966, the original meetinghouse sported a new basement, roof, and bricks that had been sandblasted clean. Today the museum holds interesting memorabilia from Mt. Healthy's past and has its doors open three days a week to those who seek historical information or a step back into history.

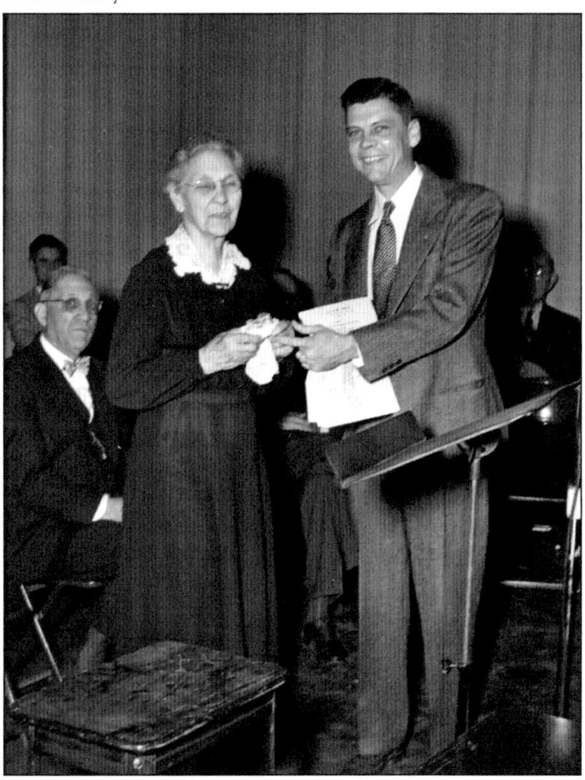

On October 24, 1951, Mt. Healthy celebrated becoming an Ohio city. Festivities included a parade, fireworks, and a special service that was held in the high school at 8:00 p.m. Gold medals were given to former mayor Pete Blum, Mt. Healthy's oldest former official at age 82, and to Harriet Herrier (center), age 90, the oldest resident. Medals were awarded by Walter Korn (right), the first mayor of the City of Mt. Healthy.

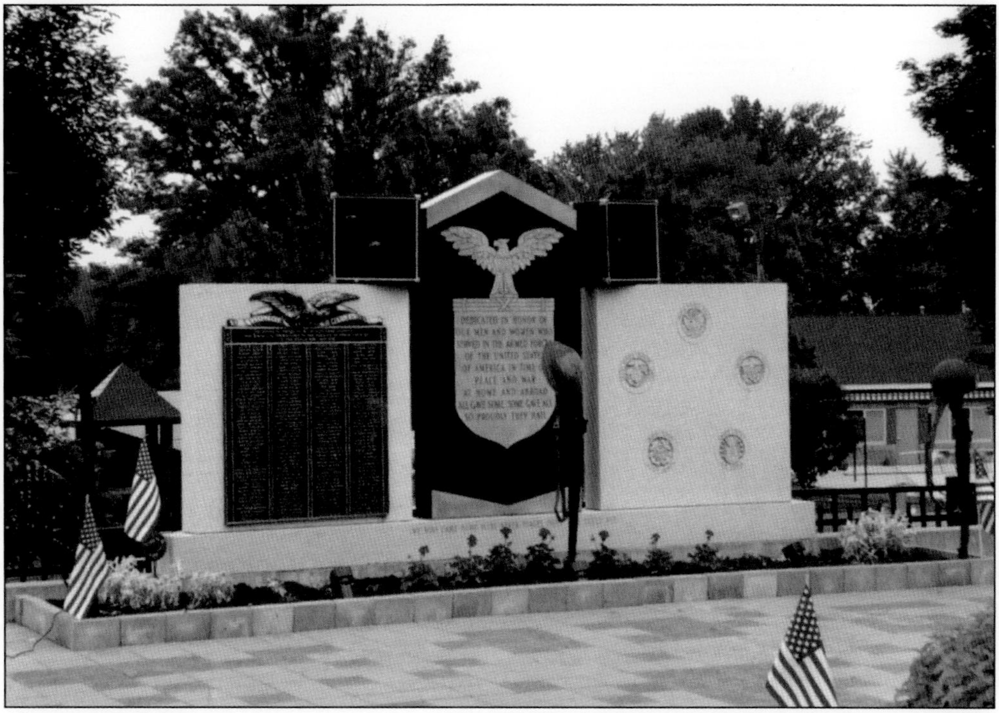

The Mt. Healthy Veterans Memorial was dedicated on May 26, 1997, to honor veterans from every branch of the service. The inscription reads, "Dedicated in honor of our men and women who served in the armed forces of the United States of America in time of peace and war, at home and abroad. All gave some, some gave all, so proudly they hail." (Courtesy of Mt. Healthy Garden Club.)

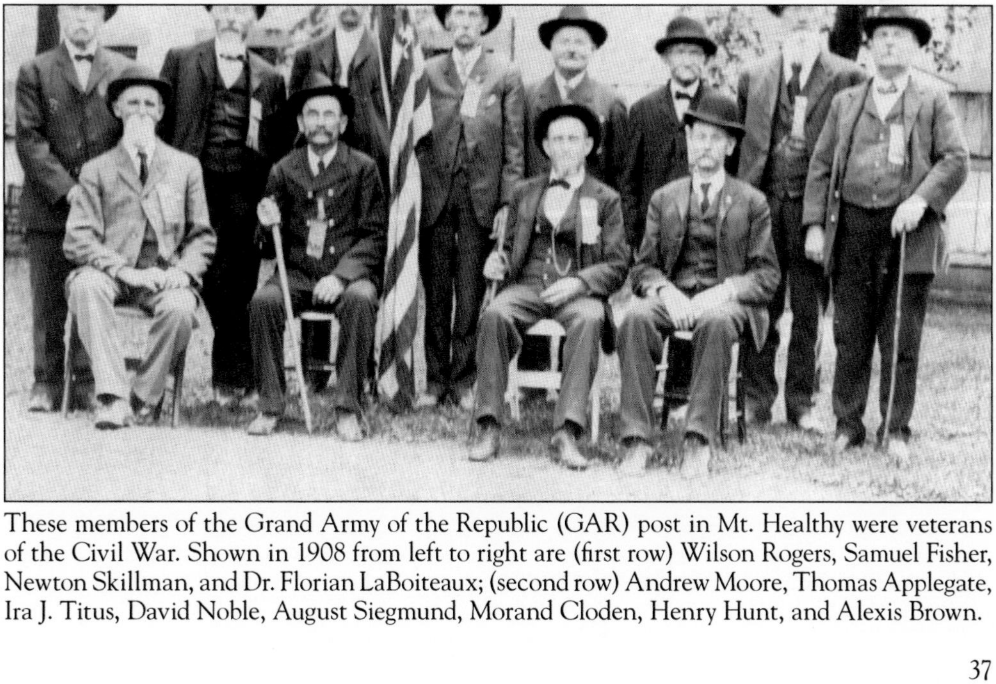

These members of the Grand Army of the Republic (GAR) post in Mt. Healthy were veterans of the Civil War. Shown in 1908 from left to right are (first row) Wilson Rogers, Samuel Fisher, Newton Skillman, and Dr. Florian LaBoiteaux; (second row) Andrew Moore, Thomas Applegate, Ira J. Titus, David Noble, August Siegmund, Morand Cloden, Henry Hunt, and Alexis Brown.

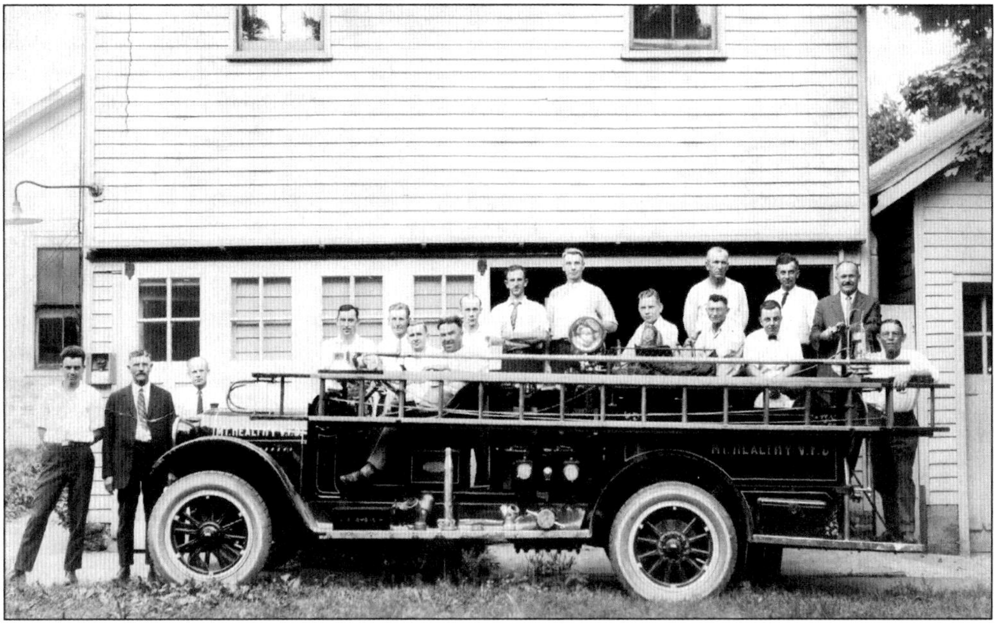

As the village grew, organized fire protection became a priority. A bell system called volunteers to action. The number of rings told volunteers what part of town needed their assistance. In the late 1800s, neighbors used hand pumps and rubber buckets to put out fires. In October 1898, the village council established the first volunteer fire department. In 1925, volunteers gathered around the first motorized pumper.

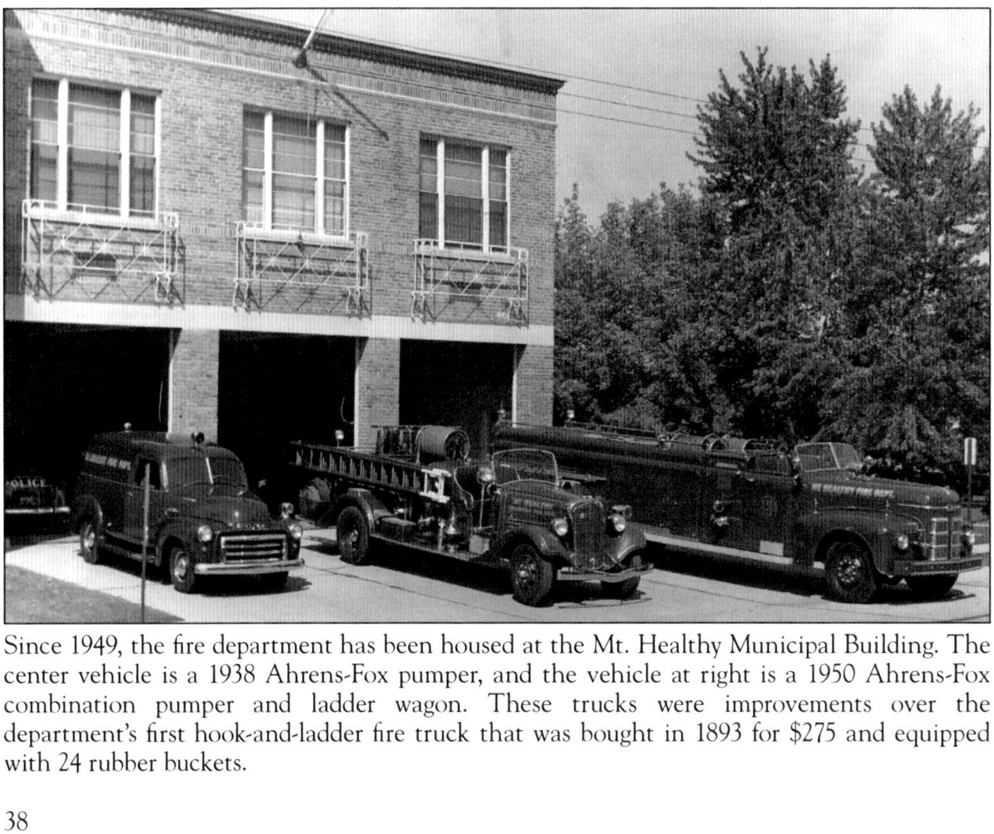

Since 1949, the fire department has been housed at the Mt. Healthy Municipal Building. The center vehicle is a 1938 Ahrens-Fox pumper, and the vehicle at right is a 1950 Ahrens-Fox combination pumper and ladder wagon. These trucks were improvements over the department's first hook-and-ladder fire truck that was bought in 1893 for $275 and equipped with 24 rubber buckets.

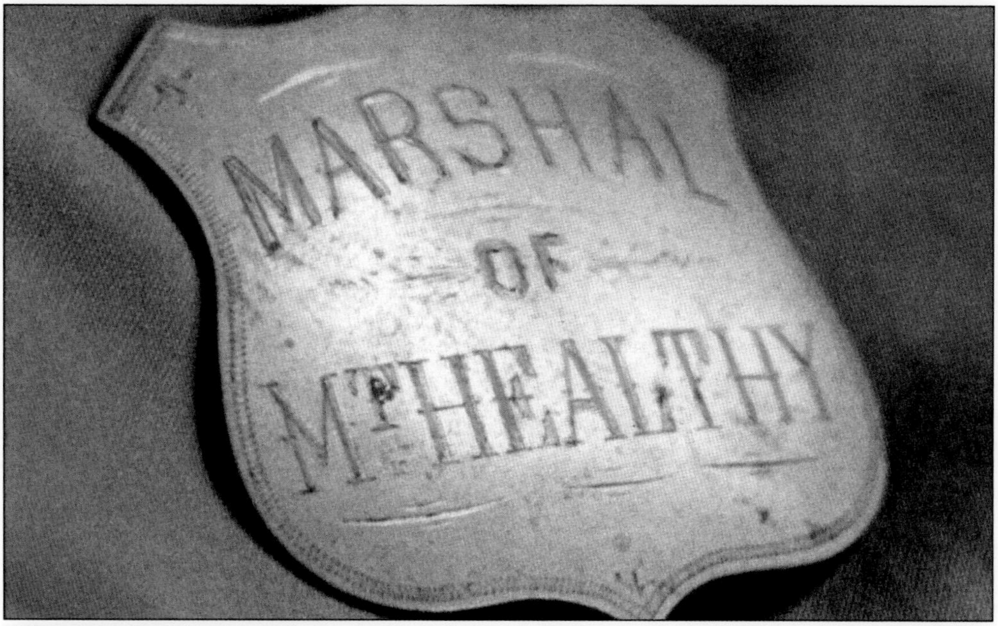

When Mt. Healthy formally became a village in 1893, community officials were elected and sworn into office. At that time, the head of the police department was an elected officer and given the title of marshal. That practice was eliminated in 1940, the title of marshal was dropped, and the department was placed under civil service. The head of the police department was given the title of police chief.

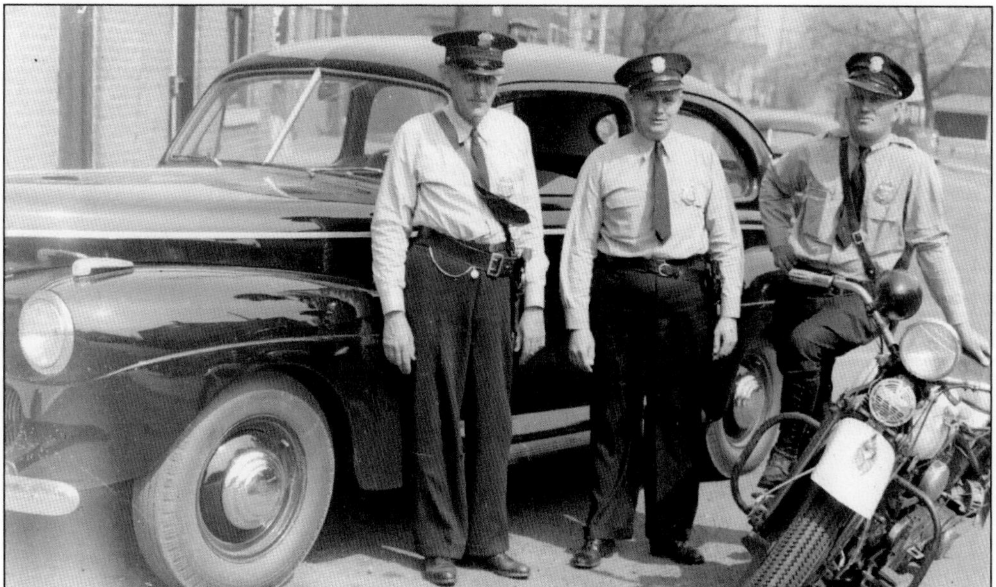

Police chief Henry "Heinie" Wirth was well loved, especially by the children. He was known by one and all as a motorcycle cop whose understanding ways settled many arguments. His diligent enforcement of the law commanded respect. Wirth (right) is leaning on his motorcycle with William Bonapfel (left) and Bill Byrd. Wirth was marshal/police chief from 1926 until his 1943 retirement. (Courtesy of Joy Cumbow Packer.)

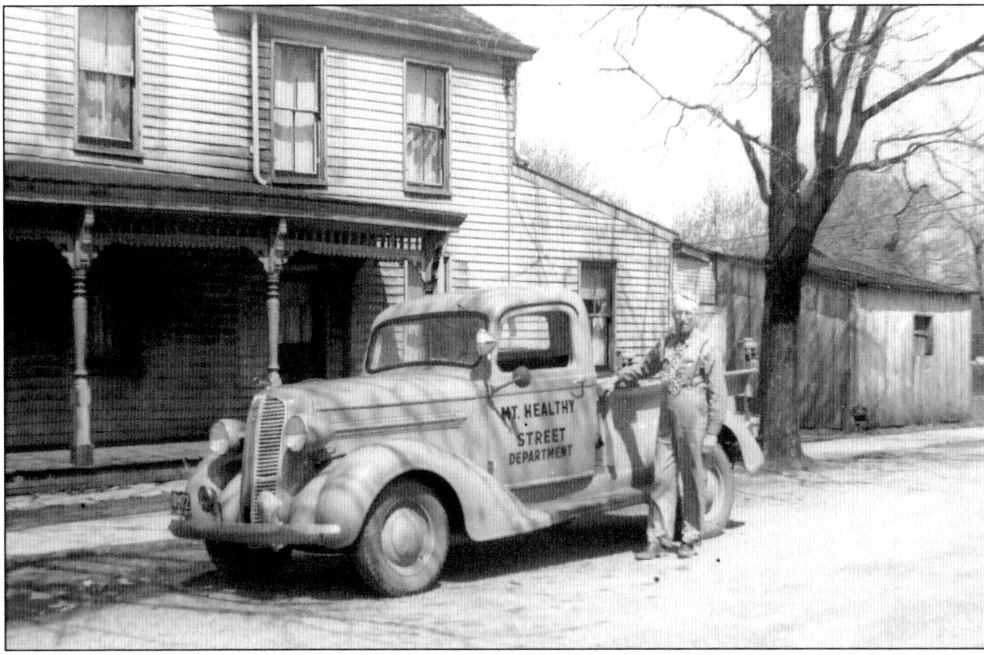

Mt. Healthy has always taken pride in the wide, tree-lined streets of the community. The job of caring for and maintaining them fell to the service director. From 1933 to 1966, Frank Denninger worked hard to keep Mt. Healthy looking beautiful. Here is Denninger posing before his city truck, ready for a day's work.

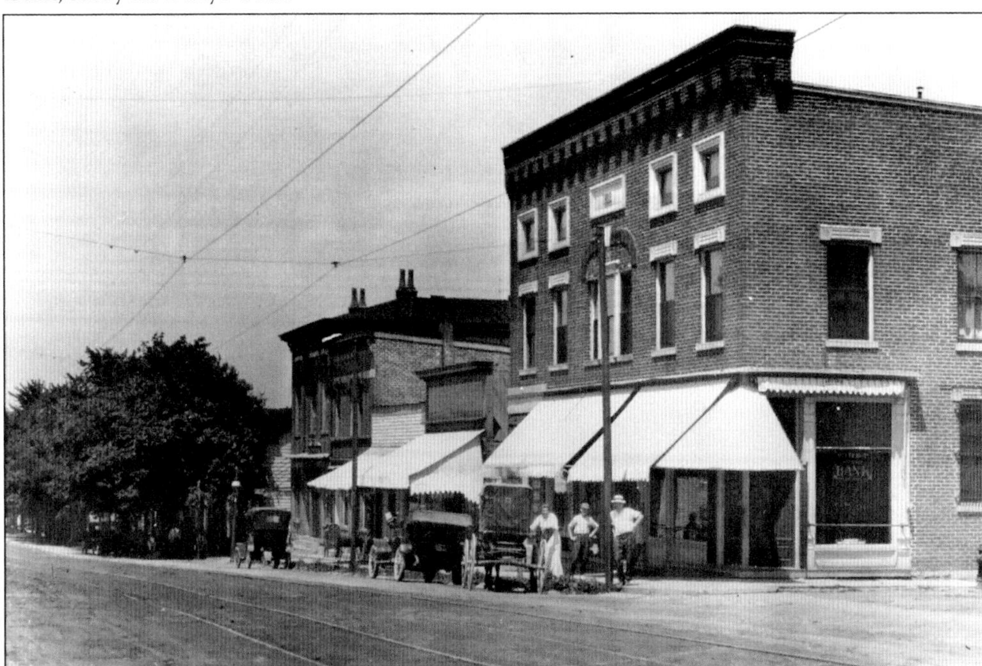

Although defeated in the October 8, 1904, special election, the Mt. Healthy Waterworks was approved in a November 24, 1908, special election four years later, with a vote of 357 for it and 12 against. One of the newly installed fire hydrants is seen to the right.

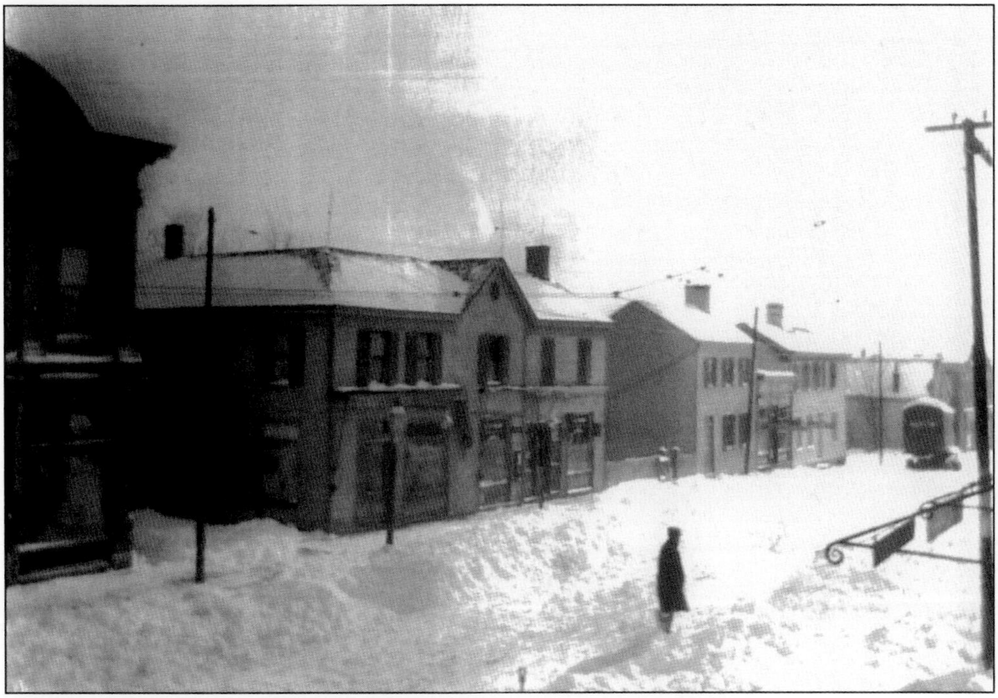

The blizzard of 1917 caused havoc all across the county. Strong winds blew snow across roads and railways, stopped travel, and downed electric lines. It took everyone who was available to clear the streets. Here is the lonely Hamilton Turnpike. Traction cars did not run their routes for a week. (Courtesy of Clayton Coleman.)

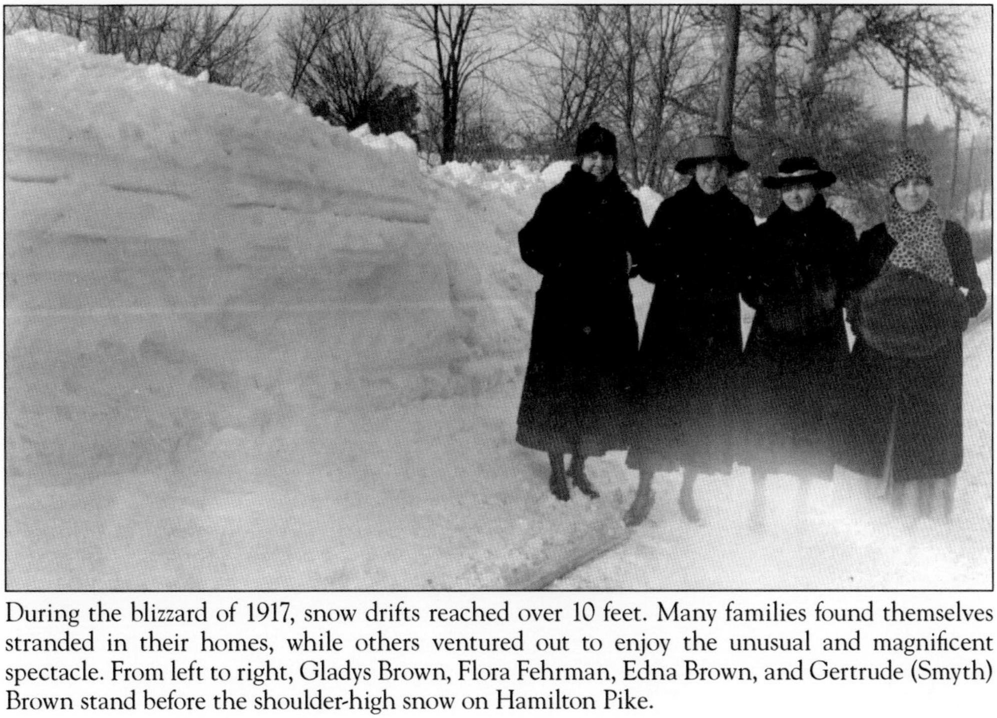

During the blizzard of 1917, snow drifts reached over 10 feet. Many families found themselves stranded in their homes, while others ventured out to enjoy the unusual and magnificent spectacle. From left to right, Gladys Brown, Flora Fehrman, Edna Brown, and Gertrude (Smyth) Brown stand before the shoulder-high snow on Hamilton Pike.

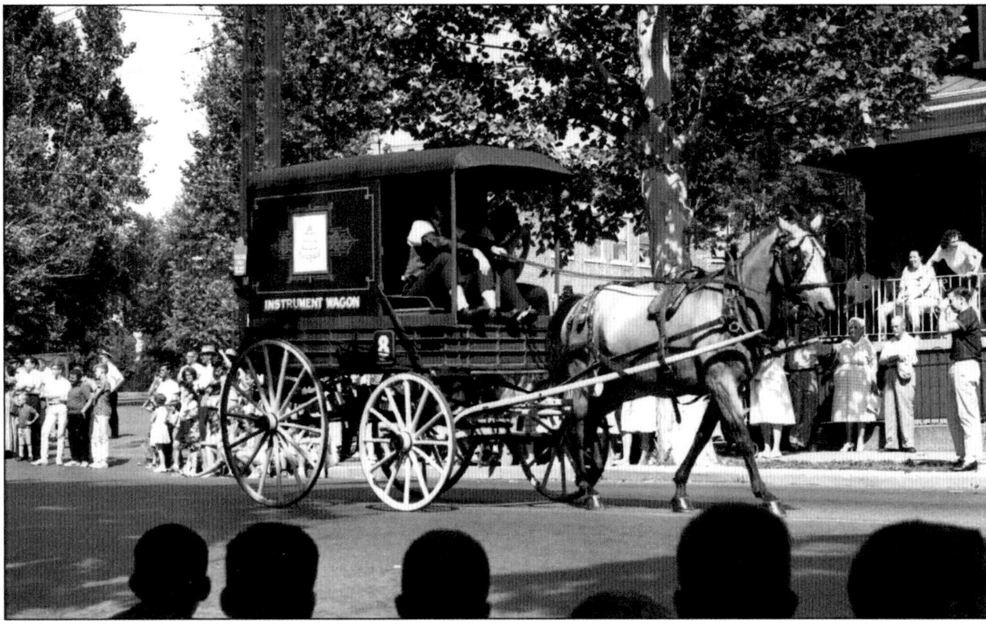

In 1912, after much delay, Mt. Healthy enjoyed full telephone service. The Cincinnati and Suburban Bell Telephone Company supplied both commercial and residential equipment to all its customers. This photograph shows the telephone repairman and his well-stocked carriage. However, the company saw the automobile as a major technological advancement and quickly replaced horses and buggies with automobiles.

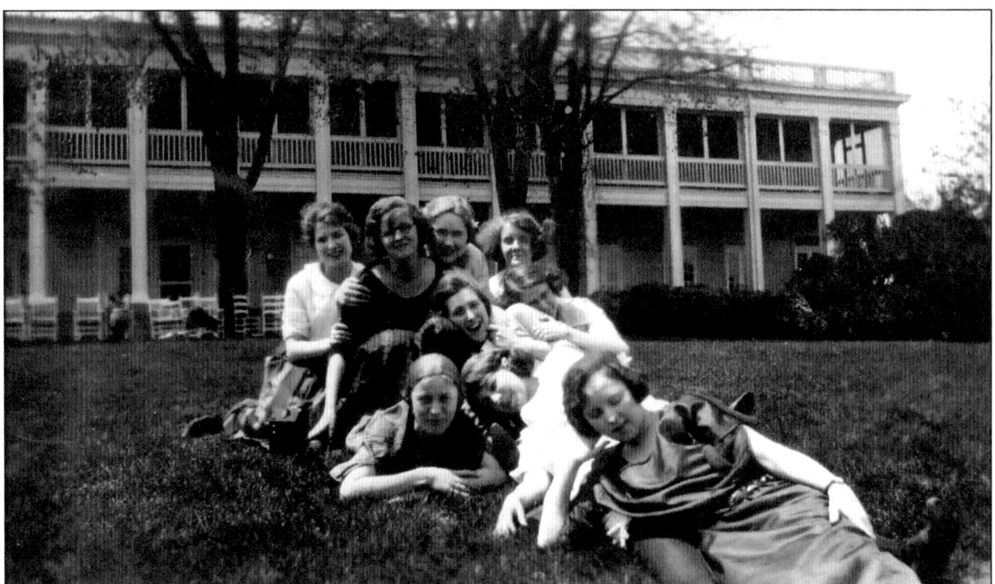

Early telephone service required telephone lines to be manually connected. For this purpose, the Cincinnati and Suburban Bell Telephone Company employed women operators they called "Hello Girls." In 1879, the first Cincinnati telephone directory was published, and the 25 "Hello Girls" recorded 145,000 calls that year. This photograph shows a few of the girls enjoying a respite from their demanding jobs while they vacationed at the company retreat called Hazelhurst.

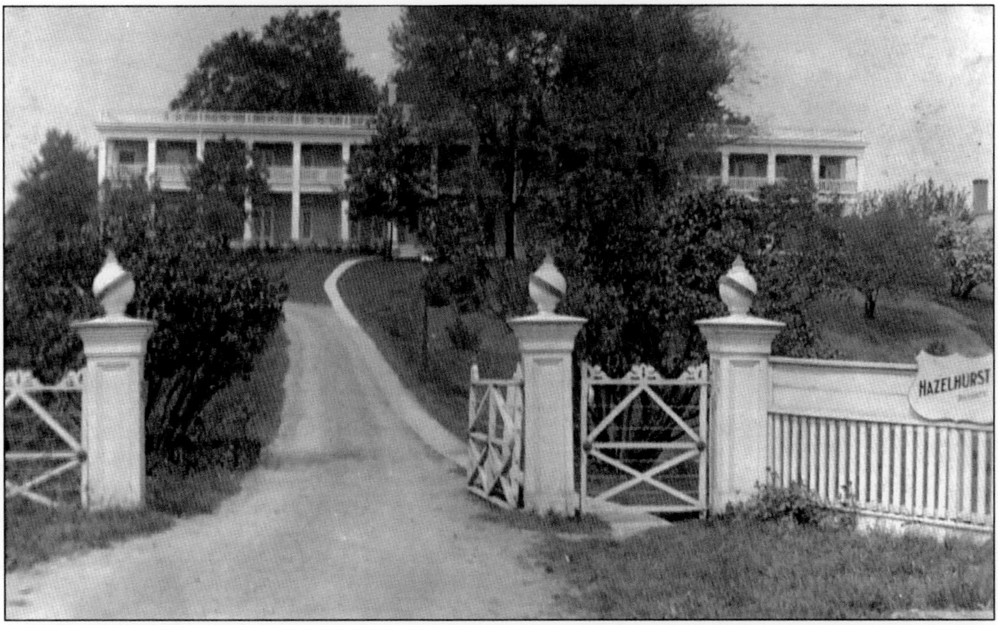

In 1914, the Cincinnati and Suburban Bell Telephone Company offered its female operators the opportunity to vacation at Hazelhurst, the company's estate. The sprawling mansion, located at 7900 Hamilton Avenue, included spacious rooms, a large kitchen, a dining area, and a living room with a stone fireplace. The grounds encompassed an orchard and floral garden. Later a pool and cabana were added. (Courtesy of Penny Huber.)

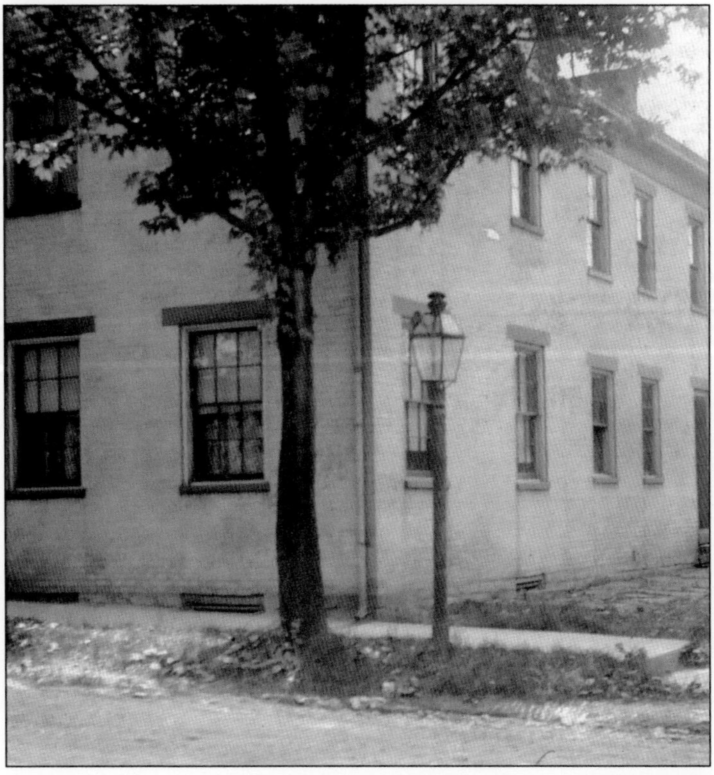

In November 1894, the village council was petitioned by 86 community members to provide "public street lighting." By December 1895, the village installed 100 gasoline streetlamps and cedar posts for $4.50 each. The light committee reported that no other village in Ohio was as well lit. Henry Hunt was the first lamplighter, earning $30 a month. Lamps were not lit during the days immediately before and after a full moon.

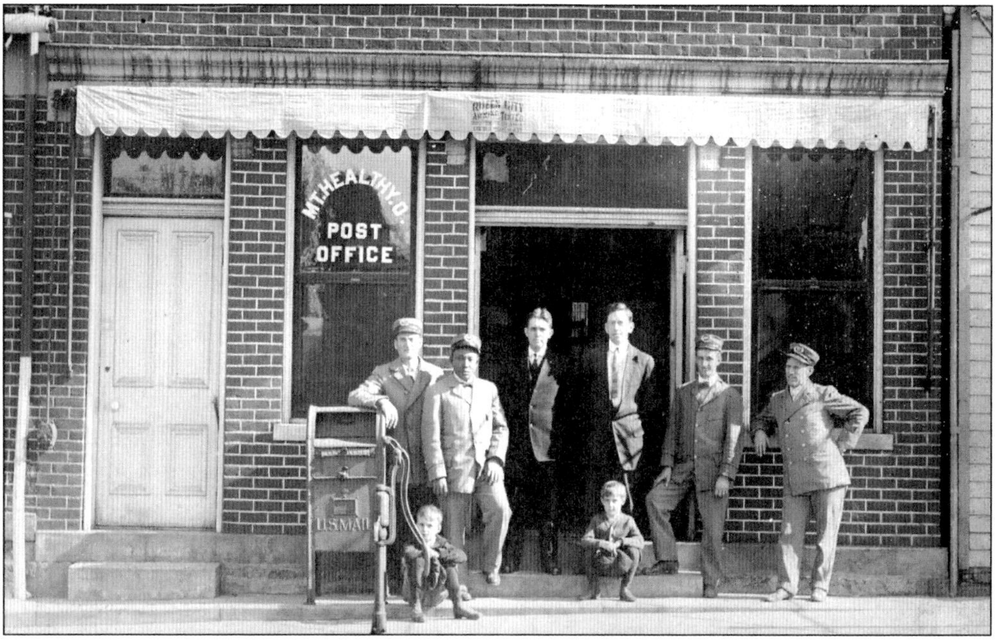

This Mt. Healthy Post Office was located on the east side of Hamilton Avenue. In 1946, the building was painted red and ivory by local painter Otto Steinbrecker. Pictured from left to right are mailmen Paul Bauer, Jim Anderson, and Ralph Ritchey, postmaster Virgil Keeling, and two unidentified men. The children are unidentified.

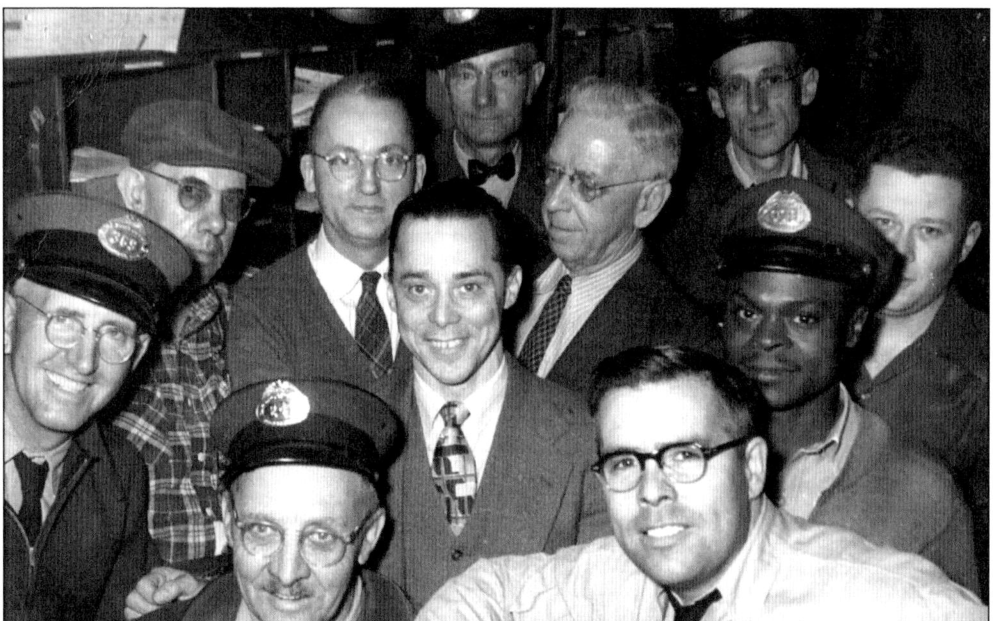

The current post office was built in 1962. It serves Mt. Healthy and surrounding areas in what is now the 45231 zip code. A large staff was required. From left to right are (first row) Paul Bauer and Arnold Schmalz; (second row) Walker Rice, George Carter, and unidentified; (third row) Art Badgley, Ralph Ritchey, Virgil Keeling, and unidentified; (fourth row) Al Blum and unidentified.

Four

SERVING THE COMMUNITY

In the early 1800s, activity in Mount Pleasant made it obvious that the settlement was destined to grow into a thriving community. The early settlers understood that regional roads must be built and kept repaired if a community was to grow. In that spirit, a toll system was constructed to pay for maintenance of the Hamilton Turnpike, the main street through the village that connected Fort Washington (Cincinnati) to Fort Hamilton (Hamilton). As roads improved, traffic between these two cities increased and commerce thrived. During the two-day trip, travelers stopped at Mount Pleasant, the mid-point, for food, lodging, and blacksmith services. John LaBoiteaux and Samuel Hill's original design for Mount Pleasant had correctly located commercial businesses on Hamilton Turnpike.

Between 1850 and 1940, the principal industry was tailoring, employing one-third of the residents. Small shops were run by German families and mostly located in the southeast corner of town.

After the Civil War, the comfort and speed of rail service made it a popular transportation choice. Goods could be transported efficiently, which gave consumers a wider selection of products. The ease of transportation allowed residents to take jobs in outside communities. Likewise, more people were eager to move to the healthier environment that Mt. Healthy offered. This increase in residents led to further growth of businesses.

By 1920, Mt. Healthy was a busy commercial center, offering all types of merchandise from groceries and clothing to banking and automobile services. People from surrounding areas reported that they shopped in Mt. Healthy for everything they needed. "You could find it all in Mt. Healthy!"

In 1997, the Ronald Reagan Cross County Highway opened with access at south Hamilton Pike. Earlier, Interstate 275, Cincinnati's beltway, opened and provided access from north Hamilton Pike. The availability of automobiles and these expressways made it easy for Mt. Healthy residents to reach jobs, shopping, and friends throughout the Greater Cincinnati area.

This chapter documents the growth of transportation and business from the simplest buggies on the Hamilton Turnpike to the height of activity in the commercial district.

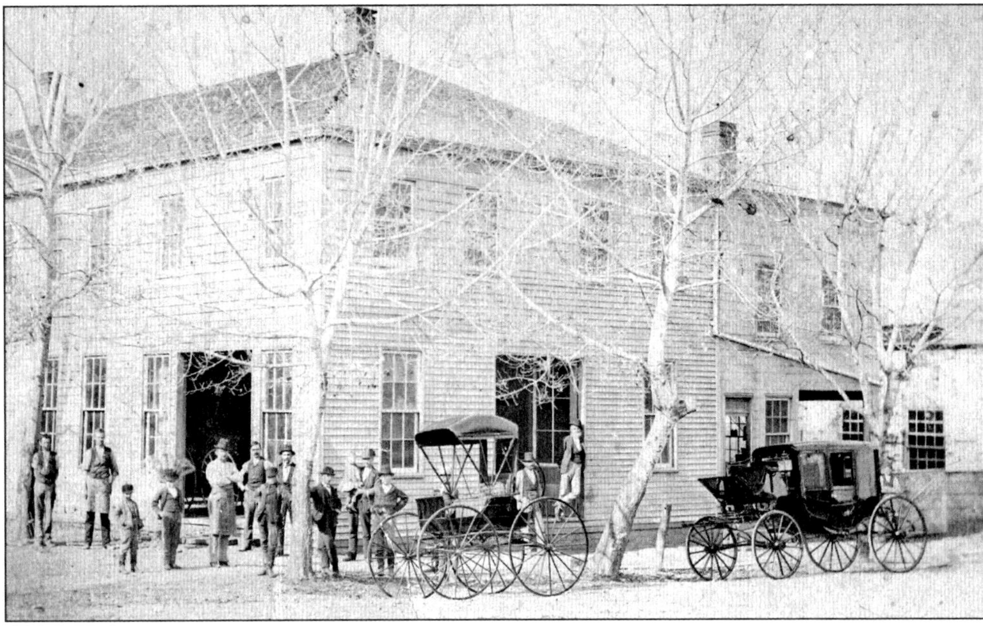

Stagecoach travel in the early 1800s was a dirty, uncomfortable, and slow experience. Because of primitive roads, many stage lines operated only in good weather and in daylight. Mount Pleasant resident George Hunt operated a line that extended from Cincinnati to Fort Hamilton. Keeping buggies and stagecoaches in good repair was the job of the Philip Dom Carriage Shop located at the northwest corner of Hamilton Turnpike and McMakin Street.

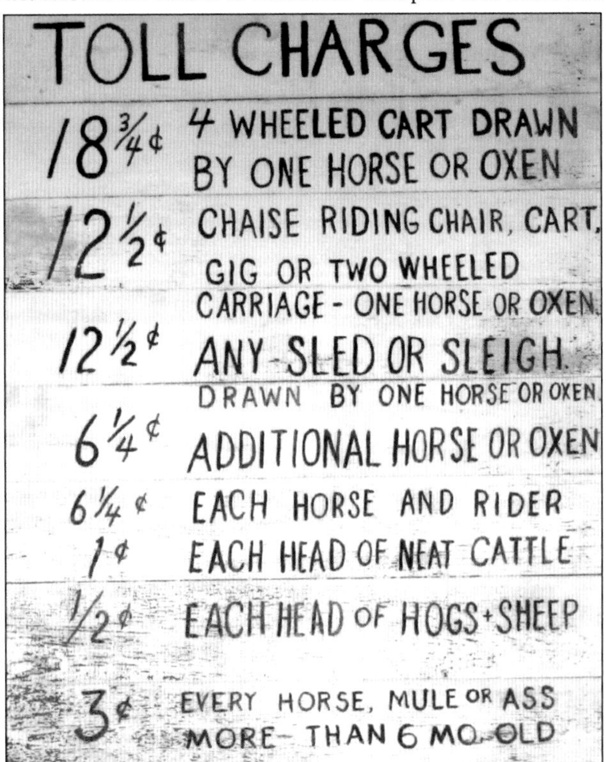

As communities developed, it became urgent for roads to become assessable. In 1803, the Cincinnati and Hamilton Turnpike Company began the construction of a turnpike between Hamilton and Cincinnati. To pay for maintenance of the road, tollgates were erected. The Mount Pleasant toll keeper lived in the tollhouse and collected money from passing vehicles. Tolls were paid based on the size of a load and the number of people in the vehicle.

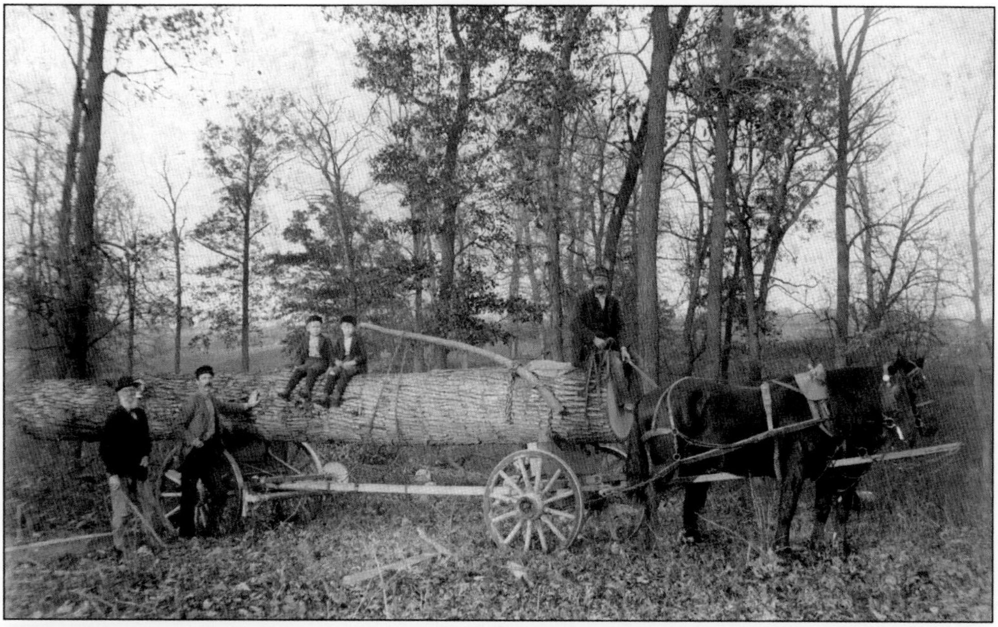

Mount Pleasant's first industry was based around travelers who stopped at local taverns and used the livery stables and blacksmiths. Another principal industry was coopering, or barrel making. Mount Pleasant's forests had large white oak trees that provided excellent wood for barrels, which were used to ship goods. Compton Road was named for cooper Reuben S. Compton, who provided upkeep to the road he used when delivering barrels.

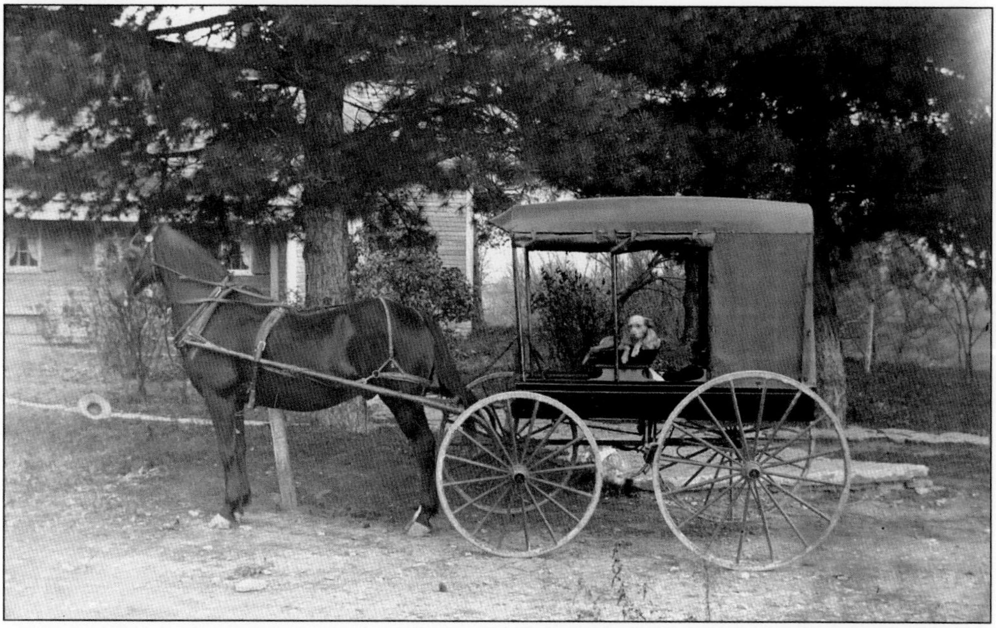

Samuel Hill owned over 800 acres of land in Springfield Township. His family used the spring wagon to navigate the bumpy roads. This versatile wagon used elliptical springs to make the ride more comfortable. It had removable seats and sported smaller front wheels to assist in turning on narrow streets. Fred, the Hill family horse, is shown hitched to the spring wagon waiting to take the Hills into town.

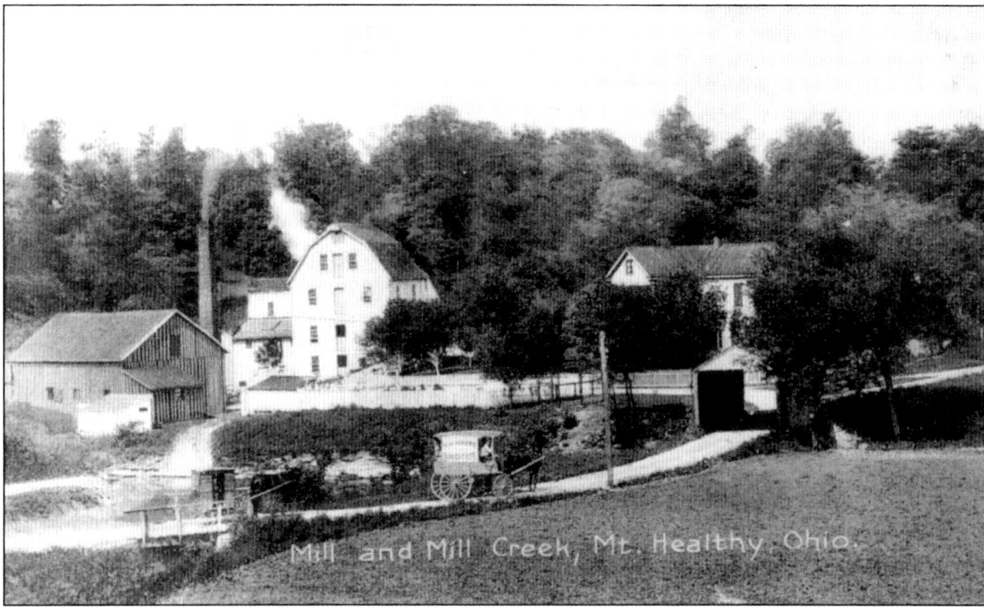

The large four-story building was the Hill sawmill, which was built in 1819 and used for over 100 years. It was originally operated by Jediah Hill and later by Henry Rogers, a son-in-law. In 1887, the mill was sold to Charles Hartman, whose family moved into the mill. When timber became scarce, Hartman began to mill flour. Farmers brought in grain and took home flour. Martin Neese, seen in the buggy (right), is delivering groceries.

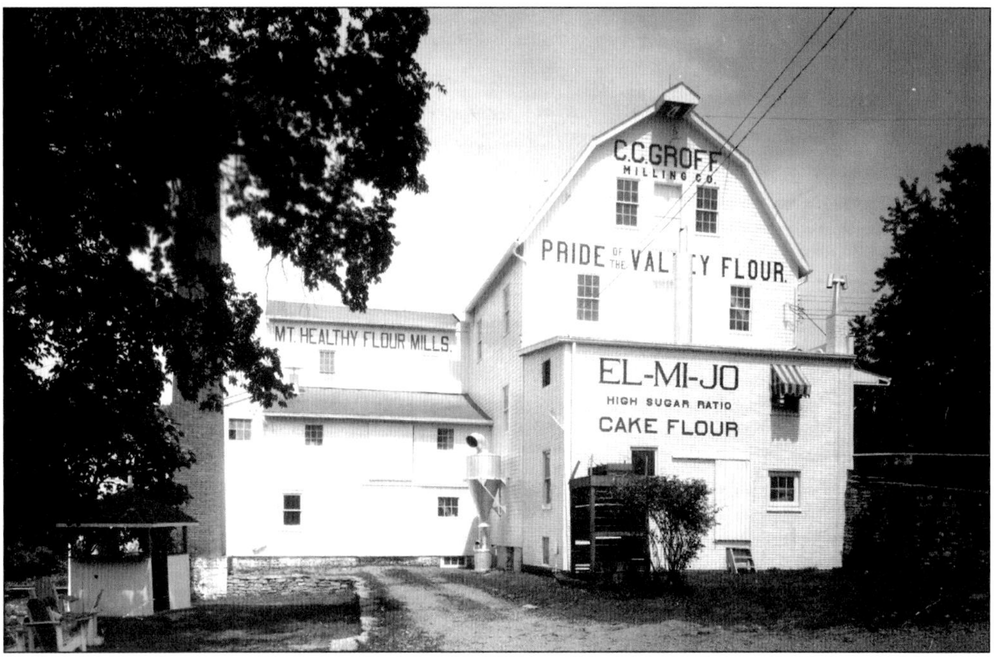

In 1898, Hartman built a home adjoining the mill and modernized the flour mill. He named his flour Pride of the Valley Flour, because the mill sat down in a valley. In 1911, C. C. Groff bought the mill and the Groff family operated it. Later the property was sold and became part of Winton Woods, a Hamilton County Park.

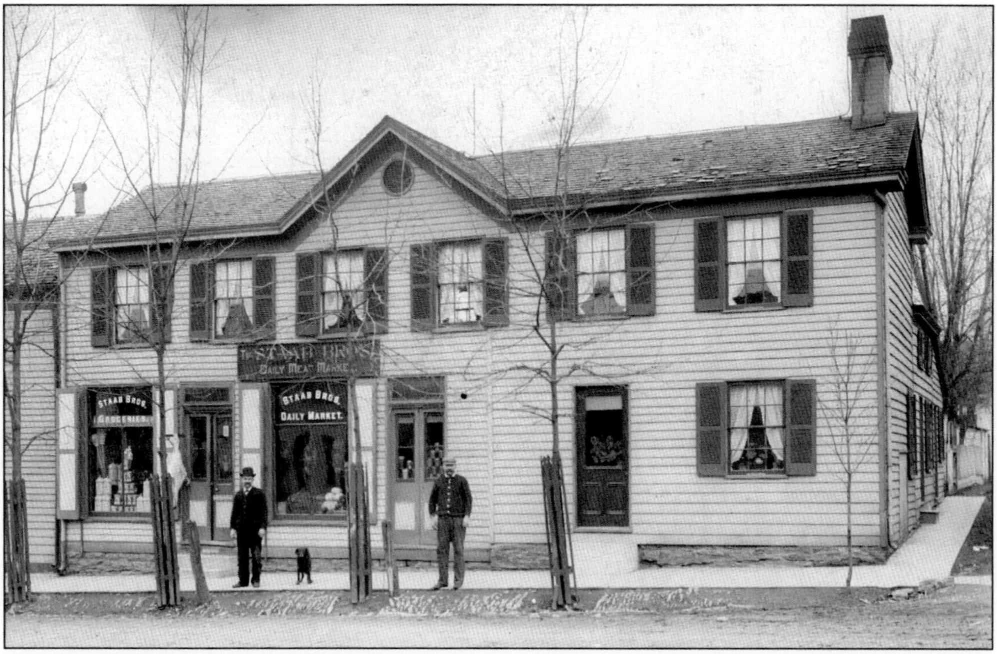

Between 1880 and 1900, the Mt. Healthy business district was centered on two blocks, providing groceries, baked items, meats, dry goods, shoes, hardware, medicines, and liquor. Like German butchers Joe (left) and Pete Staab, most proprietors lived above their stores. Proprietors believed "You can not live too close to your business."

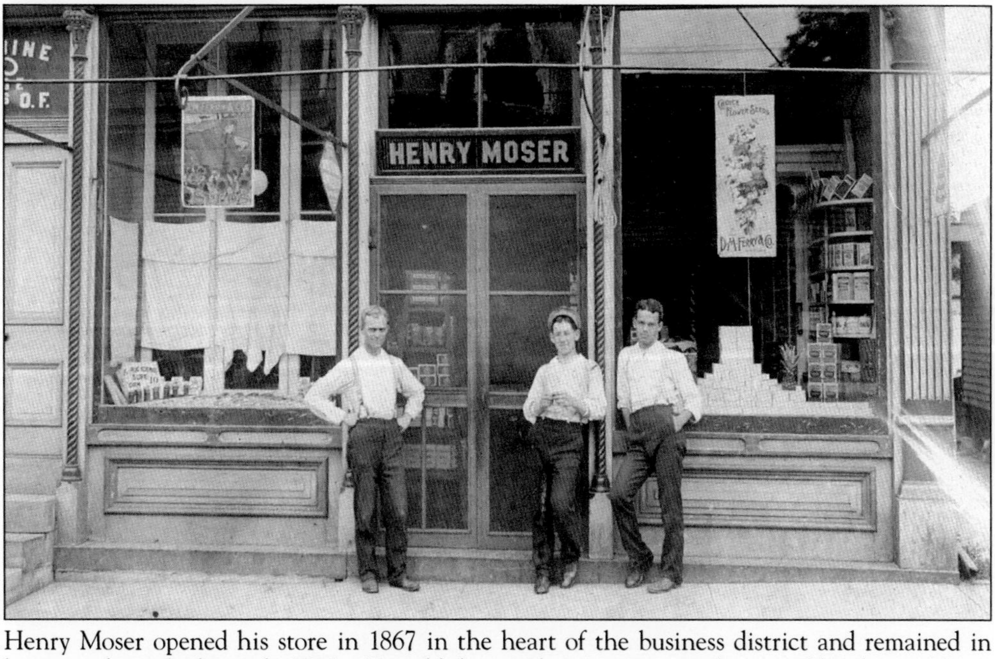

Henry Moser opened his store in 1867 in the heart of the business district and remained in business through the early 1900s. He sold dry goods, groceries, produce, and hardware. Moser built this large brick building in 1879. Over the years, the first floor housed various grocery stores operated by John Hoffner, Moser, Ben Wilger, Multner, and Wullenweber. Here stands George Moser (left), George Earl Hunt (center), and Stuart Moser.

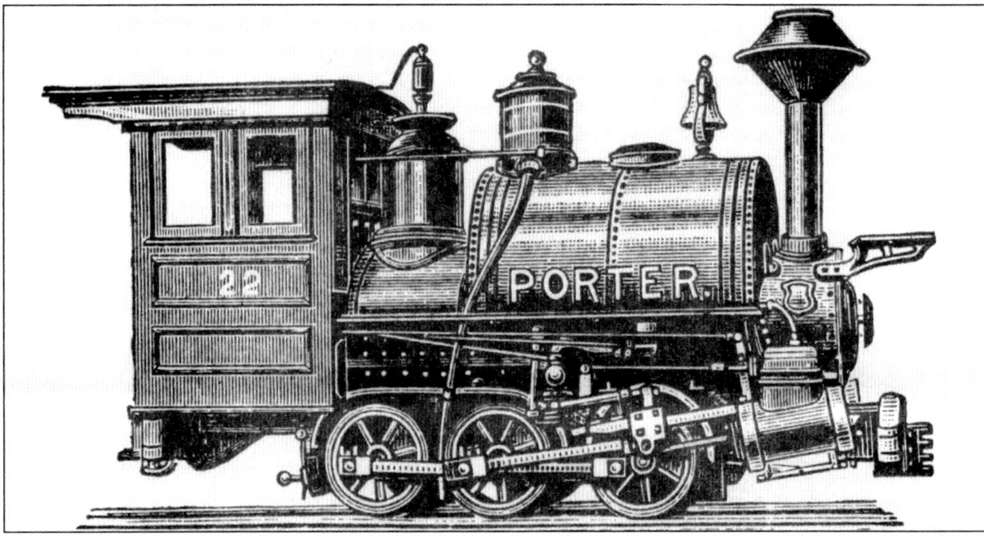

In 1873, businessmen in the neighboring community of College Hill came together to introduce rapid transit to the area. They organized the College Hill Narrow Gauge Railroad Company and in 1877 opened the line to Mt. Healthy. The small six-wheel, dummy-type locomotive enclosed in a horsecarlike body was affectionately called "the dummy line."

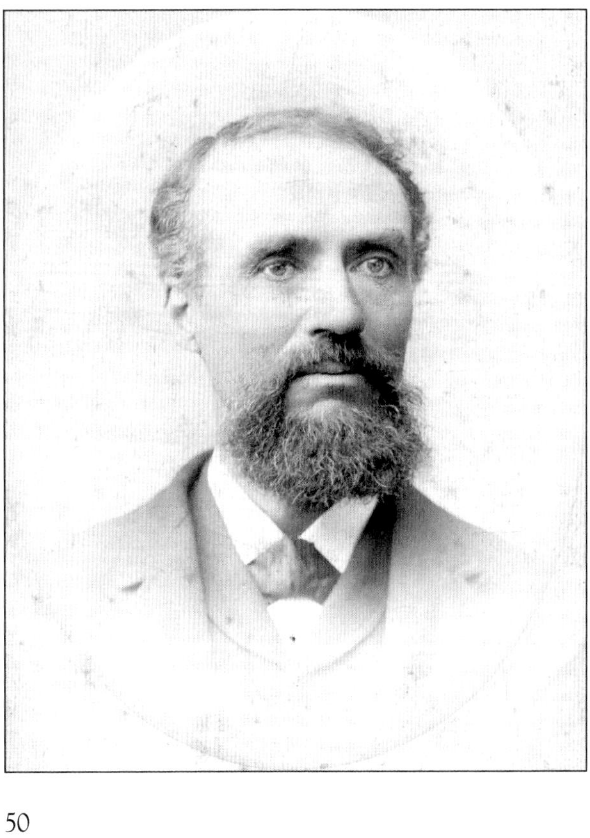

Farmer Cary Benson Johnson, grandson of early landowner Abner Johnson, took an active part in the extension of the College Hill Narrow Gauge Railroad to Mt. Healthy. For this purpose, he gave the right-of-way through a mile of his 226 acres of farmland and $1,000 in cash.

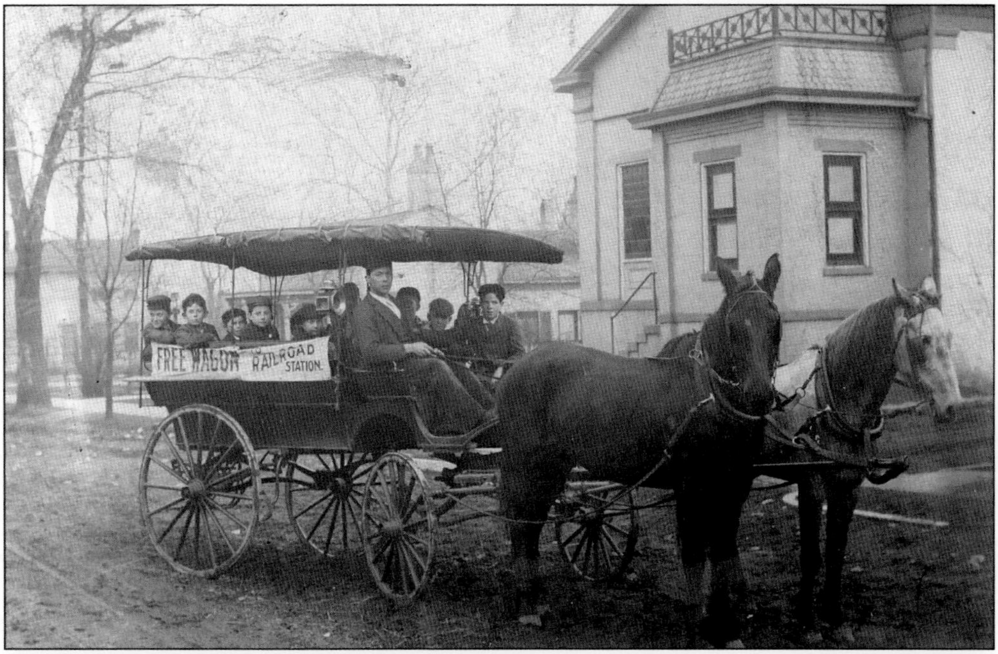

Although the dummy line train was a vast improvement over the horse and buggy, getting to the station was a challenge. To alleviate the problem, a jitney was instituted that took passengers from the center of town to the Compton Road train station. Shown here is the jitney in front of the United Brethren Church with passengers ready to be transported.

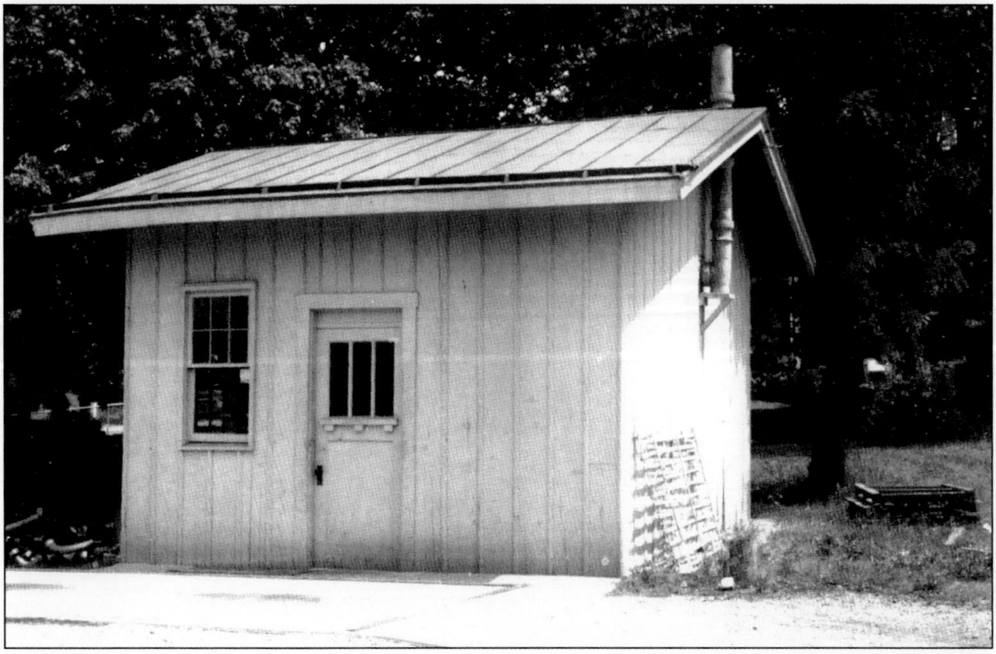

While waiting for the train to arrive, passengers of the dummy line could find shelter in the wood-framed station house, once located on Compton Road east of Arlington Memorial Gardens. The building gave shelter from inclement weather and sported a potbellied stove for warmth on cold winter days. It was very much appreciated by those folks catching the 6:20 a.m. train.

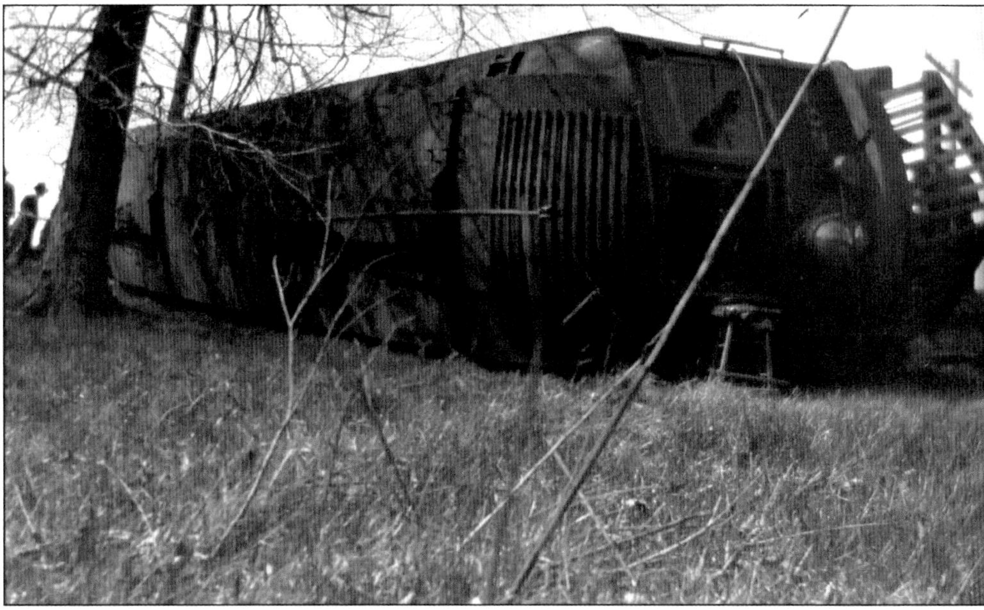

After years of struggle, the College Hill Railroad Company was incorporated into the Cincinnati Northwestern Railroad. The narrow-gauge rail was converted to standard gauge, and service continued to Mt. Healthy. This photograph shows an unfortunate accident that occurred in October 1881 when one of the trains ran off the track and turned over.

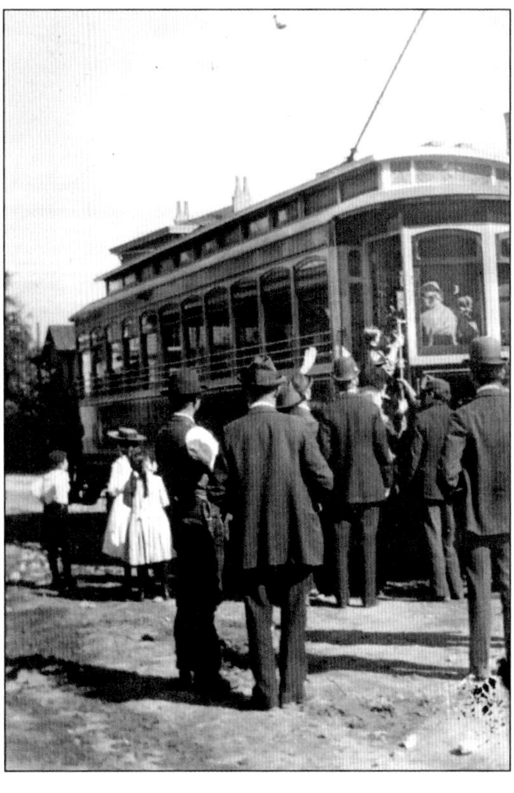

On November 1, 1898, the Cincinnati and Hamilton Electric Railway brought fast, affordable transportation to Mt. Healthy residents. Operating on tracks that followed Route 127 (Hamilton Turnpike), the train took its passengers to College Hill, where they connected to the streetcar for a trip to downtown Cincinnati. Eventually tracks were extended and the need to transfer was eliminated.

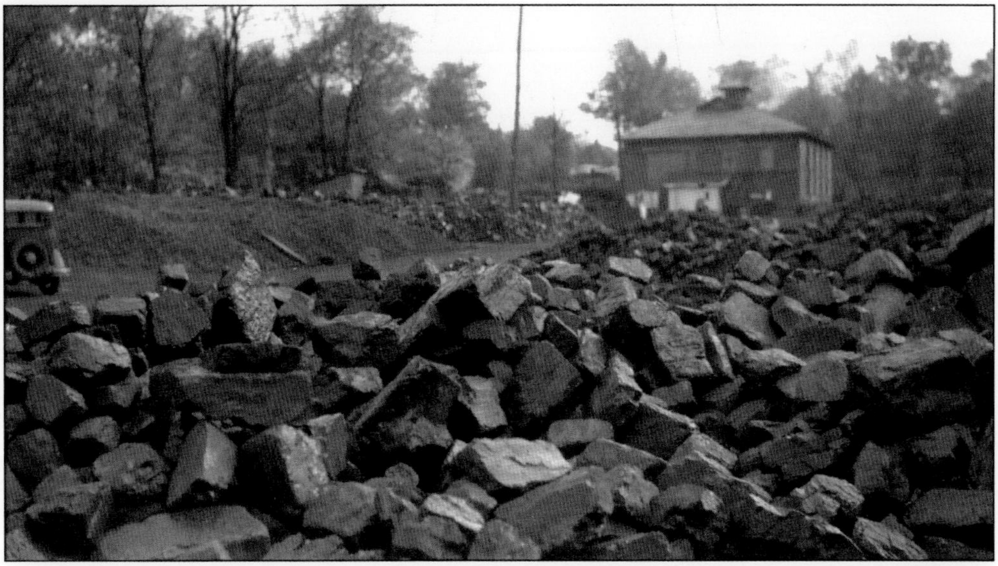

The Mt. Healthy Coal Company moved to the old railroad yard. Proprietor Dave Sunderhaus brought large blocks of Pocahontas smokeless coal to his coal yard over the old tracks. Broken coal was weighed on a large scale next to his office, the former waiting station. The old carbarn (pictured) is where train cars had been stored and repaired. (Courtesy of the Sunderhaus family.)

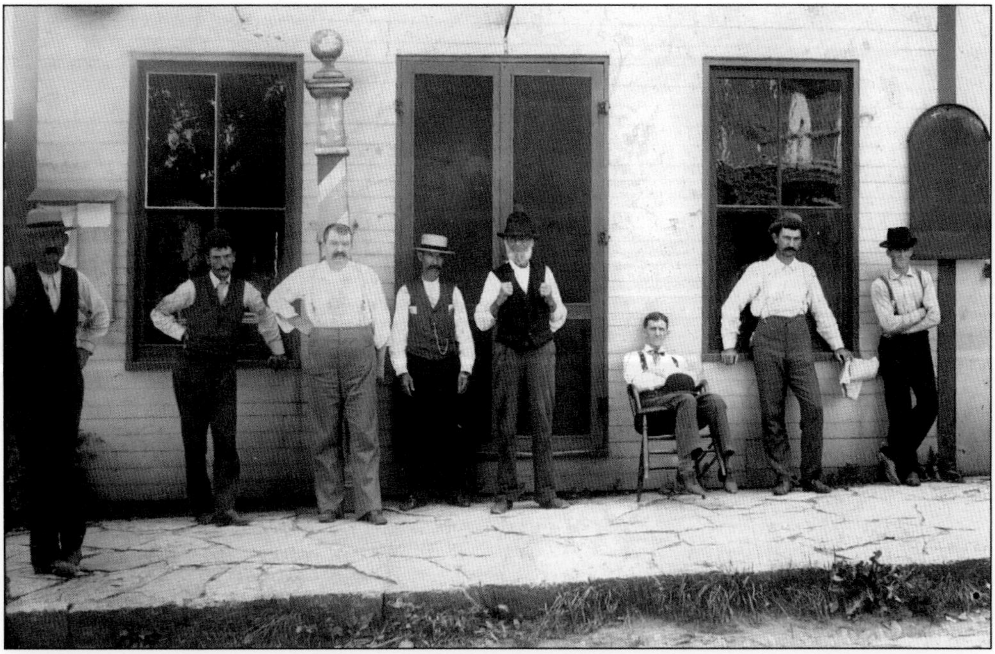

Vierlings's Barber Shop was a gathering spot for Henry Vierling's customers and friends. Pictured from left to right are unidentified, Empson Reeves, Vierling, Harry Slete, Grandpa Dom, Ben Schibi, Harry Sayre, and Ned Roberts. In 1887, Vierling rented space in his barbershop to the Mt. Healthy Savings and Loan for $1.50 a week. Vierling was one of the directors.

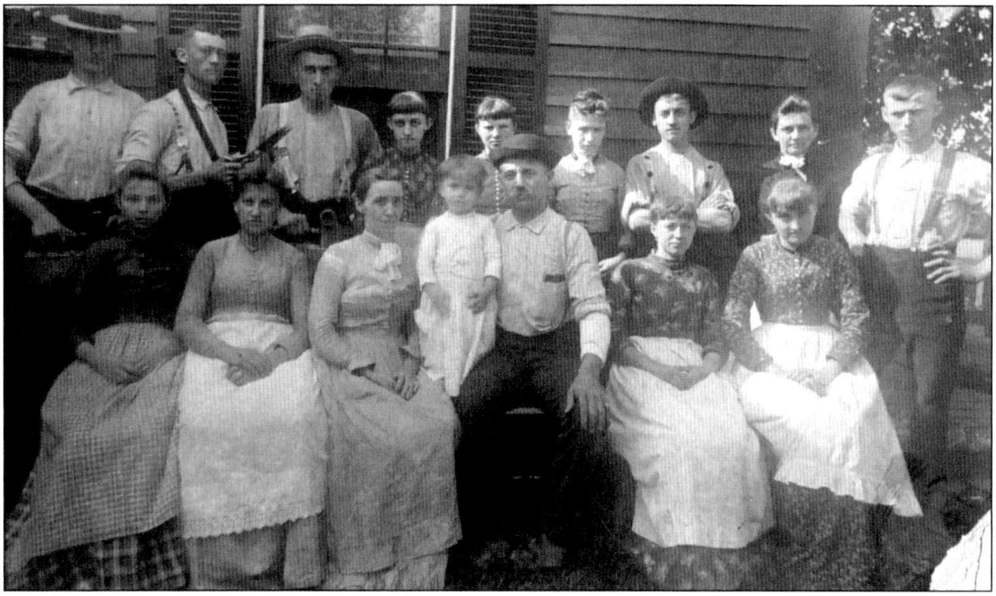

Between 1850 and 1940, tailoring was the principal industry of Mt. Healthy. During the Civil War, local shops made trousers for the Union army soldiers. Between 1880 and the early 1900s, one-third of the town's population worked in the German-dominated tailoring industry. Here in 1888 is Joe Weber's staff. Weber is pictured in the center of the front row. By 1895, Joe Hochscheid (back row, far left) and Dave Korn (back row, second from left) were operating their own shops.

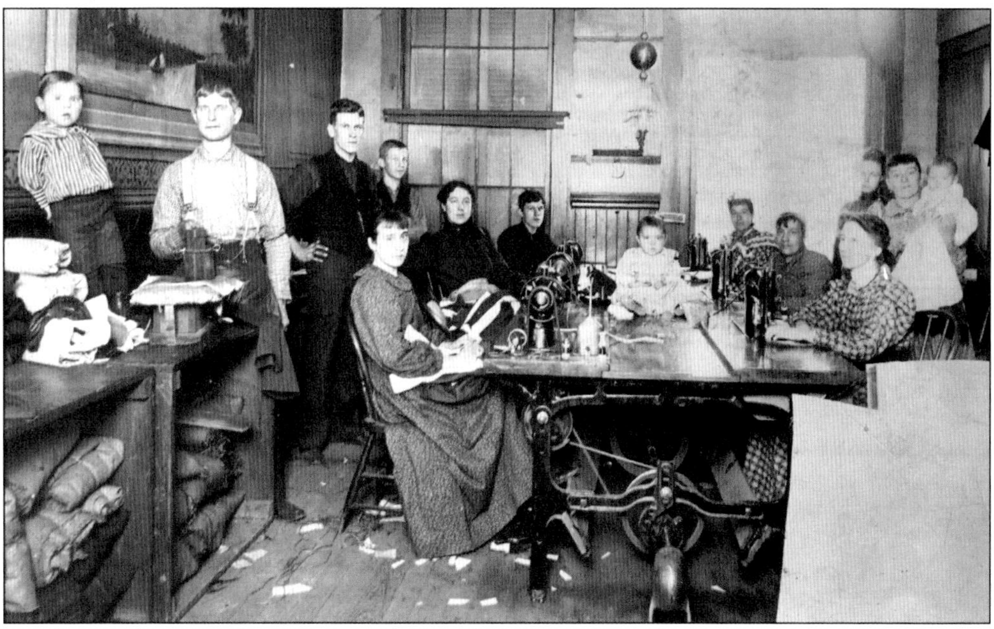

Employees of the Hessler Tailoring Shop included members of both the Hessler and Schmalz families. Fabric for pants was cut in Cincinnati but sewn and finished in Mt. Healthy. Six steam-powered sewing machines were operated at this location. Male employees worked as cutters or pressers. Large 20-pound irons were filled with red-hot charcoal that required great strength to operate.

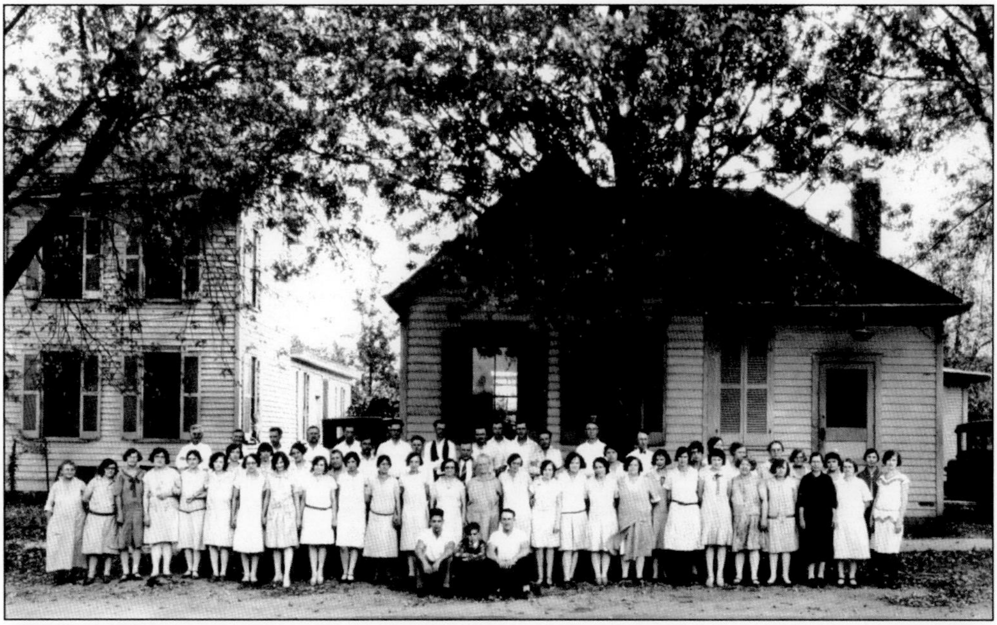

The Hochscheid family business, led by Joe, Al, and then Howard, expanded its tailoring shop, pictured in 1929, to be the largest in Mt. Healthy. Women often finished pants at home. After school, boys delivered partly finished pants to homes by bicycles and then returned finished pants to the shops. It took a seamstress one hour to add lining and buttons. It was all done for 5¢ a pair.

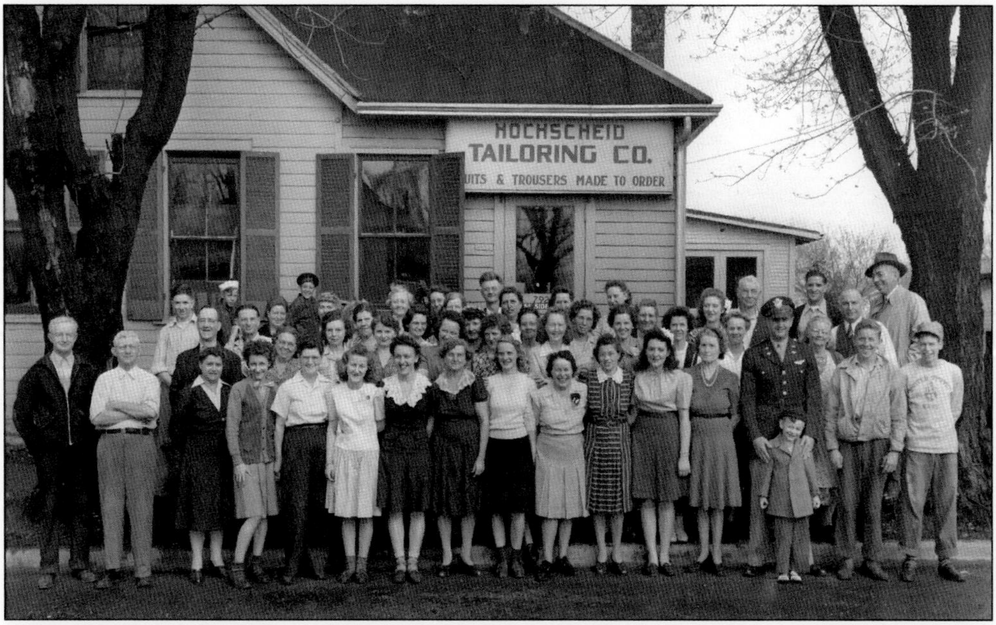

In the 1940s, Mt. Healthy produced one million trousers a year, mainly for large Cincinnati businesses. During World War II, shops such as the Hochscheid Tailoring Company had many women employees. However, centralization of large wholesale manufacturing in Cincinnati soon took over the tailoring business and forced small tailoring shops to close. Only the Hochscheid shop survived.

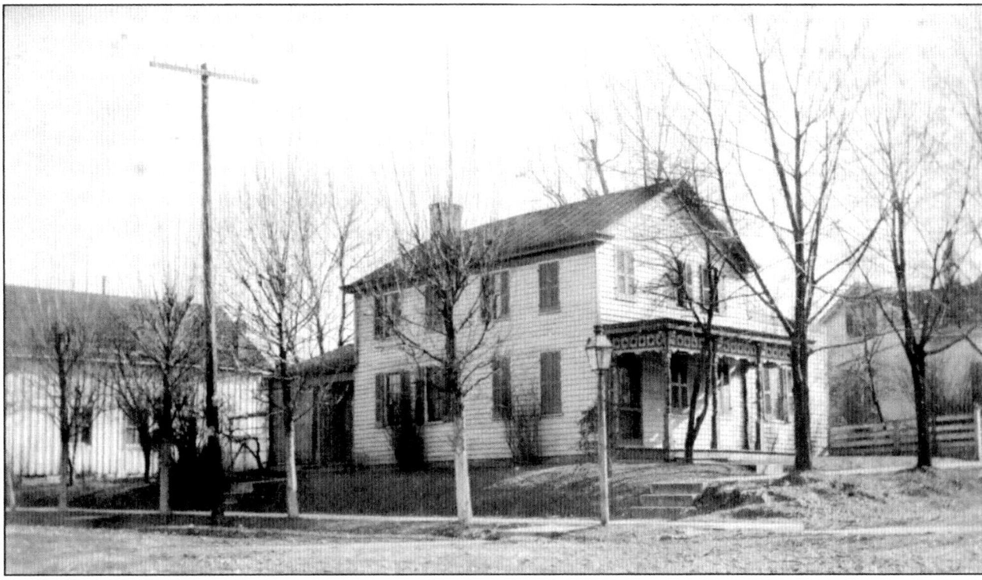

By 1880, Jacob Skillman adapted to the changing times. Skillman converted from operating a livery stable (left) to driving a passenger bus to Cincinnati. The horse-drawn bus left at 8:00 a.m. and returned at 4:00 p.m. It had a glassed-in passenger compartment. Freight was loaded on top. Before 1905, fire equipment had been housed in Skillman's livery stable, and later the stable became the Stag Café.

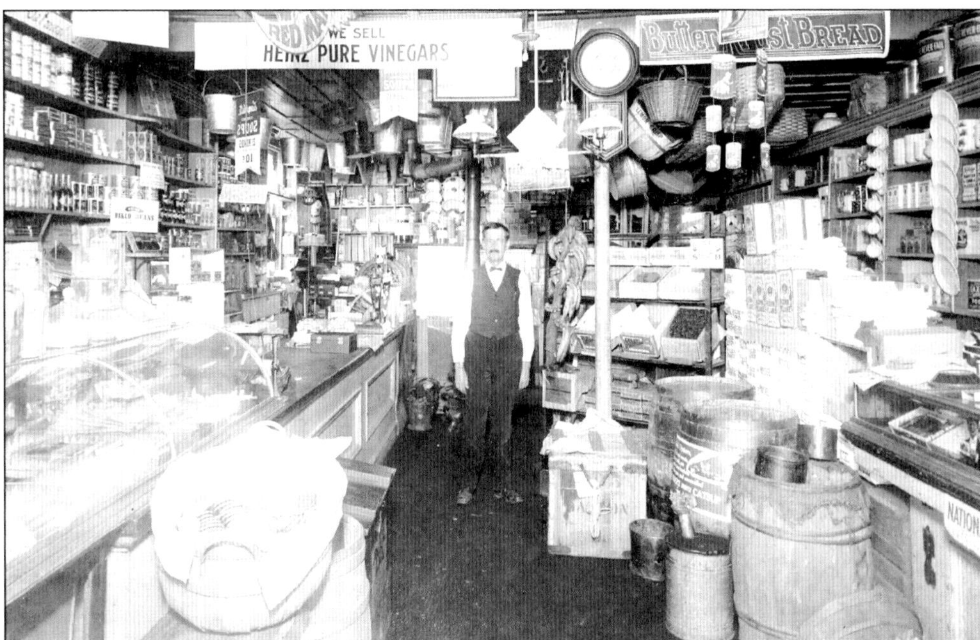

Martin Allison Neese (center) was a typical local success story. He was educated in Mt. Healthy schools then worked as a clerk at Henry Moser's store. He earned $7 a week in 1883 and took most of his wages in merchandise. By 1900, he operated his own grocery store across the street. He offered home delivery in his horse-pulled wagon.

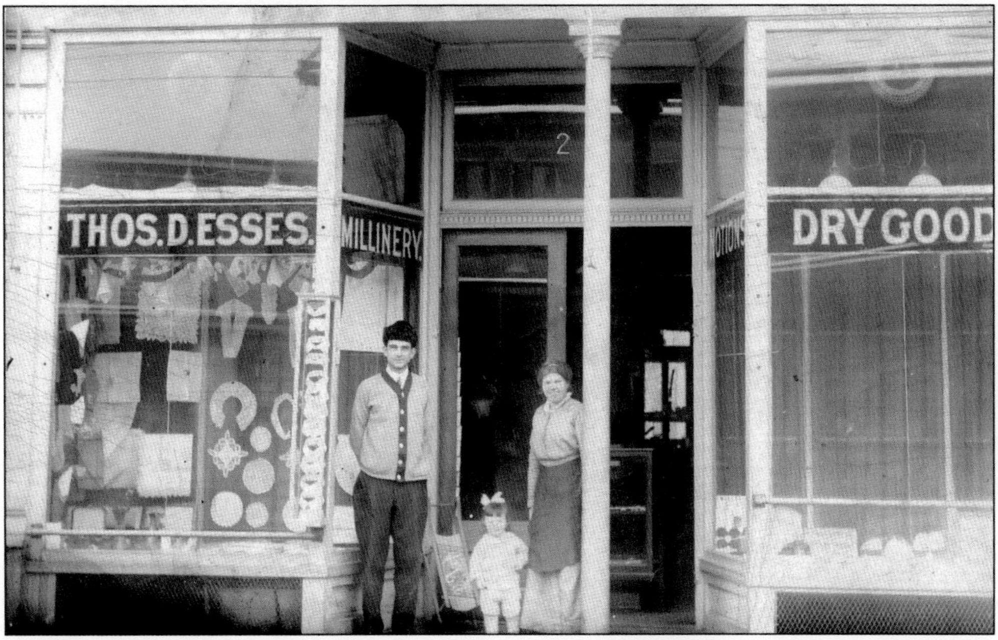

Thomas D. Esses Dry Goods Store was in business at Hamilton Pike and Compton Road over 50 years. Its cabinets and shelves were always full; there even was a back sales room. One could buy household linens, clothing, and supplies for sewing. Pictured are Thomas D. Esses (left), Maude Esses (center), and Gladys Brown.

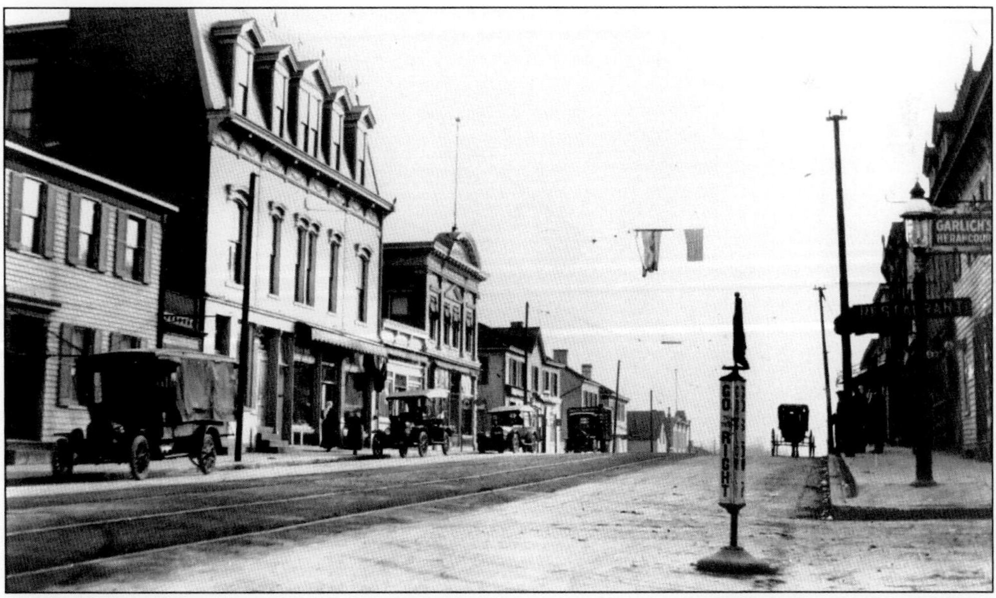

This early-1900s streetscape of the Mt. Healthy business district shows the rapid growth of the community. Gone are the trees that lined the street. In their place are concrete sidewalks and electric poles. The automobile provided efficient transportation, and the trolley lines took residents to jobs in the city. A few families and businesses held on to old-fashioned ways, as shown by the horse and buggy traveling down Hamilton Pike.

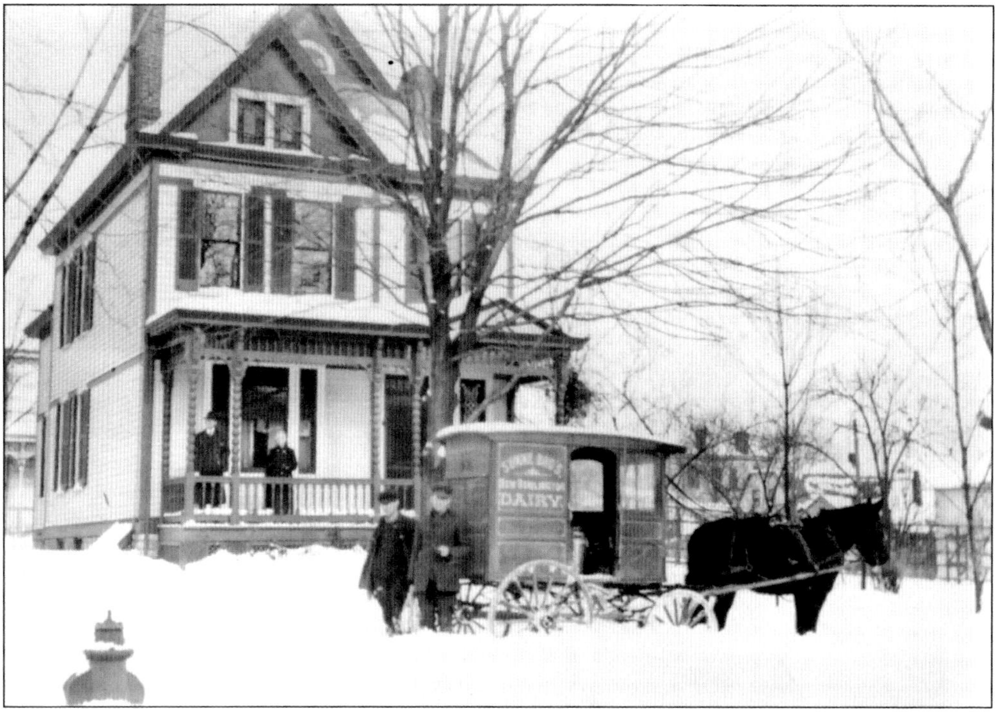

Here is proof the Summe Brothers Dairy was founded in the horse-and-buggy days. This photograph was taken between 1914 and 1917 and shows Carl Summe and probably his brother Harry faithfully delivering milk to the home of Mr. and Mrs. Joe Weber at the northeastern corner of Stevens and Harrison Avenues. (Courtesy of Lori Summe.)

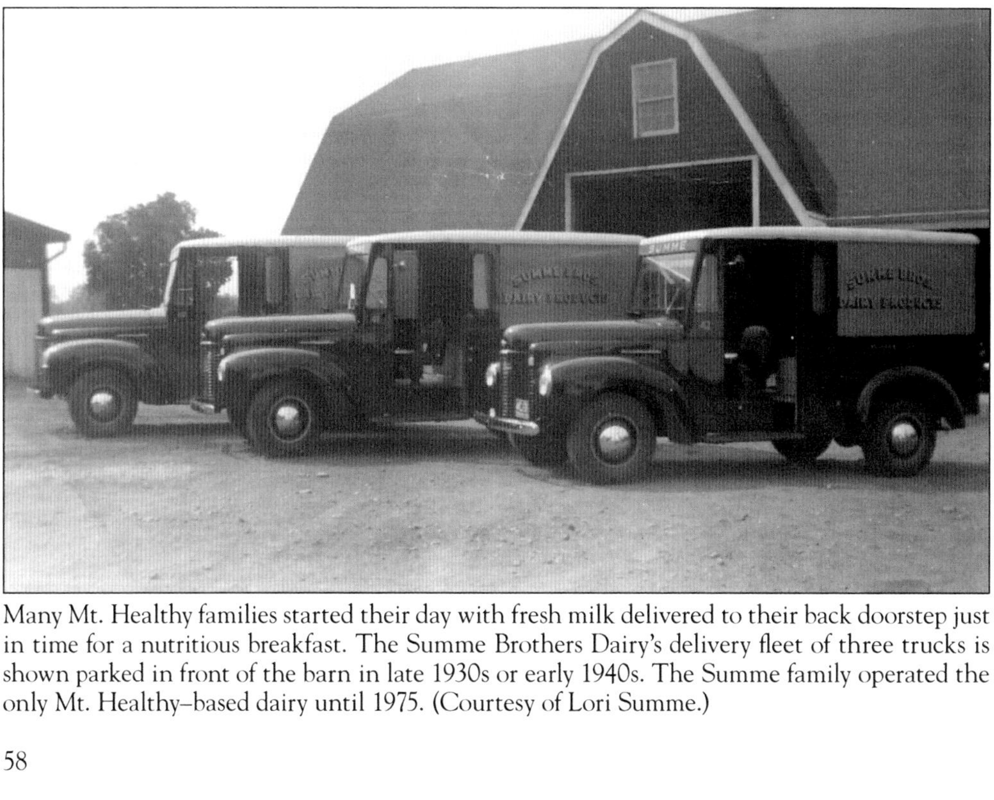

Many Mt. Healthy families started their day with fresh milk delivered to their back doorstep just in time for a nutritious breakfast. The Summe Brothers Dairy's delivery fleet of three trucks is shown parked in front of the barn in late 1930s or early 1940s. The Summe family operated the only Mt. Healthy–based dairy until 1975. (Courtesy of Lori Summe.)

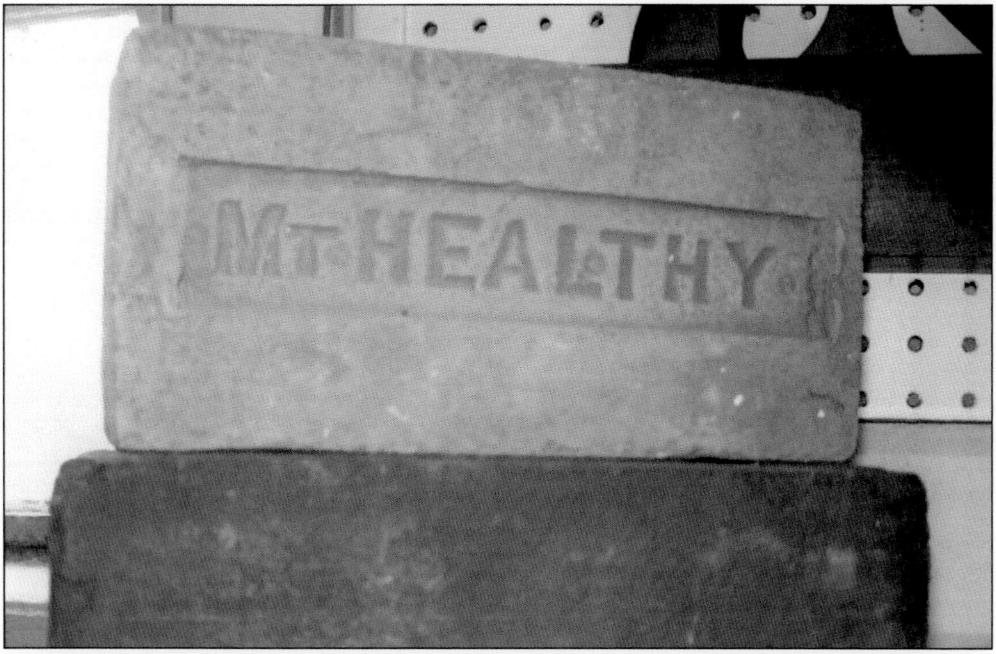

In 1887, the Mt. Healthy Brick Company was opened at the south end of Forest Avenue by Frank X. Roettele and his brothers. Each summer, they manufactured five million of the famous bricks that were stamped "Mt. Healthy." When Roettele died, his brothers raised his 10 children, who were then taken into the business as they grew older.

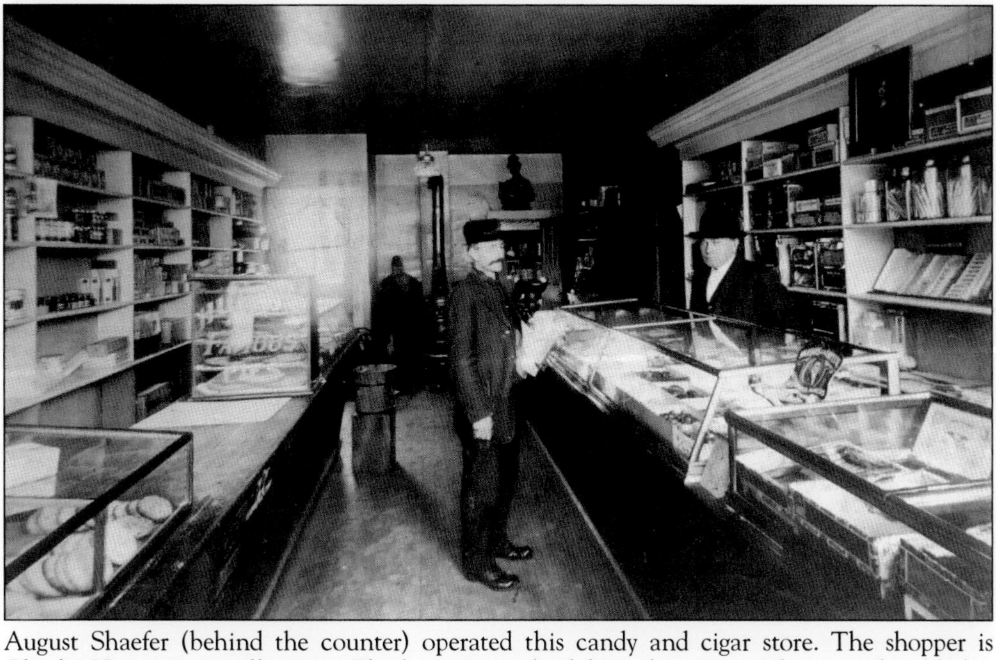

August Shaefer (behind the counter) operated this candy and cigar store. The shopper is Charlie Hartman, a mill owner. The business evolved from this store with its overhead lights and potbellied stove to the Regal Store of the 1940s. Shaefer's residence was next door at the northeast corner of Hamilton Pike and Kinney Avenue. The store and house were joined at the kitchen.

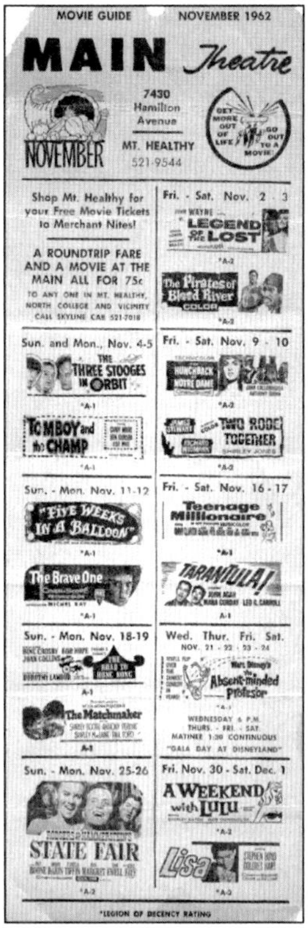

Peter Blum started the Main Theater in 1915, when "talking" movies were new. The Main Theater was the place to be. Every kid in town spent time there. The building had "Main" on the facade and on the entrance floor. Here is the November 1962 movie guide. Most weeks, there was a feature movie, an episode of a serial, a newsreel, and a cartoon.

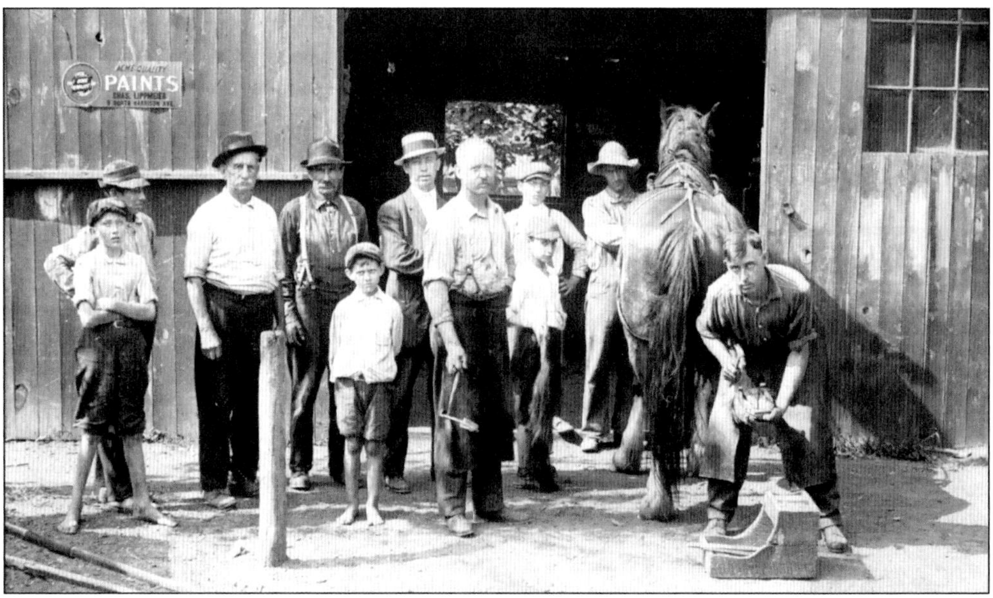

For the first 100 years, Mt. Healthy supported busy blacksmiths who serviced many horses. However, after the 1900s, the use of automobiles and trucks gradually decreased the need for blacksmiths. Here in 1925 near the northwest corner of Hamilton Pike and McMakin Street is Joe Weber's blacksmith shop. From left to right are (first row) Karl W., an unidentified boy, unidentified, an unidentified boy, and an unidentified blacksmith; (second row) Ray W., Rilie Hunt, Joe Enger, Harry Koehler in the straw hat, and two unidentified men.

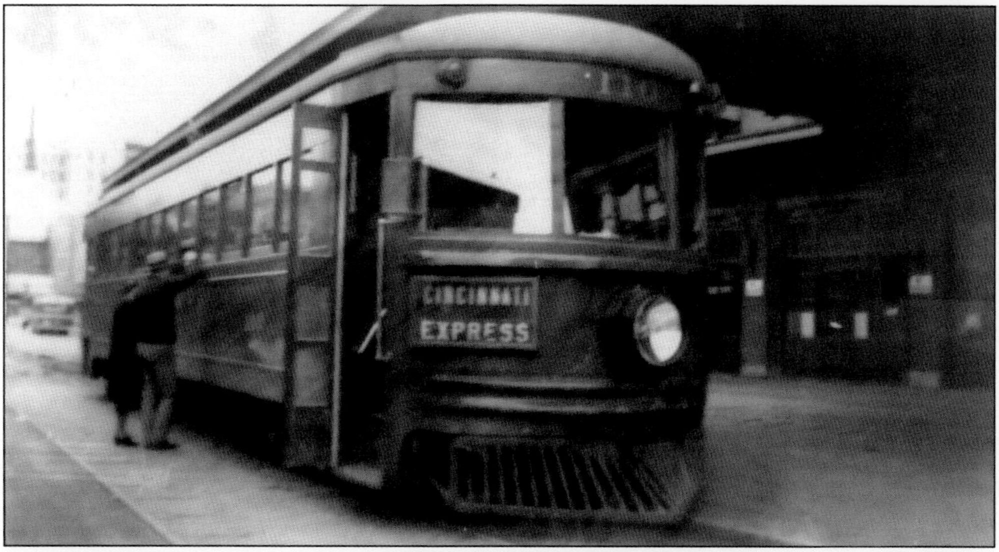

By 1926, believing that there was still a place for rail transportation, Thomas Conway Jr. restructured the former Cincinnati and Dayton Traction Company that ran through Mt. Healthy. He rebuilt the tracks and added new high-speed cars. But competition from streetcars and automobiles forced him to discontinue service. In May 1939, his company's bus subsidiary took over passenger service along the same route.

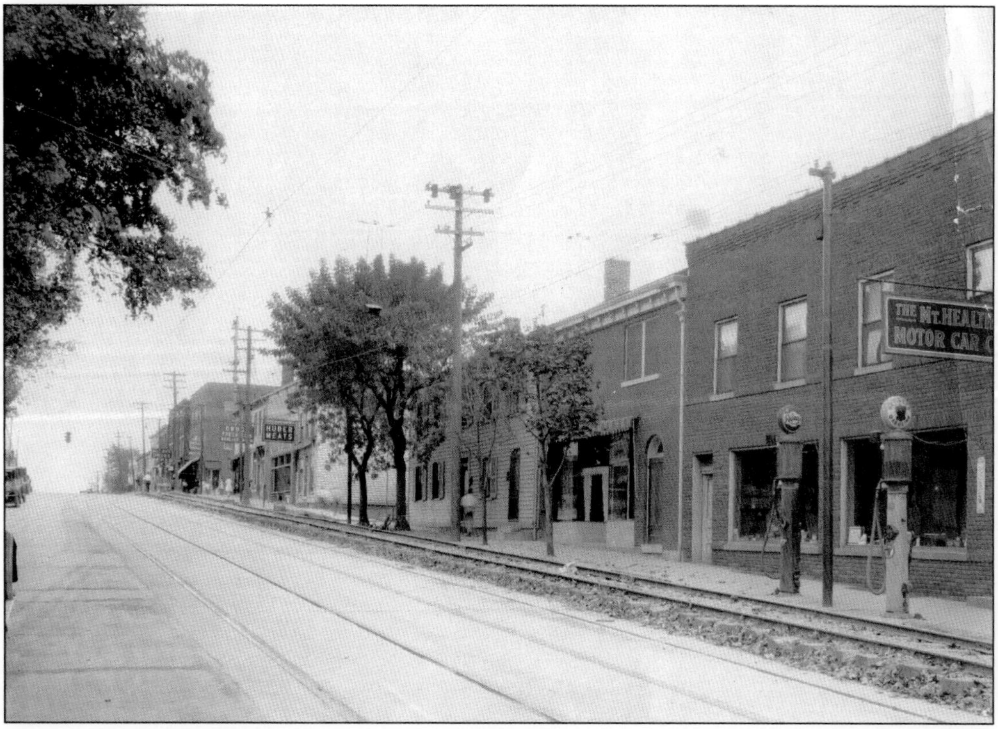

Shown are the many transportation choices afforded to local residents around 1930. There were train and electric trolley lines, gasoline pumps, and a motorcar sales showroom all located along Hamilton Pike.

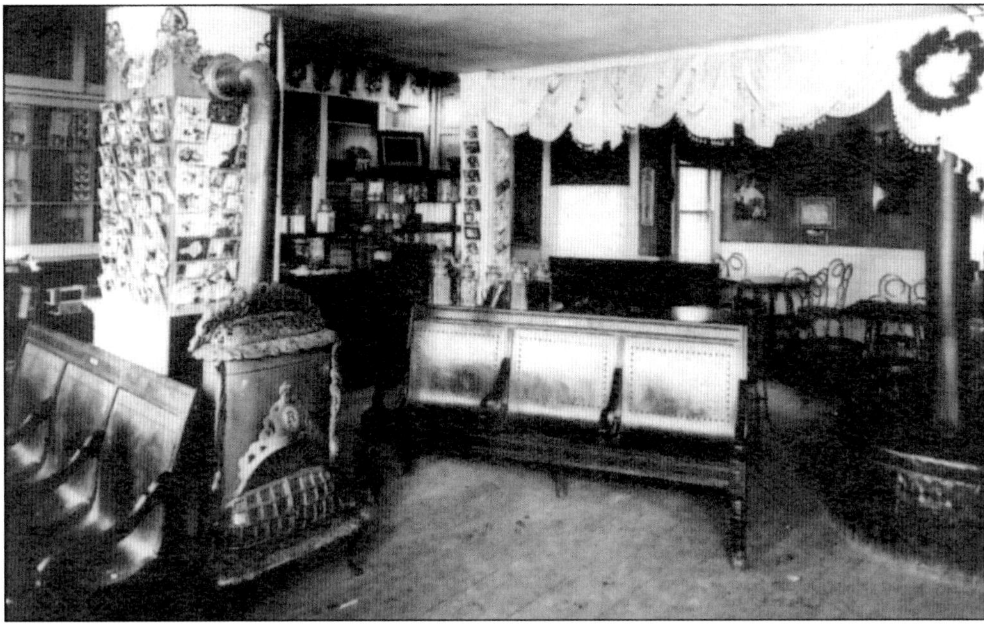

One prime commercial location was at 7519 Hamilton Pike, centered between Compton Road and Kinney Avenue. In the early 1900s, Peter's Ice Cream Shop offered cigars, cards, candy, and ice cream that could be enjoyed at the stylish ice-cream tables. Travelers bought their tickets to ride the traction car here. Benches made the wait comfortable. (Courtesy of Clayton Coleman.)

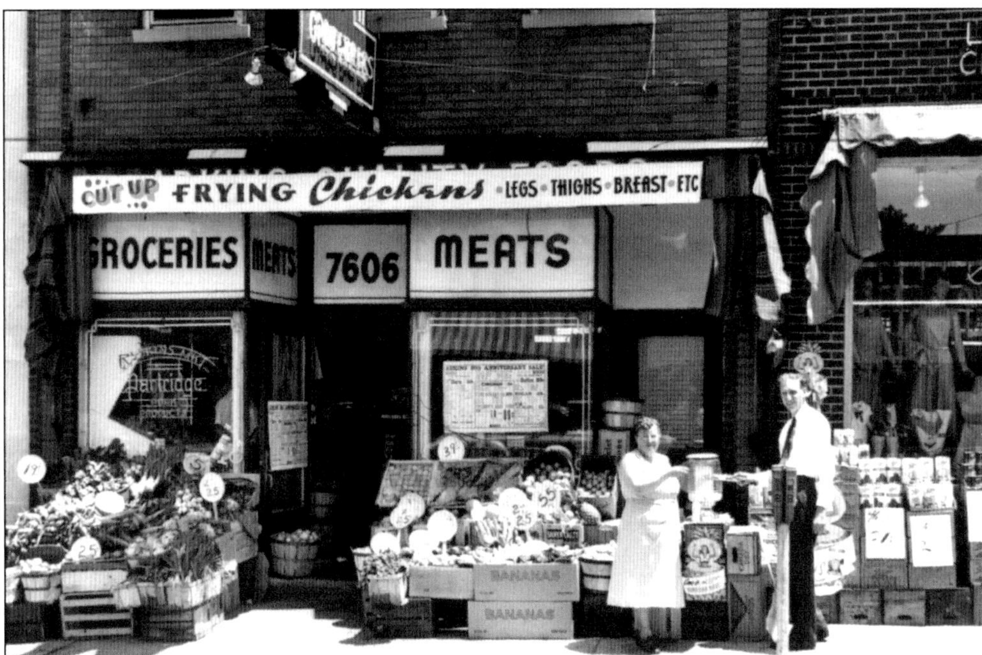

For over a quarter of a century, Adkin's Grocery Store offered its customers the freshest available groceries, chicken, meats, and produce. In good weather, it enticed shoppers by displaying farm-picked vegetables on the sidewalk. This photograph shows its 25th anniversary sale items offered with a cold cup of lemonade.

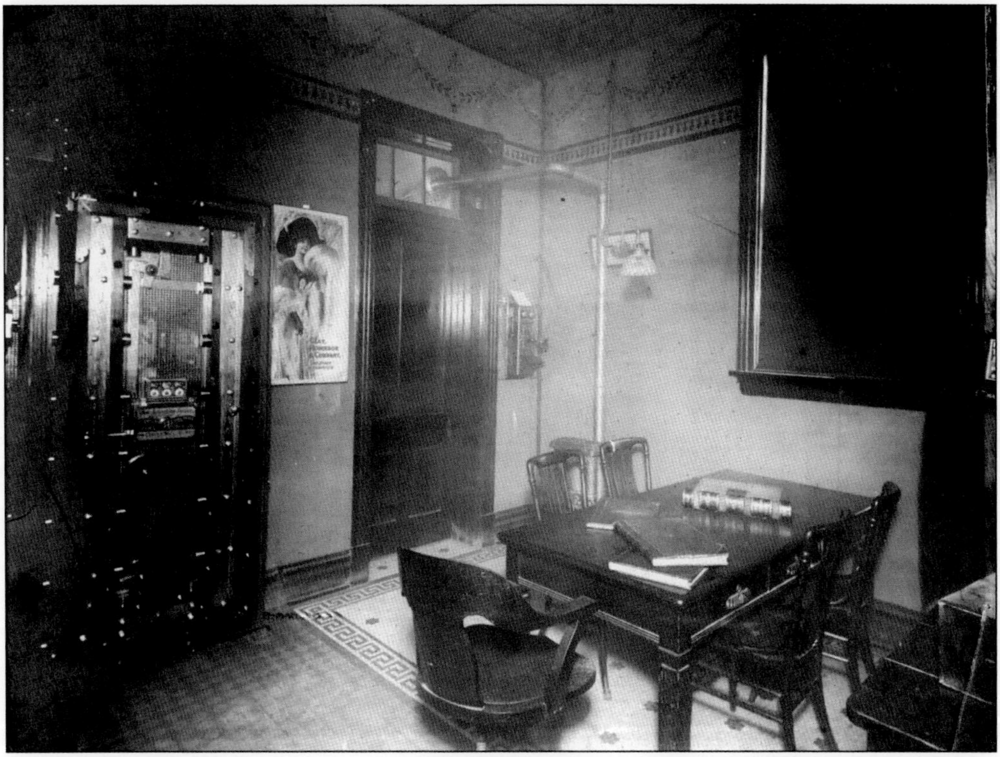

The board of directors of the First National Bank of Mt. Healthy consisted of Owen Kinney, president; Joseph Weber, vice president; Alexis Brown, cashier; Frank Nobel; Edward Seiter; Henry Bax; and Dr. L. Neufarth. Minutes from board meetings held between January 1916 and May 1921 reveal that loans were approved, and the cash in the vault was counted to see that the amount on hand agreed with the books of the bank. Between 1863 and 1935, individually chartered national banks that had government bonds deposited with the federal government could issue their own notes. Mt. Healthy issued notes of $10 and $20 to a value of $746,610. Known as Series 7661 of 1928, the notes were signed by Weber and cashier Walter R. Hartung. (Courtesy of Gene Hessler.)

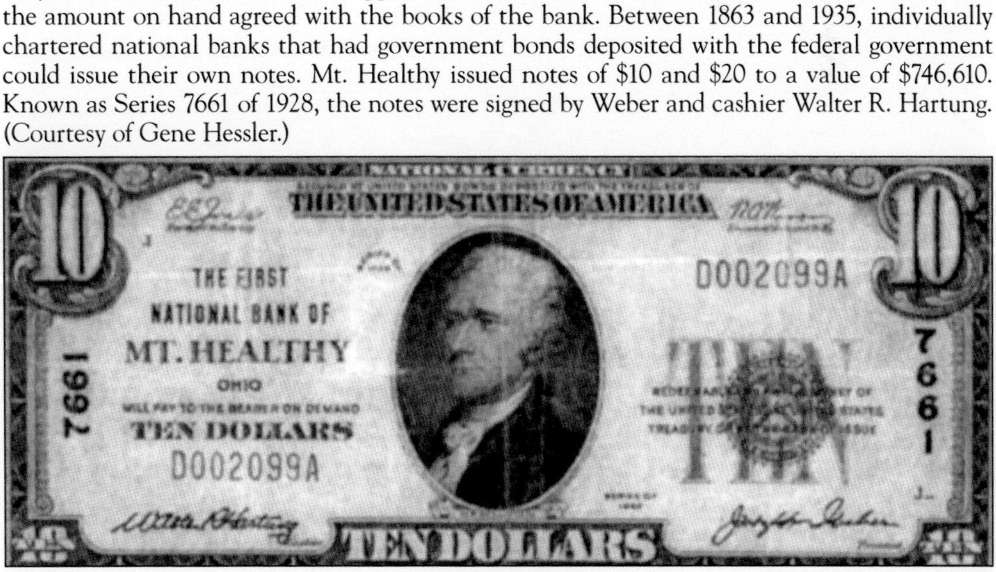

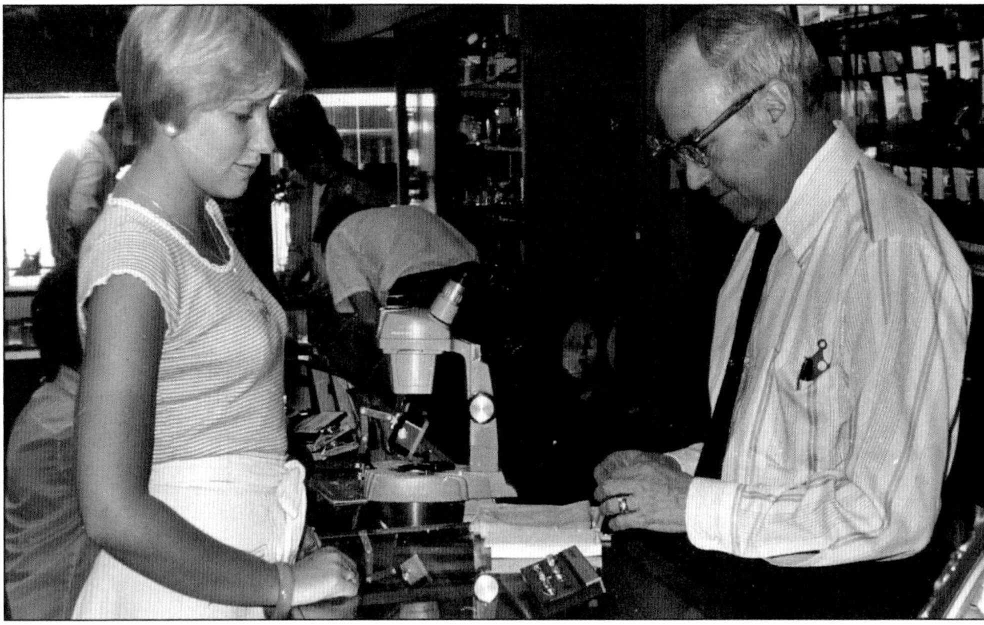

In 1920, jewelers William and Clara Effler relocated from Columbus back to Cincinnati. They found Mt. Healthy to be the perfect site for their store. Their son Bill learned the jewelry business and in 1945 became a partner. In 2003, the store changed names when the Efflers' niece Laura and her husband, James Wolf, purchased the business. Pictured is Bill with a customer. (Courtesy of Bill Effler.)

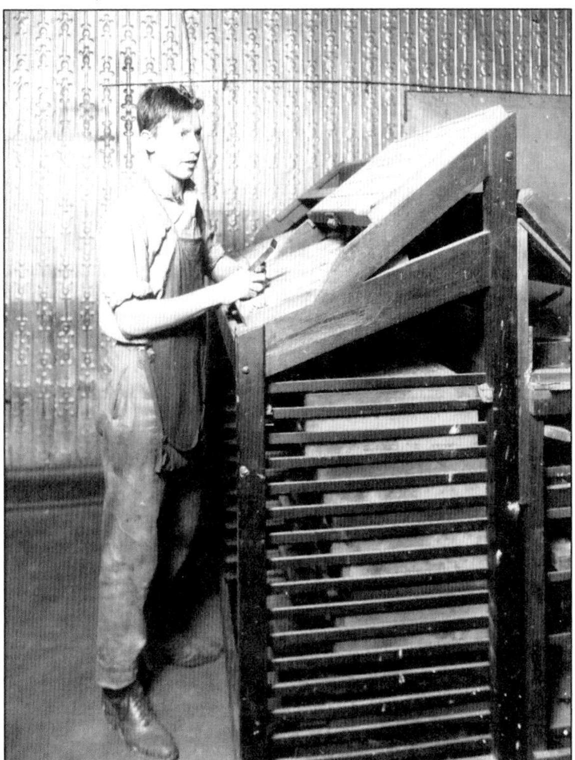

The Porter family has been in the printing business in Mt. Healthy for many years and was located on the west side of Hamilton Pike between Stevens and Kinney Avenues. Young Leroy Porter is seen setting type. Porter Printing was a publisher of weekly newspapers, including the *News Reporter*, which began in 1936. It reported typical small-town news and items of general interest.

In 1878, pioneer florist Peter Herb was the first to engage in raising prize-winning dahlias. His greenhouses were on Harrison Avenue. His sons Chris and Frank continued in the business and won additional prizes at dahlia shows. Today John Herb, son of Jack Herb (pictured), continues the family business.

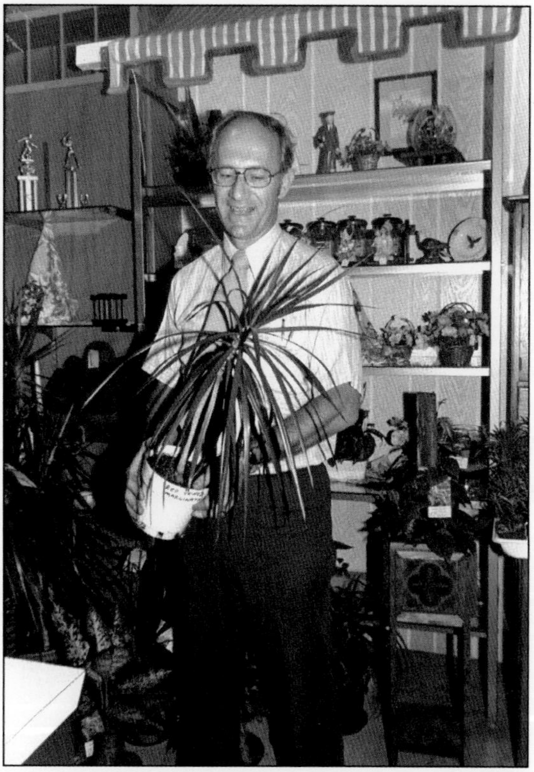

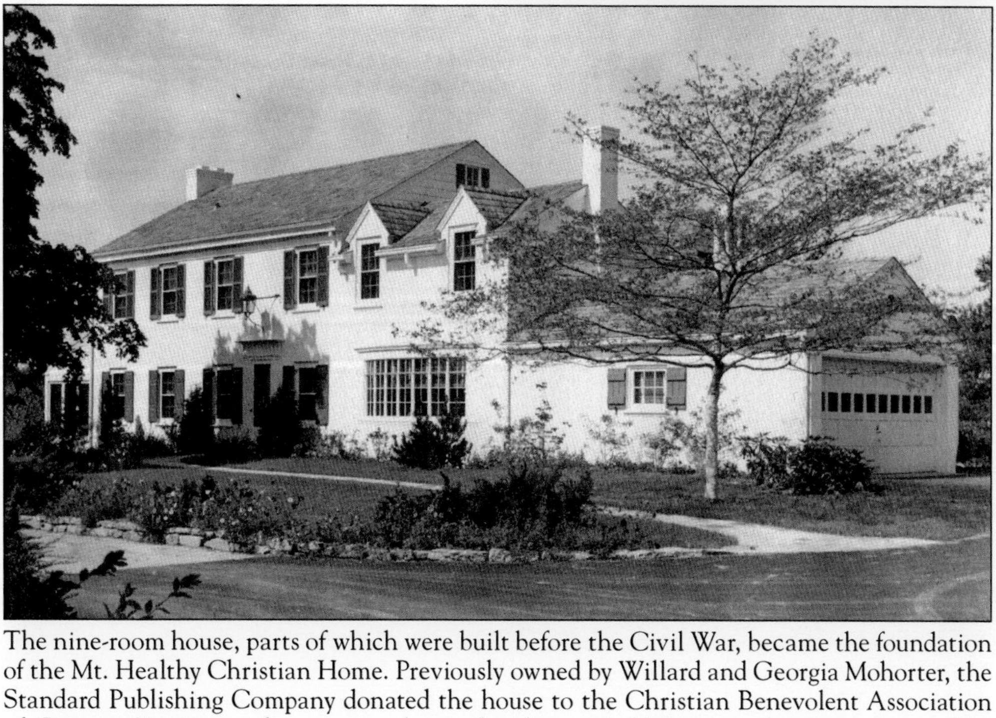

The nine-room house, parts of which were built before the Civil War, became the foundation of the Mt. Healthy Christian Home. Previously owned by Willard and Georgia Mohorter, the Standard Publishing Company donated the house to the Christian Benevolent Association of Greater Cincinnati for use as a home for the aged. Today it is home to many older Mt. Healthy residents.

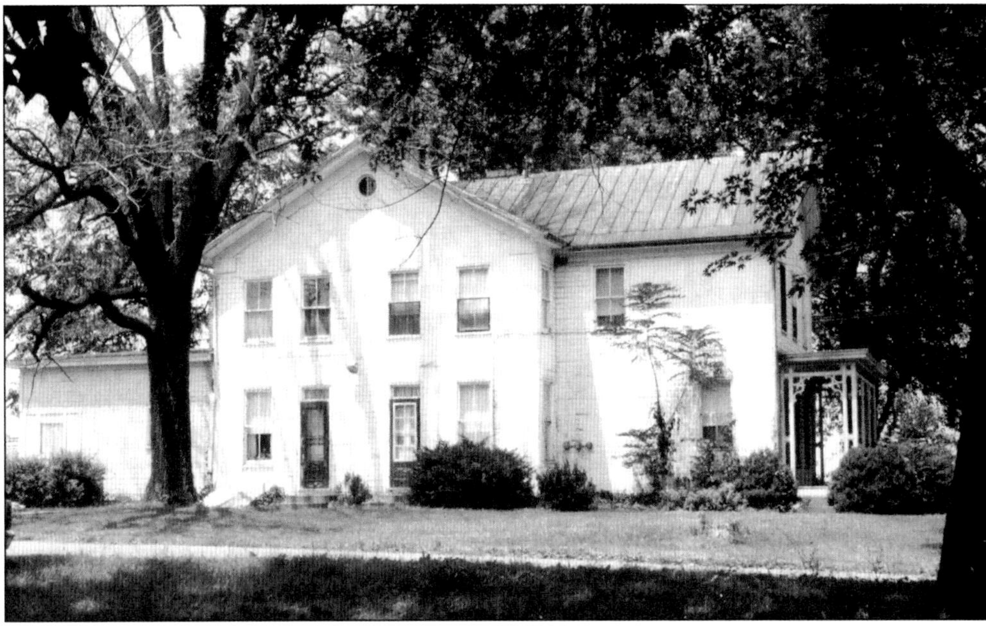

The Hamilton County Experimental Farm and office was located on 217 acres on Hamilton Turnpike north of Mt. Healthy. Experiments determined the best results for Hamilton County farmland. There were 230 plots of ground, sized one-twentieth to one-tenth of an acre, where crops were grown and tested with different combinations of seeds and fertilizers.

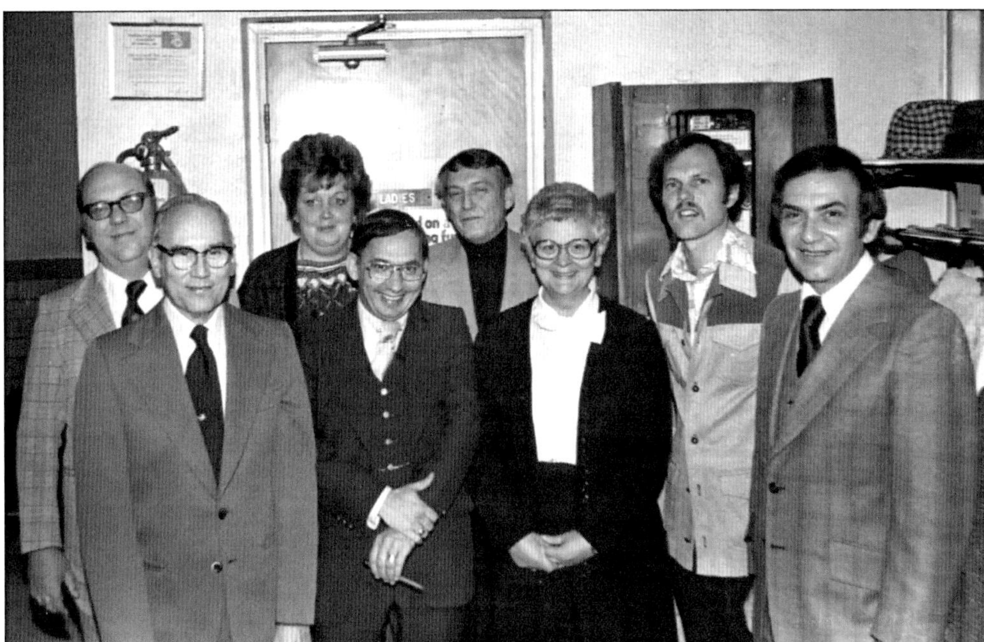

Business owners in Mt. Healthy have traditionally enjoyed the support and cooperation of the Mt. Healthy Business Association. From left to right, longtime members included (first row) Bill Effler, Bob Fezel, Betty Hutzel, and Earl Shaen; (second row) Tom Blum, Mary Arthur, Carl Schwartz, and Bob Curley.

Five

EDUCATING THE CHILDREN

Many early settlers came to Mount Pleasant possessing a useful education and wanted their children to have the advantage of a similar opportunity. Those who could not read or write also wanted an education. These early settlers took great pride in the school they created.

One of the first public buildings constructed in the village was a one-room log cabin school located at 1500 Compton Road. As enrollment grew, three larger buildings followed. In 1866, a four-room, gray brick school was constructed at the northwest corner of Compton Road and Harrison Avenue. Due to community growth, two rooms were added in 1888, and another two rooms were added in 1894. In 1910, this building was torn down to provide space for the school that was dedicated on September 30, 1911, and opened with a program for grades 1 through 12.

During the 1840s, there was dual control of the school. Springfield Township Board of Education shared control with Sub-district No. 6, as the Mount Pleasant school was called. In 1905, Mt. Healthy became an independent school district with full control over local issues. One of the first board actions was to request that a local merchant stop selling cigarettes to schoolchildren.

The high school that opened in 1929 was an outstanding school building for its day, having the largest gymnasium in the county. The building received two additions before 1962, when a new high school was built on Adams Road.

All children of Mt. Healthy had opportunities for a good education. The Church of the Assumption Parochial School was founded in 1858. The Lutheran church operated a German-speaking school. In the early 1850s, there were separate schools for African American students. It is reported that one school was on Hill Avenue between Harrison and Hamilton Avenues. Another school was located on the second floor of a building on the northeast corner of Hamilton Avenue and McMakin Street. However, there are no photographic records to confirm these early buildings.

Education has opened doors to opportunity for Mt. Healthy students. Students were well prepared to be good citizens and to assume employment that provided a productive and comfortable life.

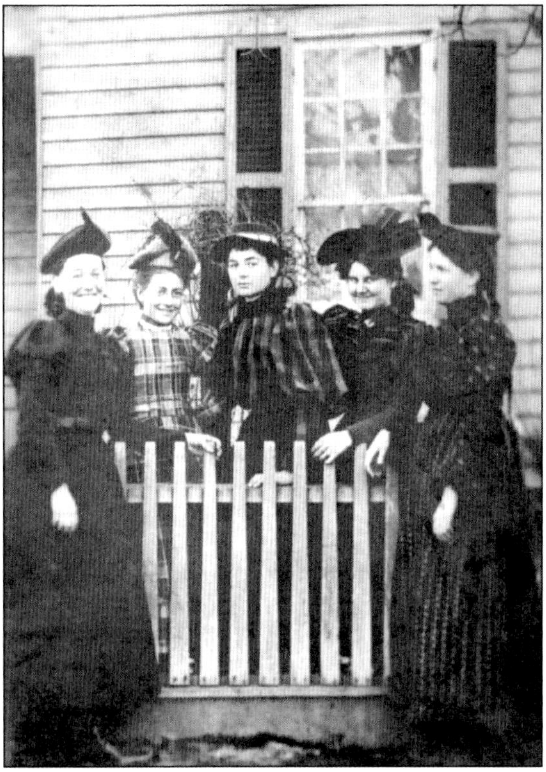

School friends, from left to right, Freda Walker, Josie Goreis, May Hartwell, May Sheehan, and Ida Yerkes enjoyed socializing. Many Mt. Healthy graduates have shared with the authors that they treasure school friends and plan regular get-togethers. They attend each other's weddings, celebrate births, and gather for funerals; others refresh friendships at class reunions.

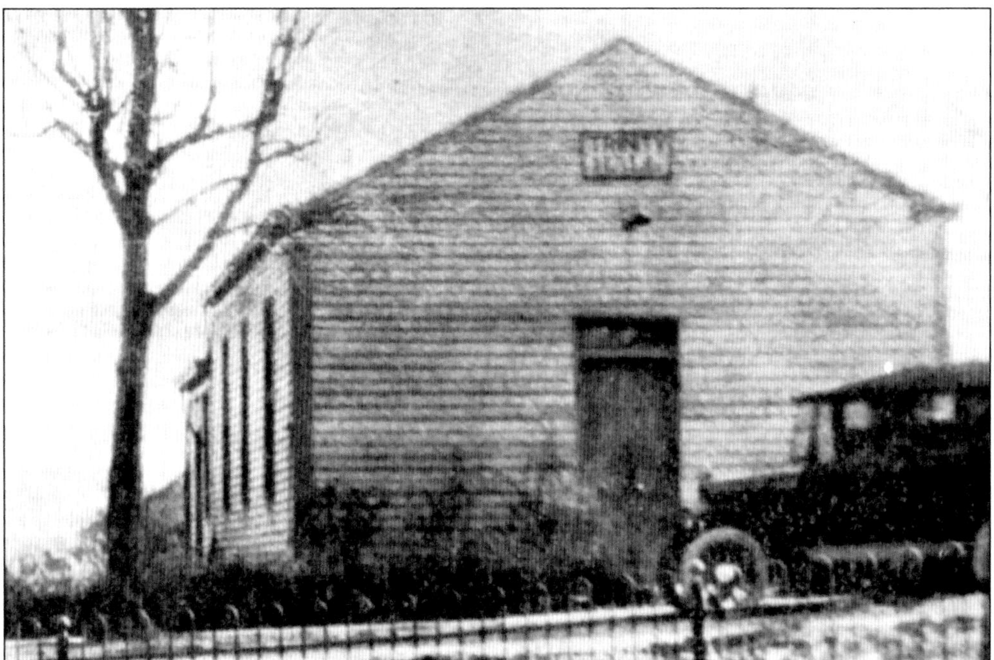

The Lutheran church established a school for students to learn in German. It is believed the school operated from 1869 until 1890. It is also believed that classes were held in the original Trinity Hall, which was a large room with a potbellied stove in the middle.

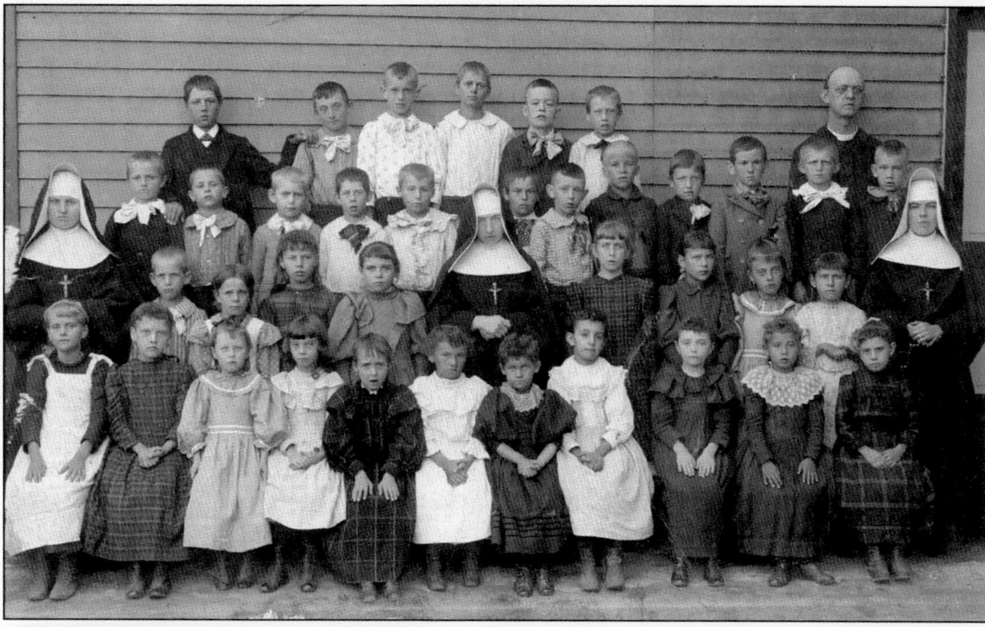

The Church of the Assumption Parochial School was founded in 1858 in a small, two-and-a-half-story frame building. One lay teacher taught all the children. In February 1894, four Sisters of Divine Providence arrived at the parish as teachers. They taught their students in the small schoolhouse until March 1909, when a new four-classroom school building was erected that included a residence for the sisters. (Courtesy of Joy Cumbow Packer.)

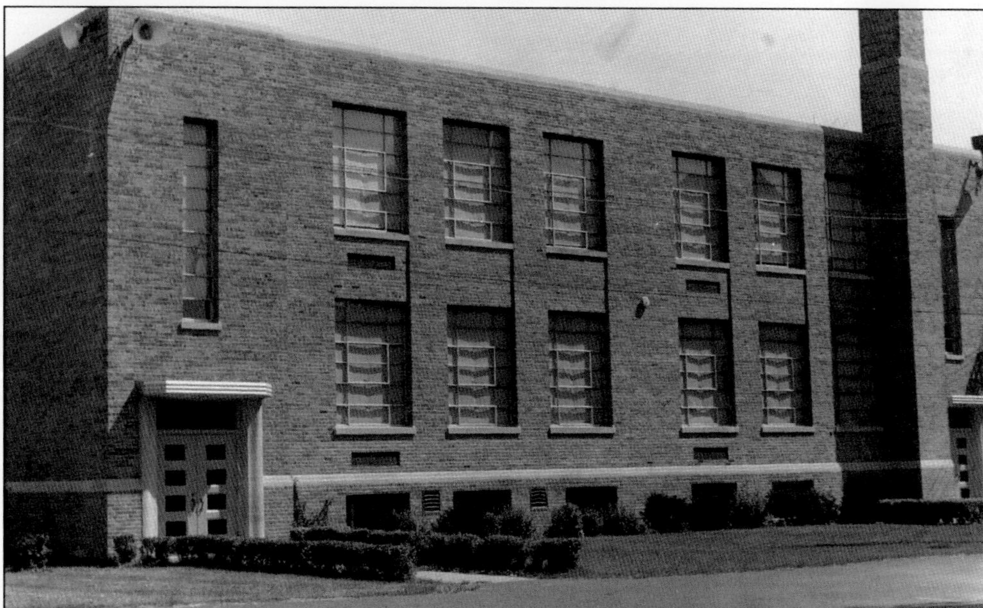

In the late 1940s, Mt. Healthy experienced a period of rapid growth. The Church of the Assumption Parochial School also grew, and its school population soared. In 1949, it was decided that a new school would be built. The building was completed for the 1950 school year. In 2008, the school merged with three other parish schools to create a regional school called Our Lady of Grace Catholic School. Shown is the 1950 school building.

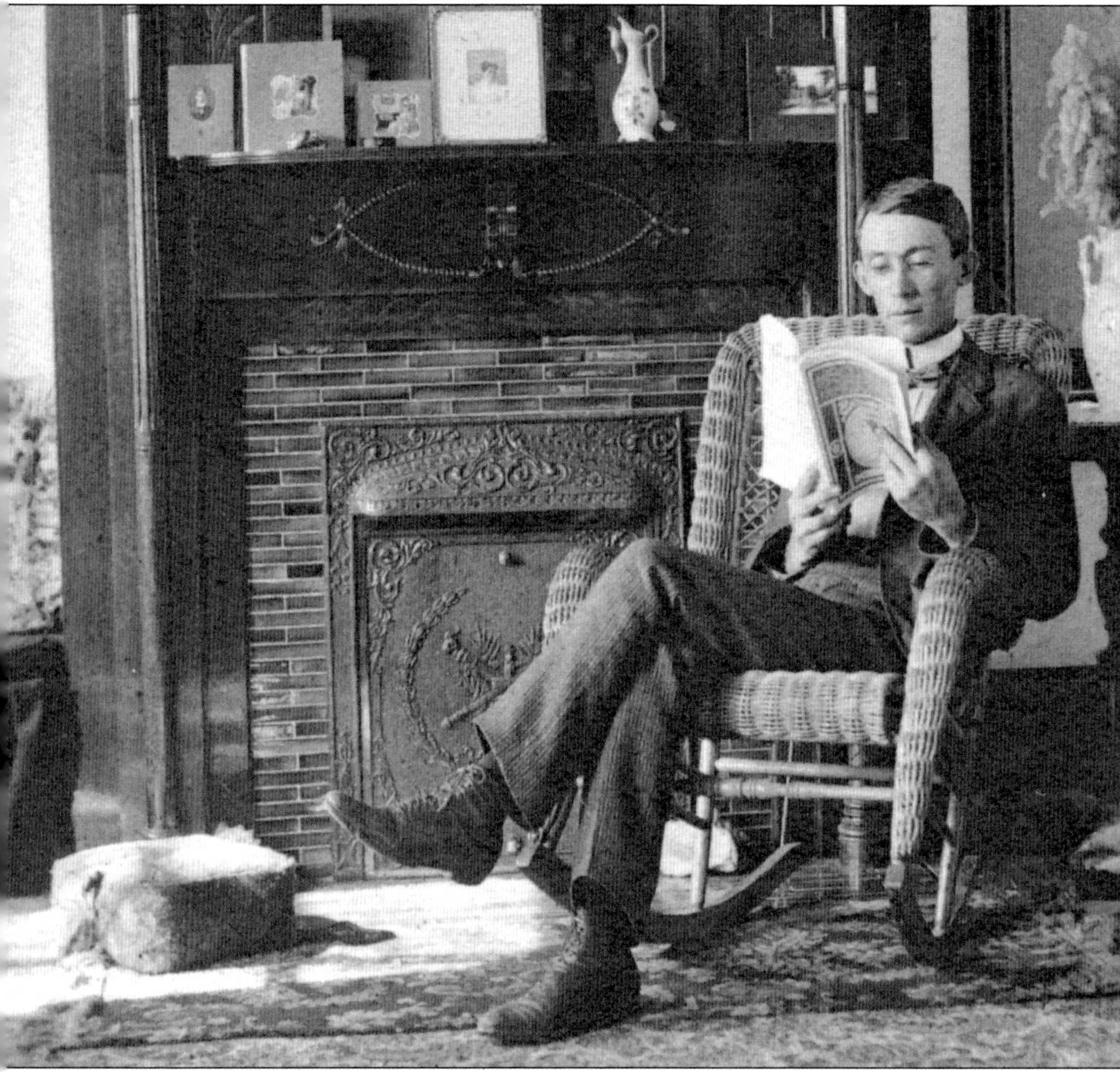

In 1897, Charles A. Hunt moved from New Burlington near the covered bridge. Hunt was a teacher, principal, and superintendent until 1912, when he resigned to open the C. A. Hunt Hardware Store. He served as master of the Masonic lodge in 1913 and was a poet. Hunt's poem "An Old Covered Bridge" was written in 1941 and recalled his childhood. "There's an Old Covered Bridge that stands today / Near the foot of a steep little hill, / Where the roadway bends as it crosses the creek / That flows by an ancient mill. / On the farther slope surrounded by trees, / Beyond where the mill race ran / Still stands the cottage where I was born; / The home where life began. / I played, when a boy, by that Old Covered Bridge, / Played in the water and sand, / Imagined the bridge was a wonderful ship / And I was the first in command. / Pretending the shadows were pirates, who crept / From the forest that stood on the ridge, / Seeking to capture my beautiful ship, / Capture that Old Covered Bridge."

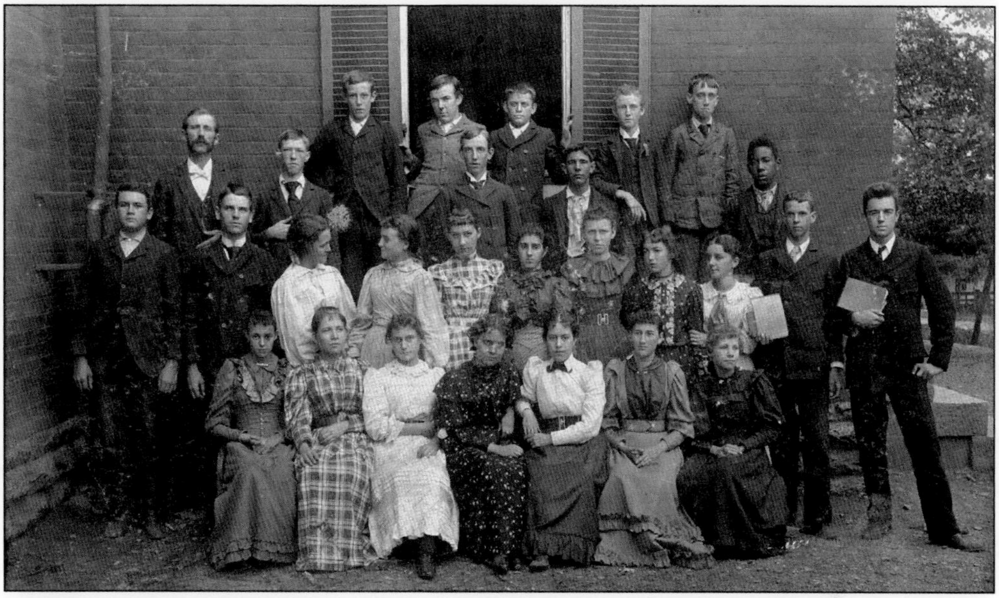

In 1892, a two-year high school program was organized. Graduating in 1895 were the first two graduates, Frank Titus and Vernon Hoffner (far right), standing proudly holding their diplomas. Also pictured are students of the upper grades and teacher and principal N. H. Bartlett (third row, left). (Courtesy of Arlette Merritt.)

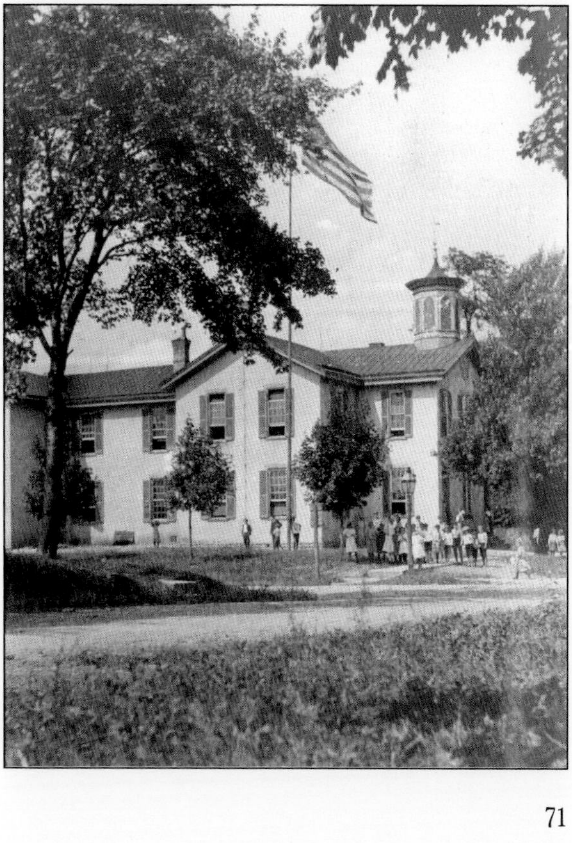

This four-room brick school was built in 1866 at the northwest corner of Compton Road and Harrison Avenue. As Mt. Healthy's population grew, two rooms were added in 1888 and another two rooms in 1894. In 1900, teachers were Lulu Greener, Grace Ludlow, Carrie McGrew, and Alice Burdge, with Hunt as superintendent. This building was razed in 1910 to make space for a new building.

DEDICATION

—OF THE—

Mt. Healthy Public School Building

SATURDAY AFTERNOON, SEPTEMBER 30, 1911

Parade of school children, societies and citizens starts promptly at 1:30 P. M., and is followed by dedicatory address and exercises in the school auditorium.

"Home Coming" Reunion, interspersed with music and five-minute addresses, in the evening at the school-house.

YOU ARE CORDIALLY INVITED

CHAS. A. HUNT } Ex. Committee.
O. N. KINNEY }

The new school building was so important that on September 10, 1910, the day of its dedication, there was a community-wide parade, which included the school band, schoolgirls in white dresses with flags, school classes, and teachers. Invitations were printed on the back of 1¢ postcards.

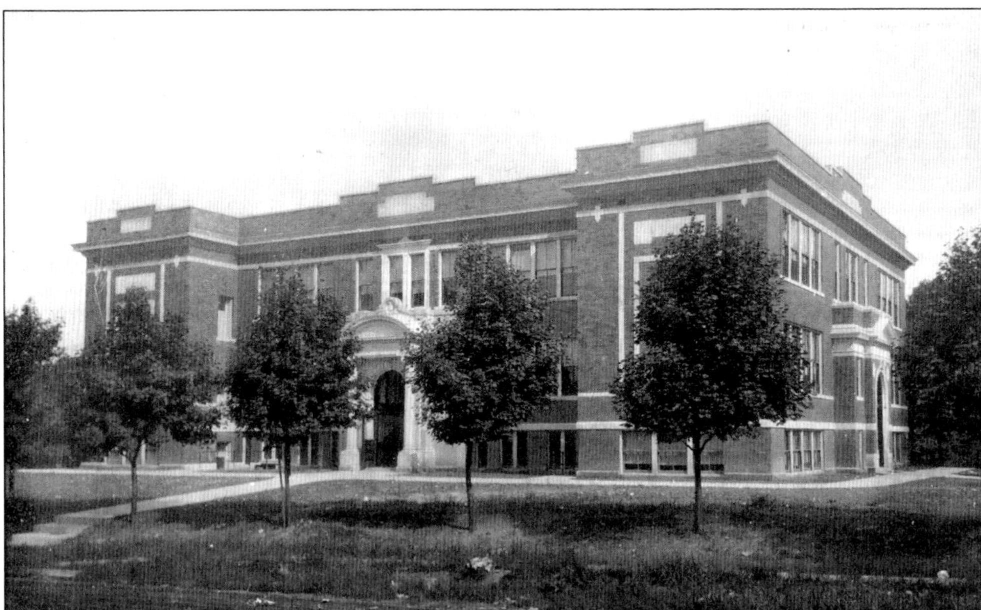

The sixth school building opened in September 1911, featuring a Rookwood drinking fountain and a stained-glass dome in the auditorium. The three-story building had the first inside gymnasium in the basement, with two large posts in the playing court. Previous basketball games had been played outside. The brick Second Renaissance Revival building was listed on the national register in 1985.

Grace E. (Ludlow) Hunt is shown as a young teacher. Hunt was a popular teacher of eighth grade and taught the first two branches of high school. As a grade-school principal, she was admired for her fairness and her ability to smoothly fill in when a teacher was out sick. The 1911 building was later named in her honor.

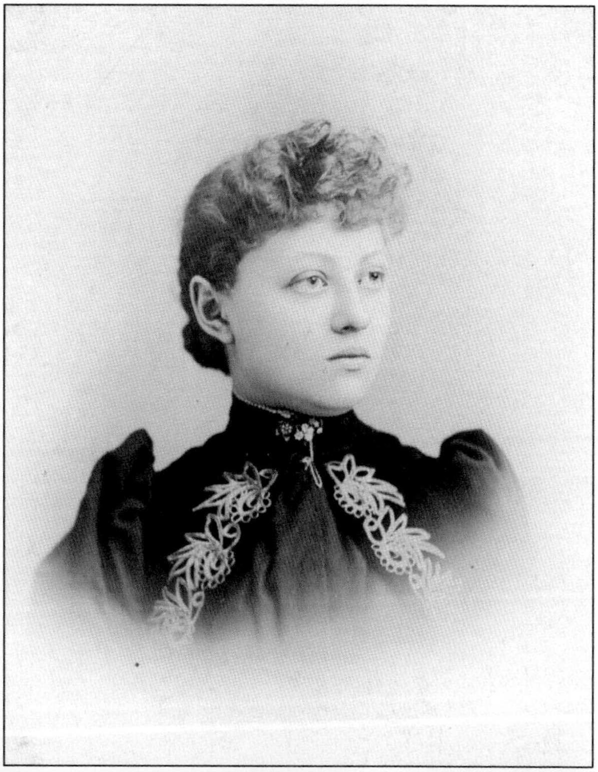

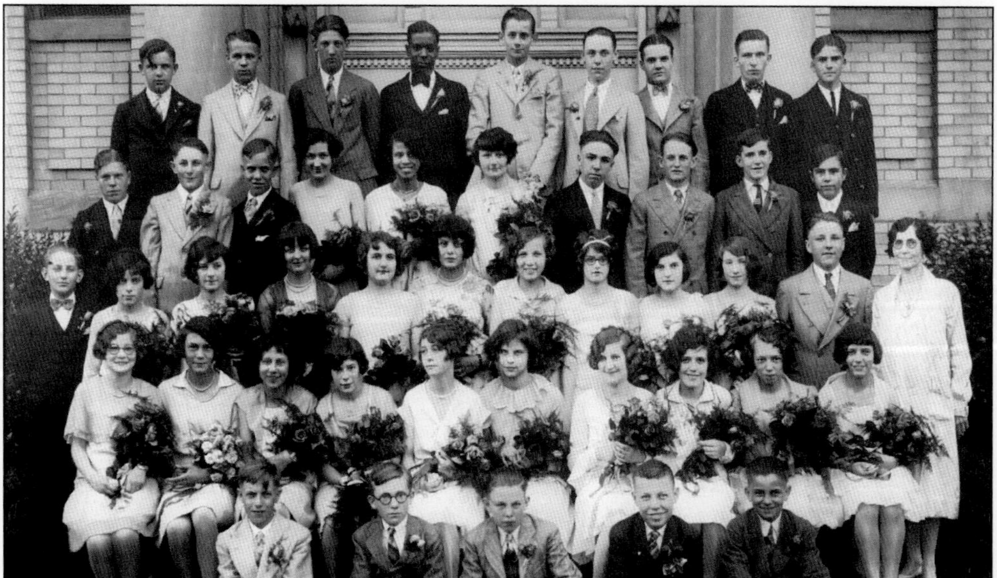

Eighth-grade graduation was a big accomplishment in the early 1900s. The eighth-grade class of 1928, along with its teacher, Nellie Finch, invited family and friends to the graduation with the following announcement: "The Eighth Grade of the / Mount Healthy Public School / request your presence at the / Graduation Exercises / Tuesday, June Twelve / at eight o'clock / Auditorium / Motto - Work and Win / Colors-Blue and Gold / Flower-Rose." (Author's collection.)

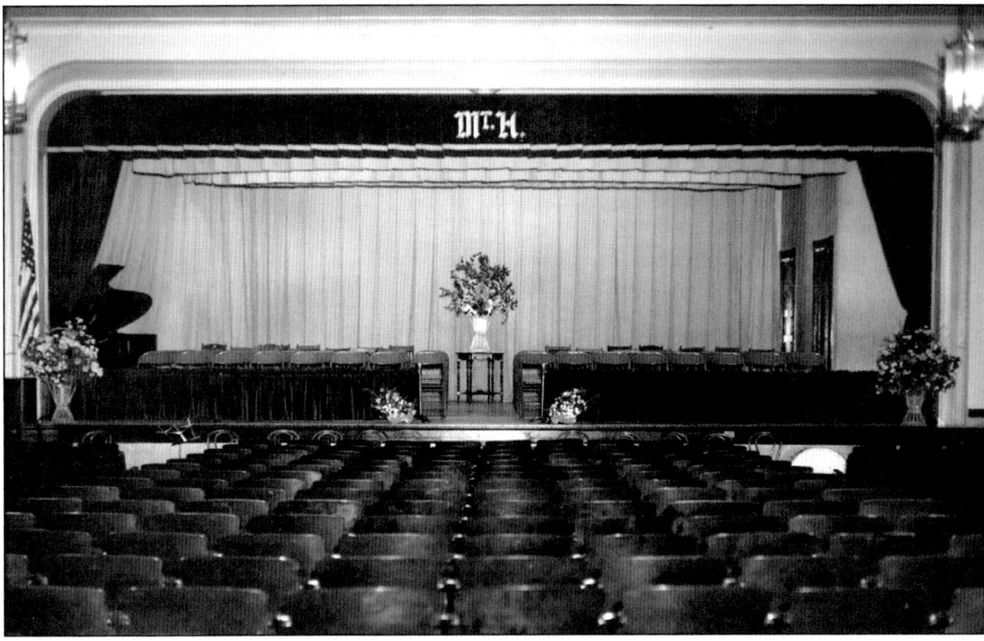

The functional auditorium was used for concerts, plays, student assemblies, and outside group meetings. Shown between 1948 and 1951, the Mt. Healthy Garden Club school committee decorated for high school commencement and baccalaureate sessions. The following ladies worked on the school committee: Mrs. C. Rittenhouse, Alta Droste, Mrs. R. Mallette, Mrs. Carl Schaeuble, Ruth Auburn, and Stella Wade. (Courtesy of the Mt. Healthy Garden Club.)

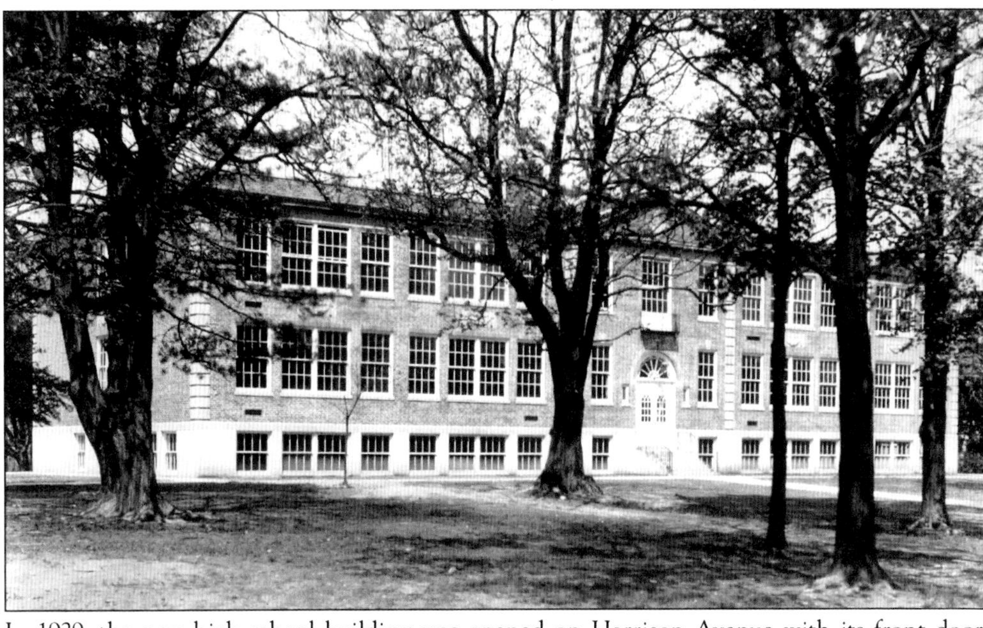

In 1929, the new high school building was opened on Harrison Avenue with its front doors opening toward McMakin Street. It was considered to be one of the finest buildings with the largest gymnasium in the county. Land had been purchased from the Sampson family in 1909 for $2,350. The building was designed by architects Samuel Hannaford and Sons and built by contractor Ed Honnert. This image includes the additions.

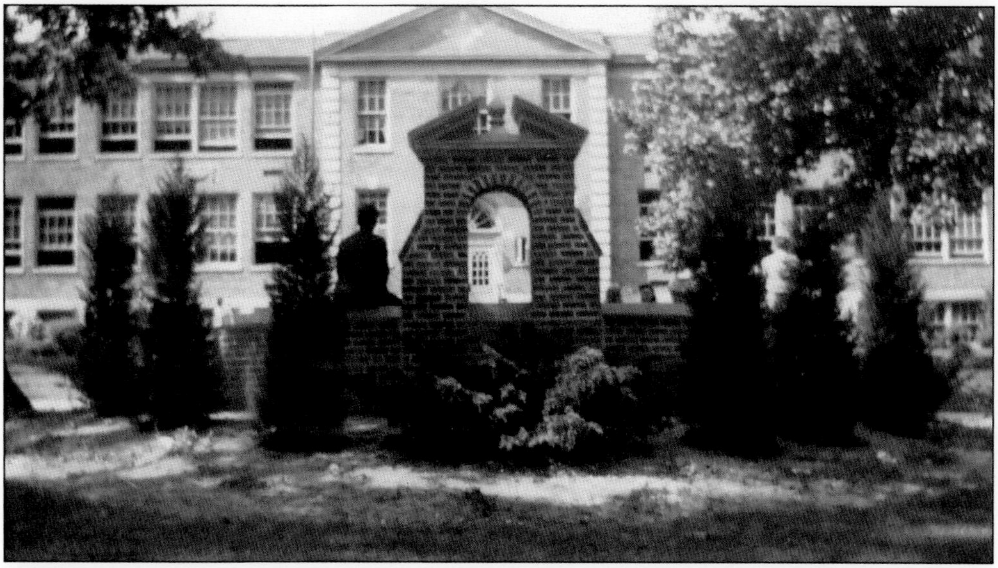

The fountain in front of the high school is a local landmark. It was the meeting place for many students and provided the background for numerous photographs. The fountain was given to the Mt. Healthy High School Foundation by the classes of 1936 and 1937 and Spotlight Club of 1938 and 1939. It was landscaped and planted by the Mt. Healthy Garden Club in 1939. (Courtesy of the Mt. Healthy Garden Club.)

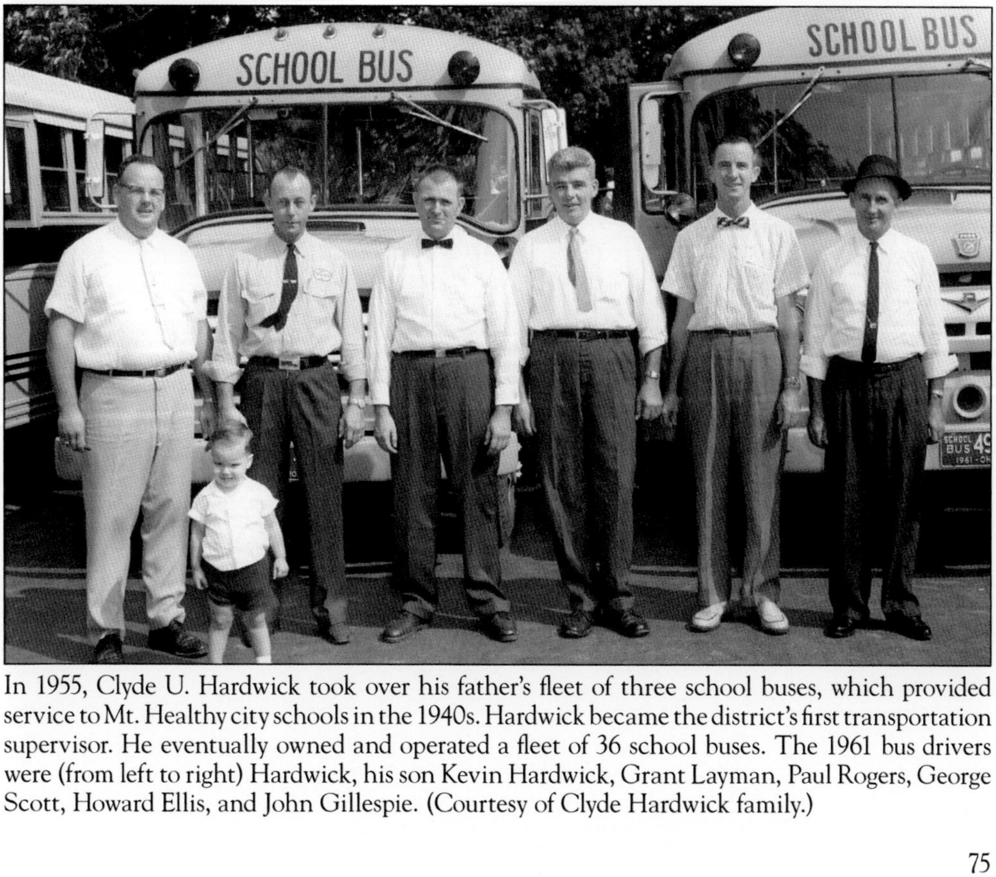

In 1955, Clyde U. Hardwick took over his father's fleet of three school buses, which provided service to Mt. Healthy city schools in the 1940s. Hardwick became the district's first transportation supervisor. He eventually owned and operated a fleet of 36 school buses. The 1961 bus drivers were (from left to right) Hardwick, his son Kevin Hardwick, Grant Layman, Paul Rogers, George Scott, Howard Ellis, and John Gillespie. (Courtesy of Clyde Hardwick family.)

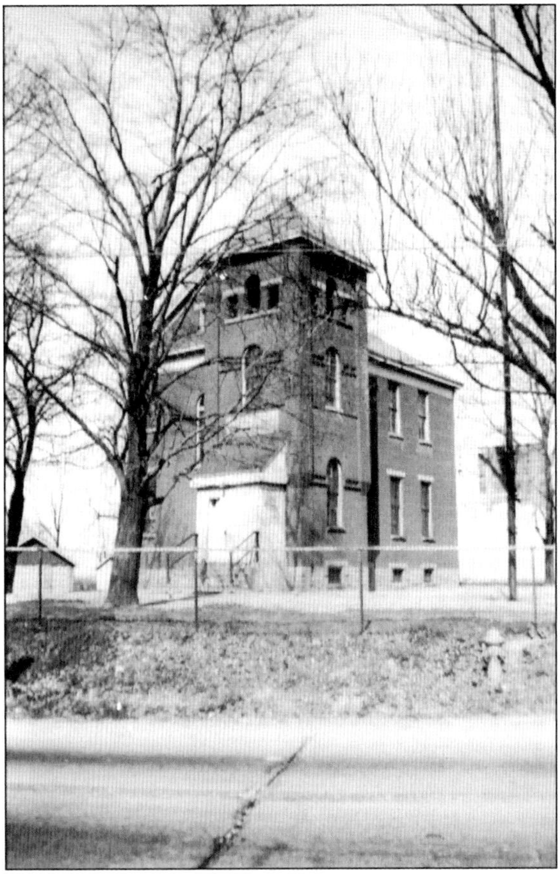

In May 1920, the Mt. Healthy School Board voted to form a centralized high school program. School districts in the surrounding communities were invited to send students to Mt. Healthy High School. The seven invited school districts included Clovernook, Finneytown, Liberty, New Burlington, Newell, Pleasant Run, and Science Hall. The surrounding districts welcomed this opportunity because during this era, most districts were not offering a high school program. Some operated very small one-room schools, such as Liberty, Newell, and Science Hall. In 1920, students typically ended their education at grade eight and went to work. On the other hand, attending Mt. Healthy High School was comfortable for the students because they were used to coming to Mt. Healthy for church and shopping.

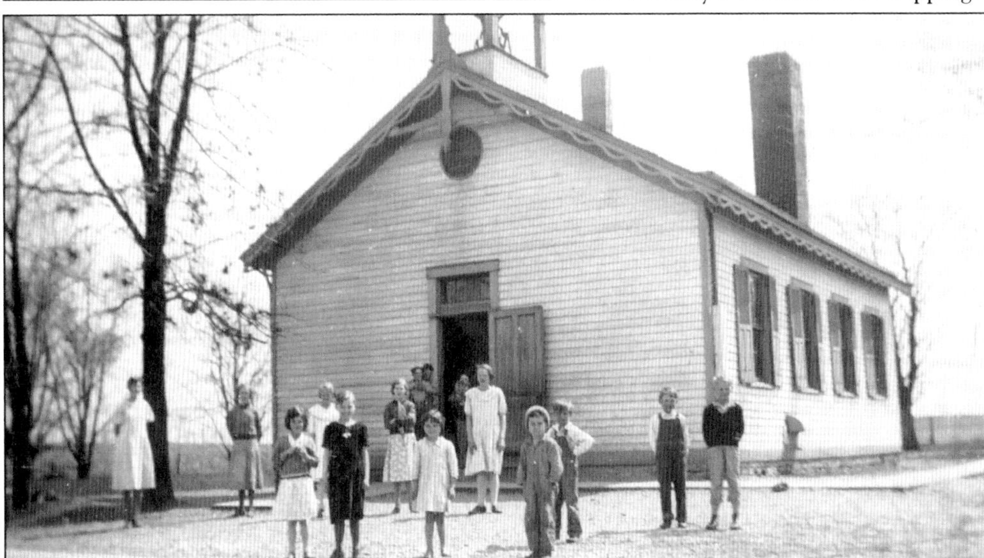

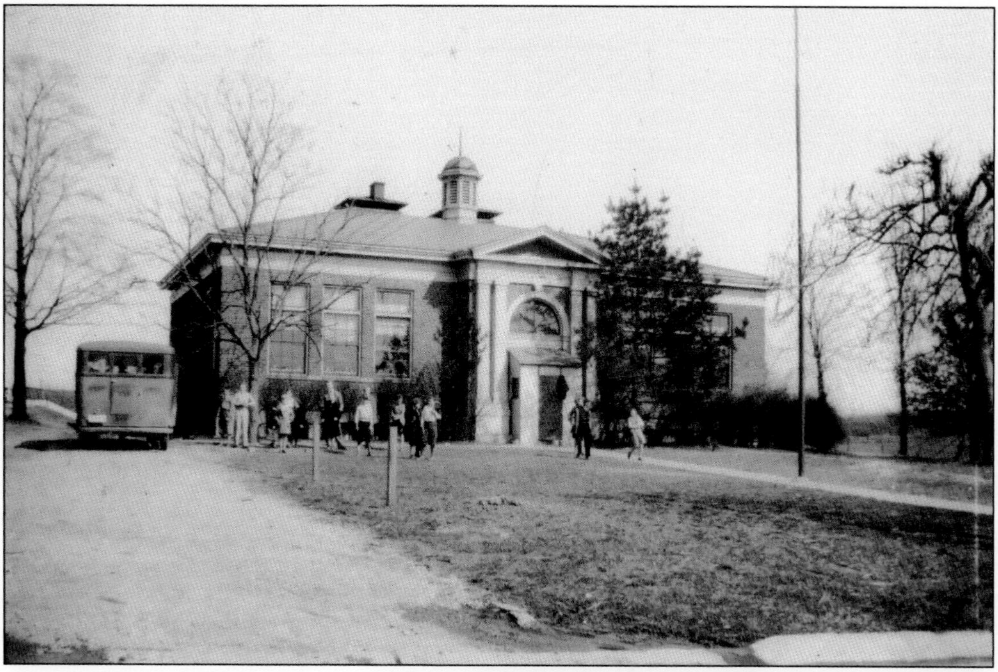

Beginning in September 1922, tuition was set at $80 per year for 10 months. For many families, attending high school was expensive. Costs included tuition and transportation to and from school plus lost wages. By school year 1930–1931, 11 school districts were represented among high school students. Mt. Healthy contributed 124, then North College Hill with 76. The others were as follows: Monfort Heights, 41; New Burlington, 16; Finneytown, 5; Newells, 2; Science Hall, 3; Liberty, 2; Pleasant Run, 2; Colerain, 1; and Cincinnati, 2. North College Hill sent students until its building was opened in 1931. Mt. Healthy remained a central high school until the 1960s; by then most districts had built their own high school buildings.

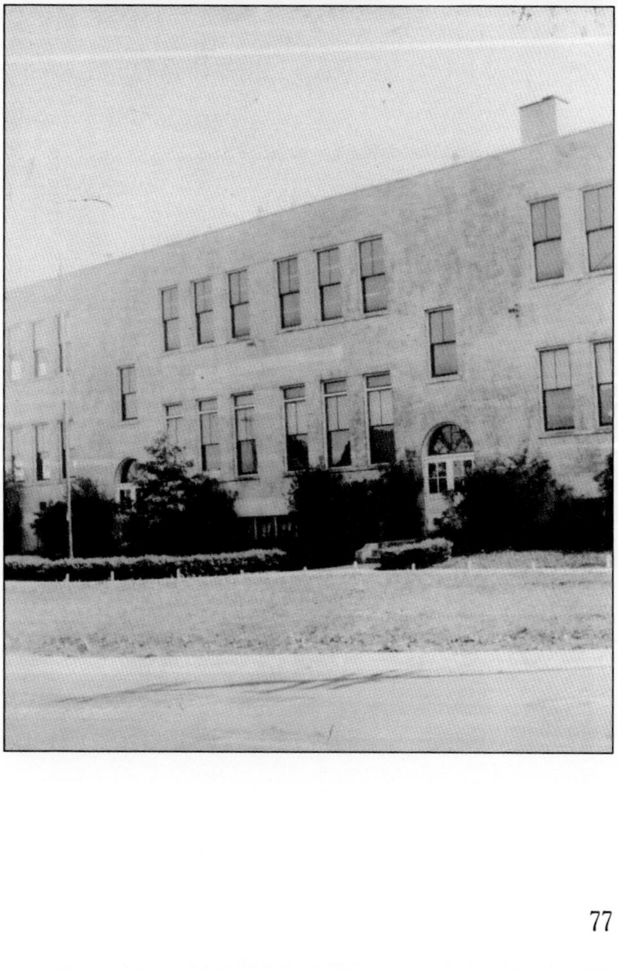

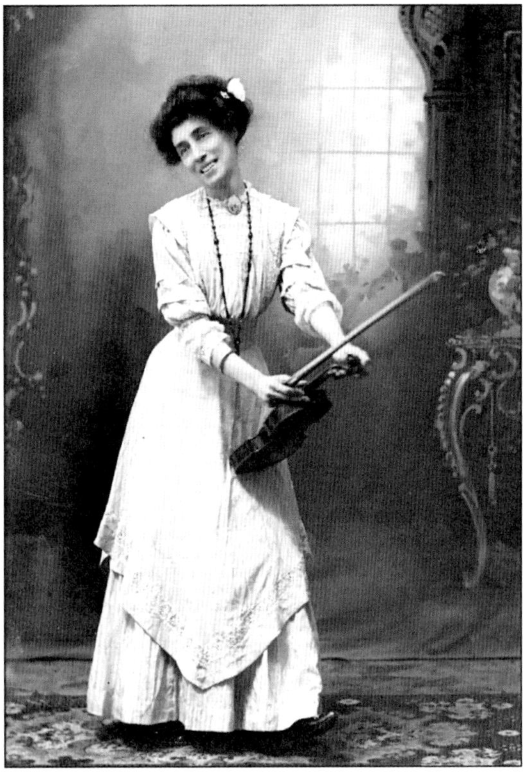

Mt. Healthy loved its music. During the early 1900s, Lulu Greener taught two days a week and created a respected music program. This special program was enjoyed by students and brought pride to parents. By the 1930s, Greener taught full time. She operated the Lulu Greener School of Music, where she expanded students' musical skills. Greener also published poetry in the *Cincinnati Times-Star* newspaper.

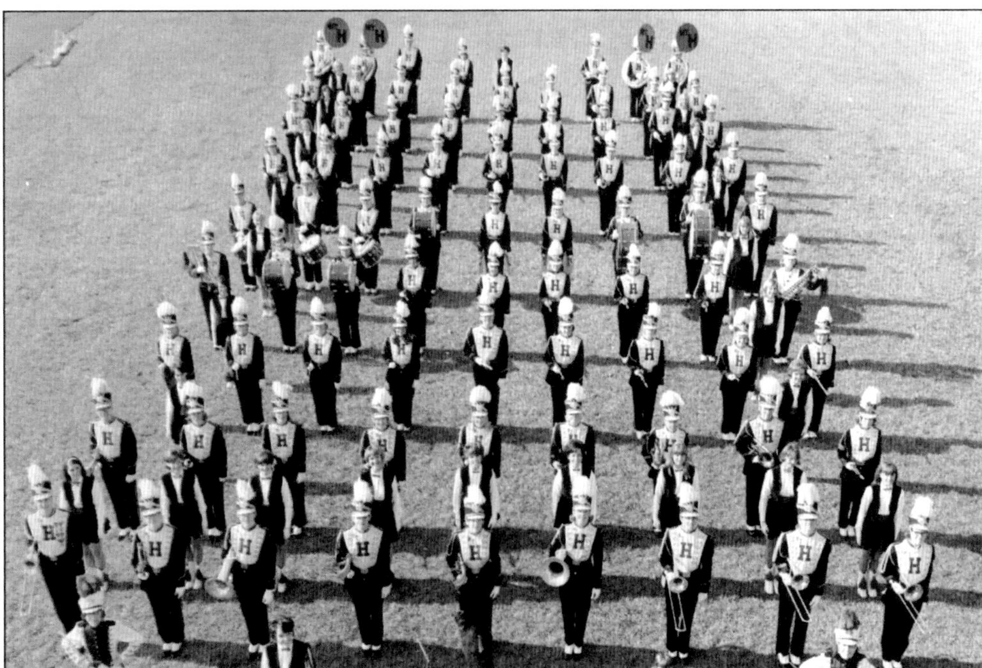

Many students enjoyed the high school music program. Here in the 1970s is the Mt. Healthy High School marching band. With Russell Hinkle as director, the band performed and marched for many events.

In later years, the district grew to include New Burlington. This map shows the location of school buildings that existed during the mid-1900s when the community experienced an influx of new residents. Over a 20-year period, the district built the Jane Hoop, Matthew Duvall, Lulu Greener, New Burlington, and Ethel Frost Elementary Schools; the North Junior High; and the high school on Adams Road. (Courtesy of Mt. Healthy School District.)

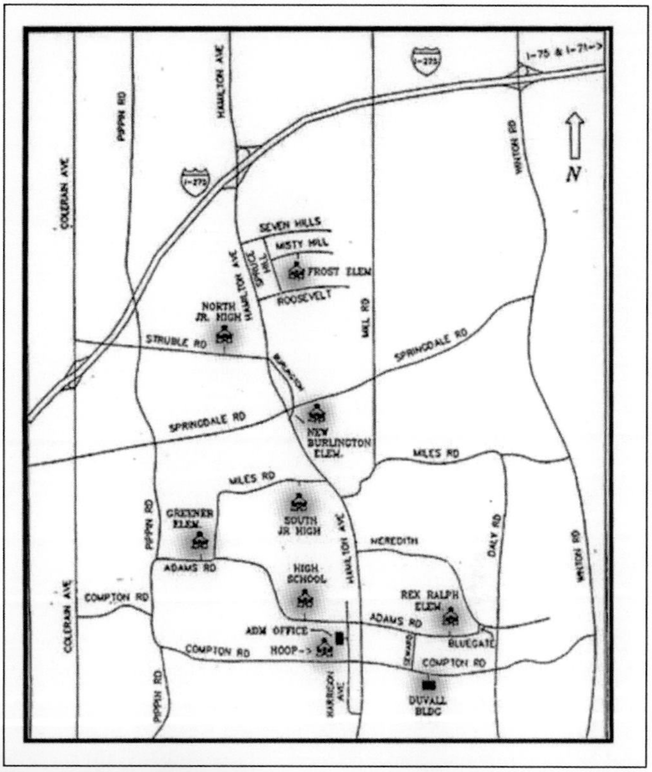

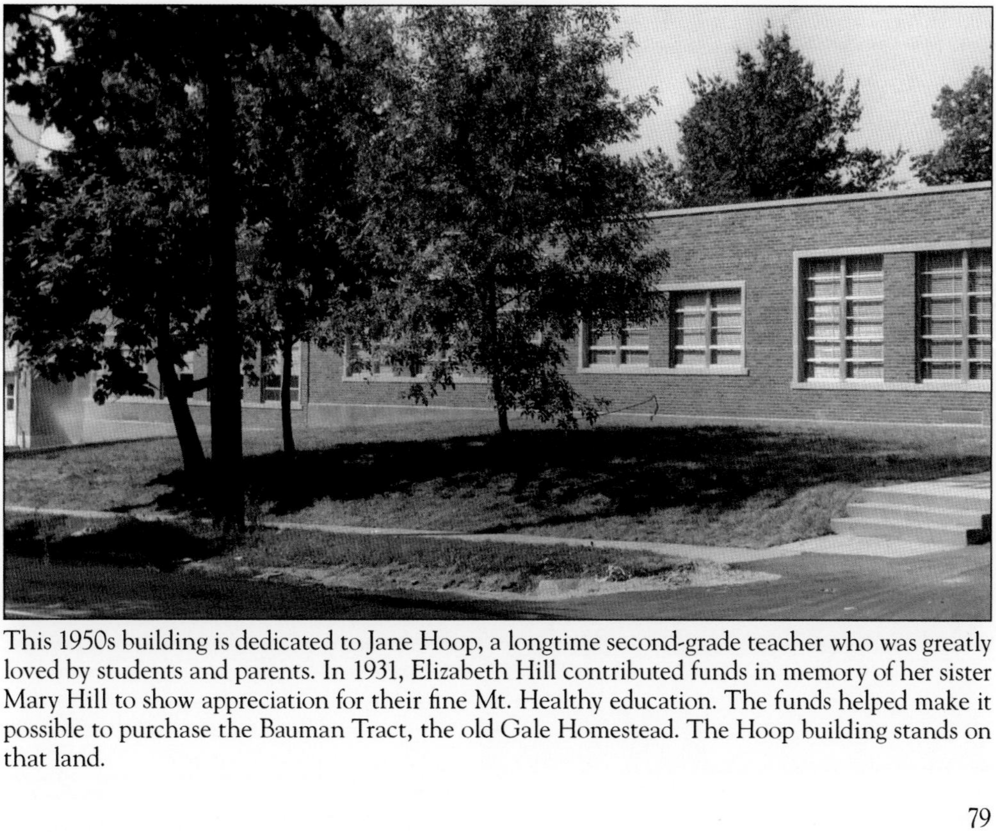

This 1950s building is dedicated to Jane Hoop, a longtime second-grade teacher who was greatly loved by students and parents. In 1931, Elizabeth Hill contributed funds in memory of her sister Mary Hill to show appreciation for their fine Mt. Healthy education. The funds helped make it possible to purchase the Bauman Tract, the old Gale Homestead. The Hoop building stands on that land.

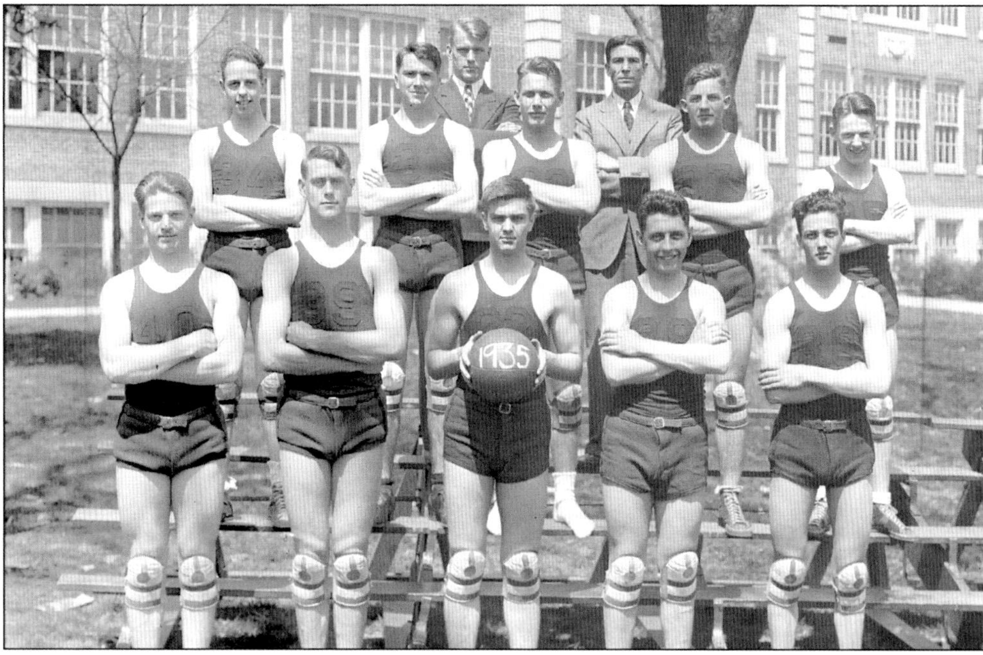

Motivated by their modern gymnasium, Mt. Healthy basketball teams won many championships. Teams were coached by Matthew Duvall (back row, right) for 28 years. This 1935 team was the last team that he coached. Duvall served 45 years in education, 36 of those at Mt. Healthy. He worked as a teacher, and between 1912 and 1943, he served as superintendent. A school was named in his honor.

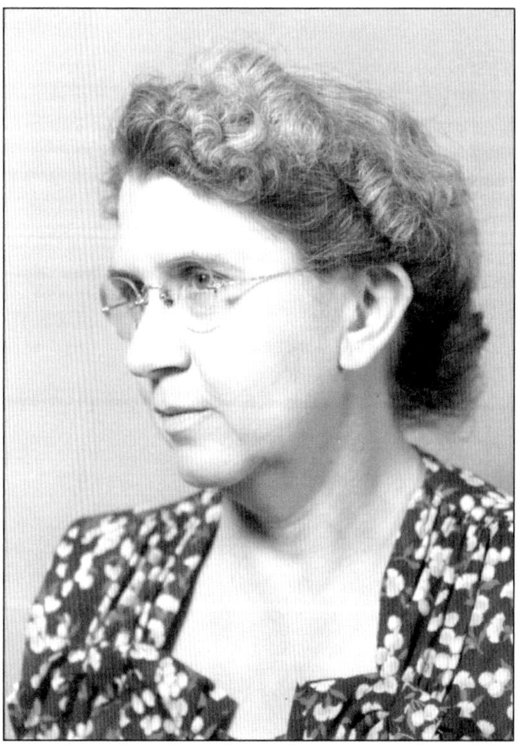

The Ethel L. Frost elementary building, located in Seven Hills, was dedicated on September 5, 1965. Beginning in 1921, Frost taught in the Mt. Healthy schools for 44 years. Generations of Mt. Healthy students knew her as their high school English and Latin teacher and as the advisor to the *Zem-Zem* staff.

Six

SUPPORTING FREEDOM FOR ALL

Because the Northwest Ordinance of 1787 stated that slavery was not permitted in the territories north of the Ohio River, Ohio became crucial to the antislavery movement. The Underground Railroad was a system of transportation routes over which fugitive slaves were secretly taken to Canada. There were many points along the Ohio River where fleeing slaves could cross and be met by folks willing and able to help them move toward freedom. It is estimated that there were approximately 3,000 miles of Underground Railroad trails existing in Ohio.

By 1850, the Fugitive Slave Law made the work of the Underground Railroad even more dangerous. Those who were found to be involved were subjected to jail and heavy fines.

The title *abolitionist* was given to those individuals actively working to abolish slavery. Early settlers such as the LaBoiteaux and Cary families spoke out vigorously against slavery. Five homes in Mt. Healthy have been positively identified as safe houses. These homes harbored slaves as they journeyed toward Canada. Two of them stand today and have evidence of rooms or tunnels where slaves were concealed.

The issue of slavery pulled the nation apart. Even school-age children were involved in the debate. The story goes that those children whose families were against slavery wore an American flag on their lapel while those who felt that slavery should be permitted wore a butternut pin. The issue became so heated that several churches in Mt. Healthy closed their doors until the end of the Civil War.

The Liberty Party, formed during the 1830s, hoped to elect people to political office who agreed with its beliefs that slavery should be outlawed. It nominated James Birney as its candidate for president in both 1840 and 1844. Its political conventions were held in Mt. Healthy and caused many debates among residents.

The involvement of families in the movement to end slavery is an example of the diversity that has traditionally been found in Mt. Healthy. Many of the original settlers had fought in Gen. George Washington's army, were independent, and believed in freedom for all.

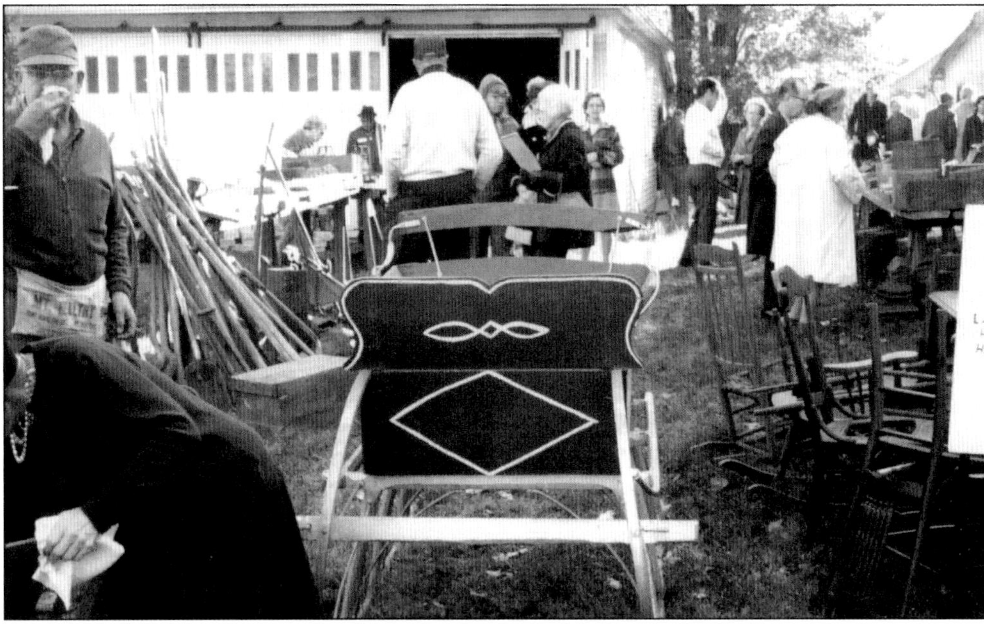

Dr. Alexander B. Luse was a respected physician who served the community from 1830 to 1892. Patients posted their names on a bulletin board located outside the Scott House. Luse traveled to their homes on horseback and by sleigh during winter. An ardent abolitionist, he also cared for the fleeing slaves as they moved through the Underground Railroad. His sleigh was discovered at a garage sale in 1970.

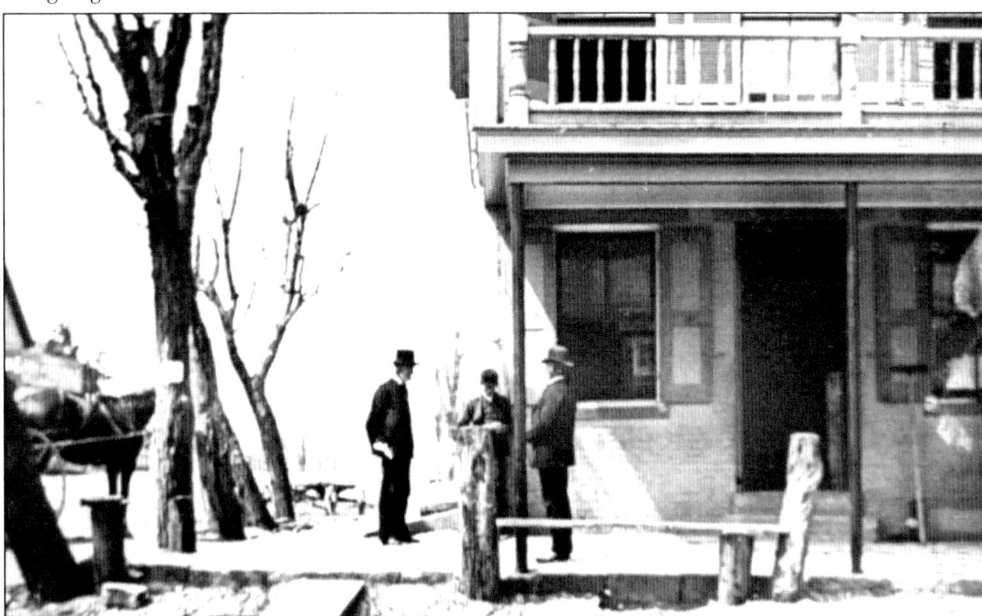

John Scott, a professor at the Farmer's College, was an active member of the Underground Railroad. His Mt. Healthy home was located directly on Hamilton Turnpike and to this day contains traces of tunnels and rooms once used to hide runaway slaves. This photograph shows Luse standing in front of the Scott House checking the bulletin board for names of residents needing medical attention.

The Liberty Party, formed by a splinter group of the American Anti-slavery Society, ran a candidate for president of the United States in both 1840 and 1844. It held its conventions in the Mount Pleasant Union Meeting House and each time chose James Birney, publisher of the *Philanthropist* as its presidential nominee. An active abolitionist, Birney's publication called for the immediate end to slavery and demanded equal rights for African Americans.

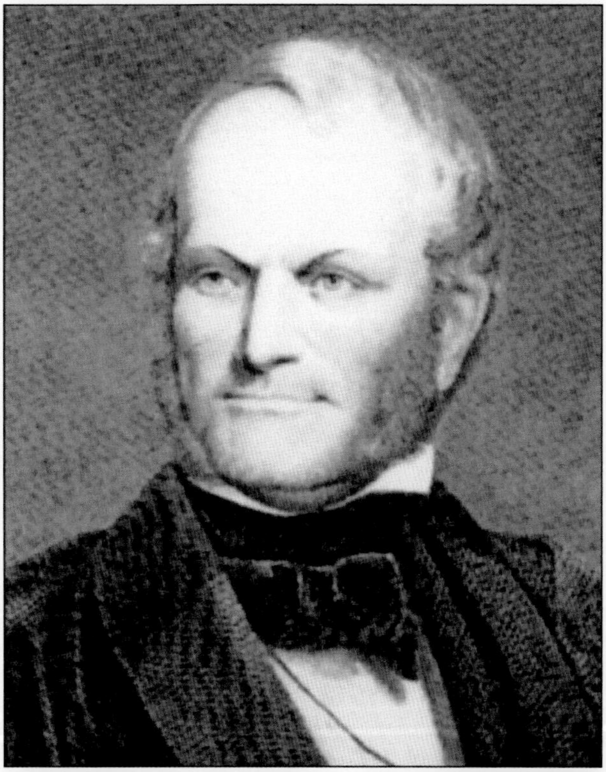

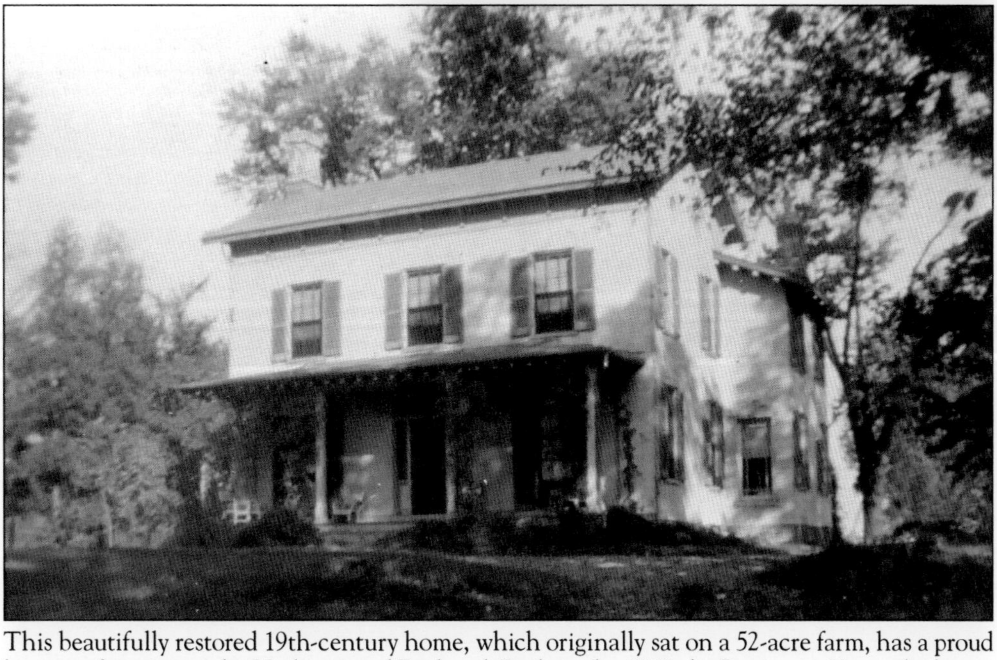

This beautifully restored 19th-century home, which originally sat on a 52-acre farm, has a proud history of service to the Underground Railroad. Built in the 1840s by Benjamin Hunt, the house faces Hamilton Turnpike. Rooms in the attic and basement as well as the barns and outbuildings were used to hide fleeing slaves. The 1840 census records also list two "free men" living in the house at that time.

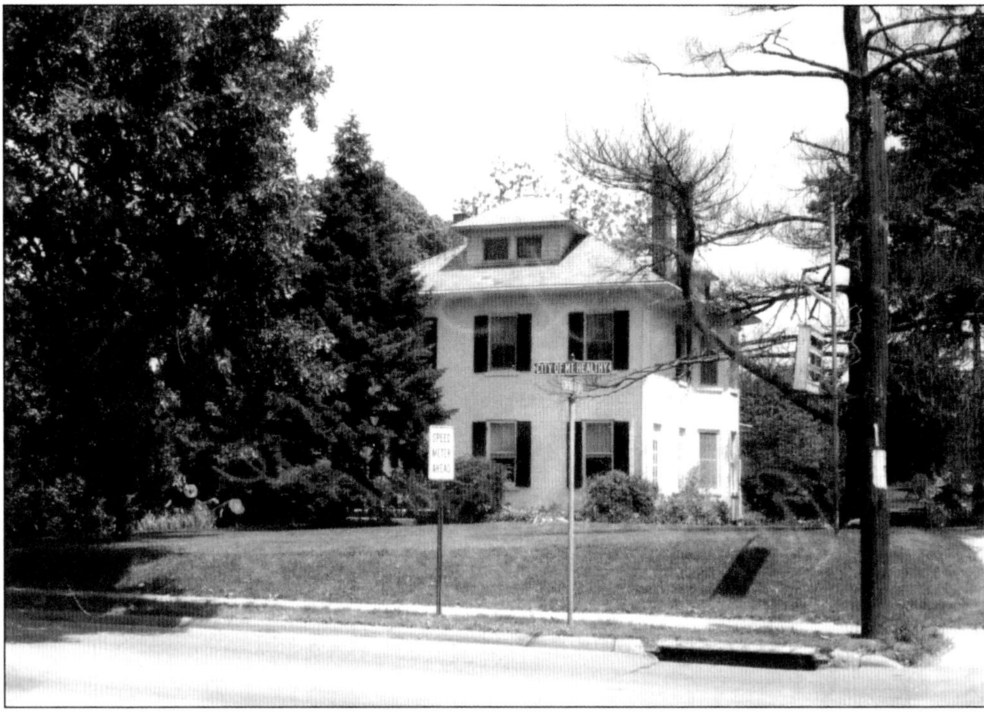

Sitting next door to the Benjamin Hunt house was the home of the Aiken family. Known as strong abolitionists, it is said that an escape tunnel ran from the basement of the Aiken house to a nearby creek. A slave yoke was found hidden in an old summer shed located behind the house. This home was demolished in the mid-1970s to make room for the Ronald Reagan Cross County Highway.

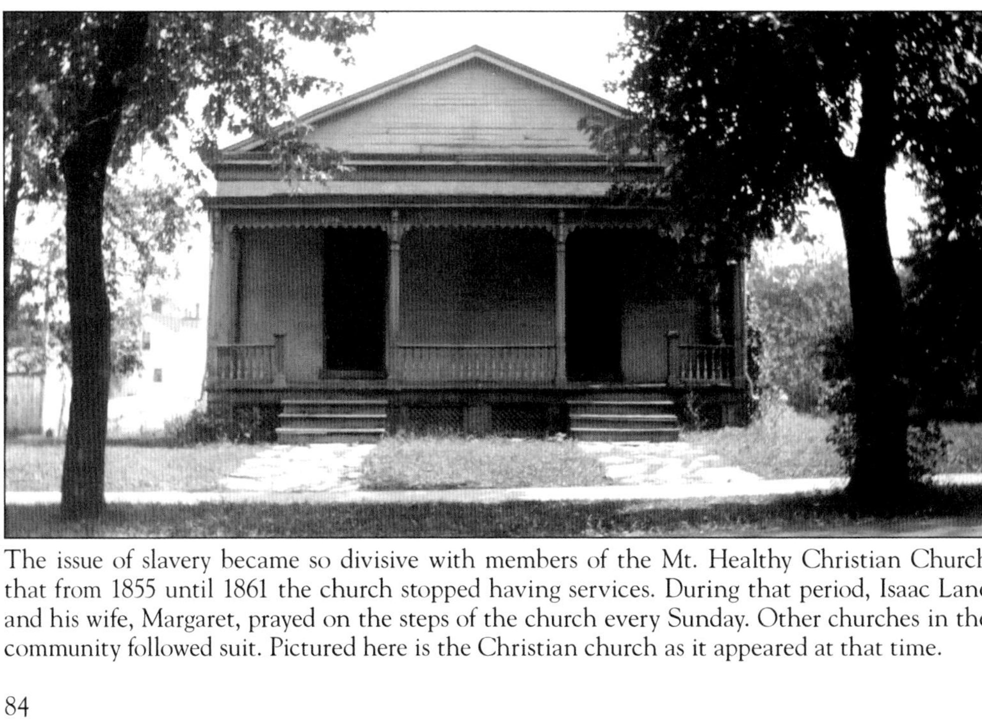

The issue of slavery became so divisive with members of the Mt. Healthy Christian Church that from 1855 until 1861 the church stopped having services. During that period, Isaac Lane and his wife, Margaret, prayed on the steps of the church every Sunday. Other churches in the community followed suit. Pictured here is the Christian church as it appeared at that time.

In 1859, Anthony Nelson, a freed slave, brought his wife, Rebecca, granddaughter Rachel Nelson, and other family members from Indiana to Mt. Healthy. After purchasing three lots from Gilbert LaBoiteaux, he built his home. The family became active in the Underground Railroad and helped slaves navigate the trails to safe houses. Nelson's descendants continue to live in Mt. Healthy to this day. Rachel is pictured here. (Courtesy of Arlette Merritt.)

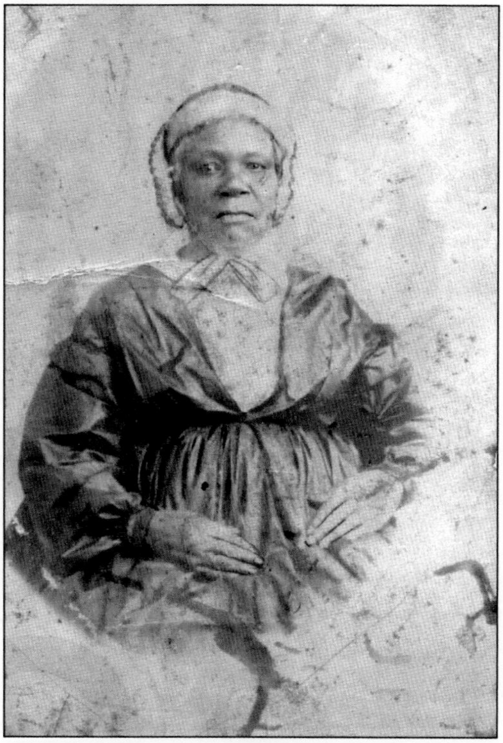

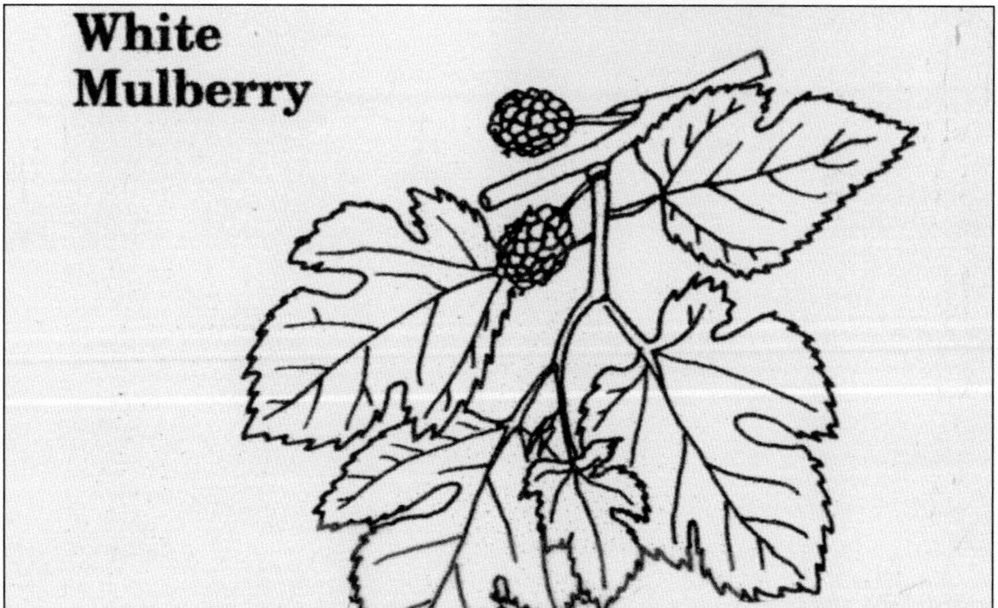

In 1835, Charles Chaney came to Mount Pleasant from Manchester, Connecticut, to start the Mulberry Grove Silk Growing and Manufacturing Company. A strong abolitionist, Chaney and his family hid fugitive slaves in their home until it was safe to drive them to another safe house farther north. Jim, a free black man who worked for the Chaneys, drove the wagon with Chaney's son Frank riding alongside.

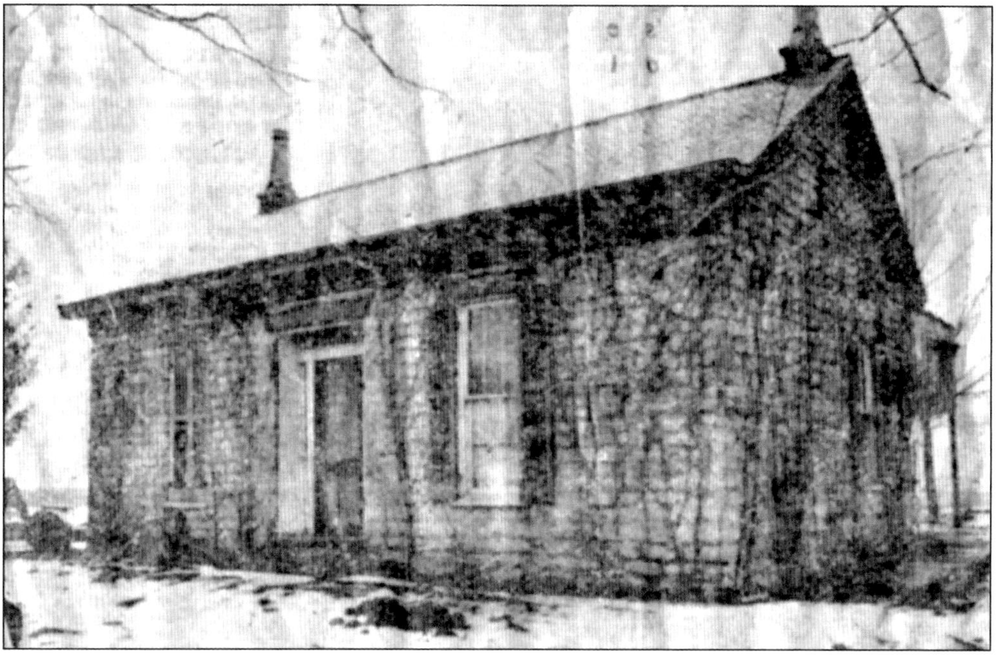

John Lane, an early pioneer, built this home in 1813 on Mill Road. The Lane family was very involved in the abolition movement and the Underground Railroad. They harbored slaves in their home and on their farm while being vocal on the need for emancipation. Their son Clark became a successful businessman who continued to speak out against slavery.

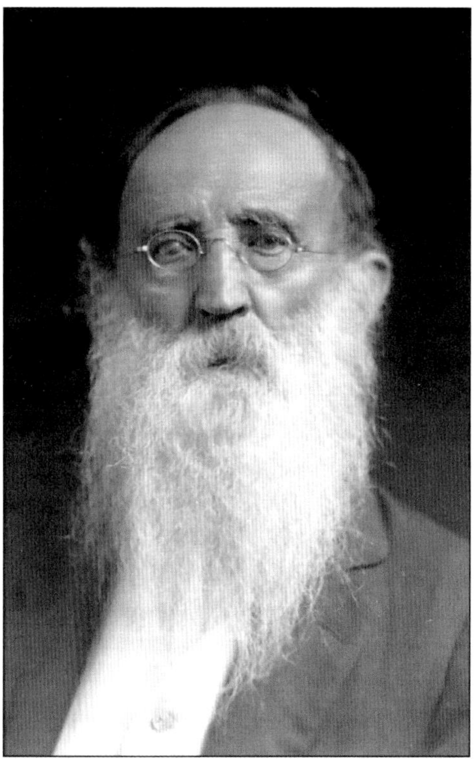

Gilbert LaBoiteaux, the son of early settlers, spoke out strongly on social issues. He collaborated with other abolitionists in the community and hid runaway slaves in his home. Among his close friends was Robert Duncanson, a prominent black artist who lived directly across the street from his home. Because of Duncanson's frequent travels abroad, LaBoiteaux cared for his son while he was away.

Seven

Building a City

Originally Mount Pleasant had many large farms that were gradually replaced by homes on newly dedicated streets. Often called an addition, the process involved the farmer dividing his property into lots and selling the lots to new residents. There was an influx of new residents between 1860 and 1880, around 1920, and again in the late 1940s. After the Civil War, many current residents moved west to Indiana, Illinois, Missouri, or Iowa where land could be purchased for $10 an acre instead of Mt. Healthy's price of $100 an acre. At this time, African American families moved toward Canada to be located away from the South.

Early houses were log cabins, soon followed by the rectangular Colonial-style house. Houses were placed near the front edge of the lot with deep backyards used for kitchen gardens and the barn. Early settlers helped each other out by coming together for house and barn raisings.

Older houses are located near the center of town, and newer ones were toward the outskirts. The varied architectural styles represent the time period when the houses were built. The majority of existing houses were built between 1915 and 1960.

During the early 1900s, Mt. Healthy was a bustling commercial center located along Hamilton Turnpike. A shopper could buy anything he wanted. Mt. Healthy has an outstanding and rare historic business center, where the old buildings are treasured and admired. In 1876, Henry Moser's brick building started the construction of the large commercial area. Today there is a balance of newer and older buildings with the majority being fine two-or-three-story structures built between 1876 and 1930. A walk along Hamilton Turnpike reveals modern uses for these unique antiques. The storefronts have been altered, but the upper floors retain original details.

This chapter will show the architectural evolution of the community from its earliest houses and will highlight some of the key commercial buildings in the distinctive business district.

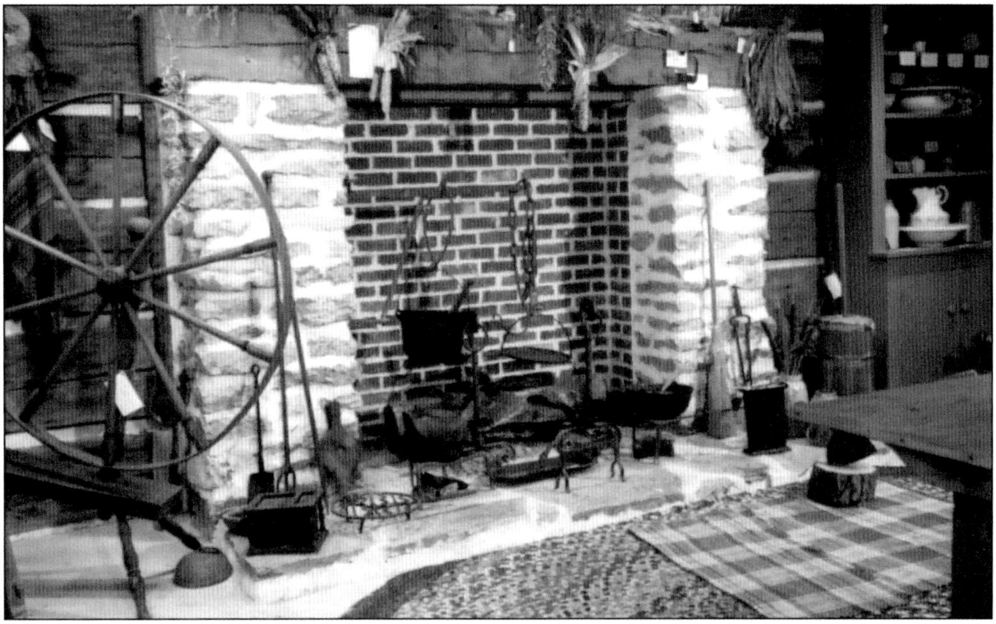

The Mt. Healthy Historical Society Museum houses many artifacts from early Mount Pleasant homes. Of particular interest is a reproduction of an early kitchen area. Around the pioneer hearth are placed authentic cooking equipment, woven rugs, and a spinning wheel. Early settlers in the area grew flax on their farms to make linen. Pioneer women had many talents and accomplished much with local resources.

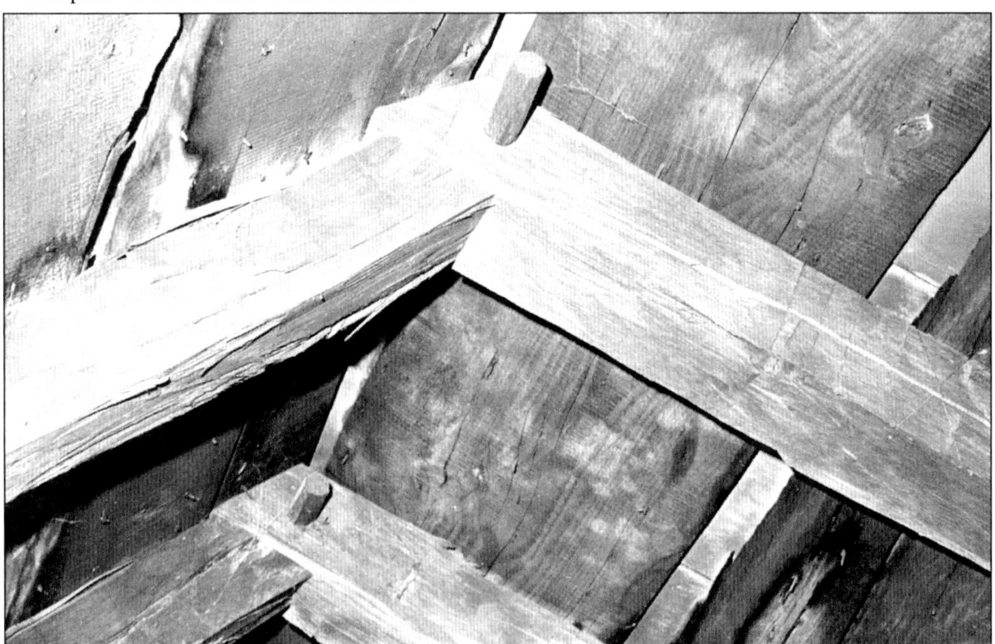

These beams support the roof of the Mount Pleasant Union Meeting House. The wood beams were dried for a year before being brought together to create the building's frame in 1826. They were connected by sliding the left beam, a tenon, into the square, the mortise, at the right. A wooden peg, or trunnel, was then pounded into the joint to hold the beams together.

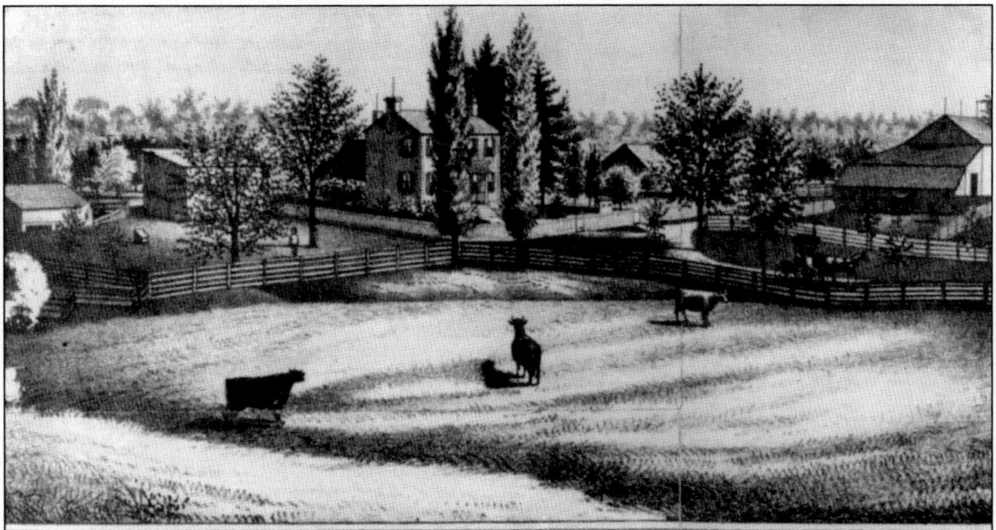

RESIDENCE OF C. B. JOHNSON, (BUILT IN 1821.) NEAR MT. HEALTHY, HAMILTON CO., O.

In 1804, Cary Johnson, son of Abner Johnson, built this farm on 236 acres of land awarded to his father for his service in Gen. George Washington's army. Johnson's first task was to construct a log house for his new bride, Rachel Jessup. After 16 years of living in the cabin, Johnson enlisted the help of his brothers to build a larger Colonial-style home for his growing family. Native stone was used for the basement walls, and wood was harvested from the property and dried prior to construction. The bricks were formed and fired on site. The cabinets and woodwork throughout the house were hand crafted by Johnson and are a tribute to his carpentry training. Today the Johnson homestead stands as the administrative building for the Arlington Memorial Gardens. (Courtesy of Arlington Memorial Gardens.)

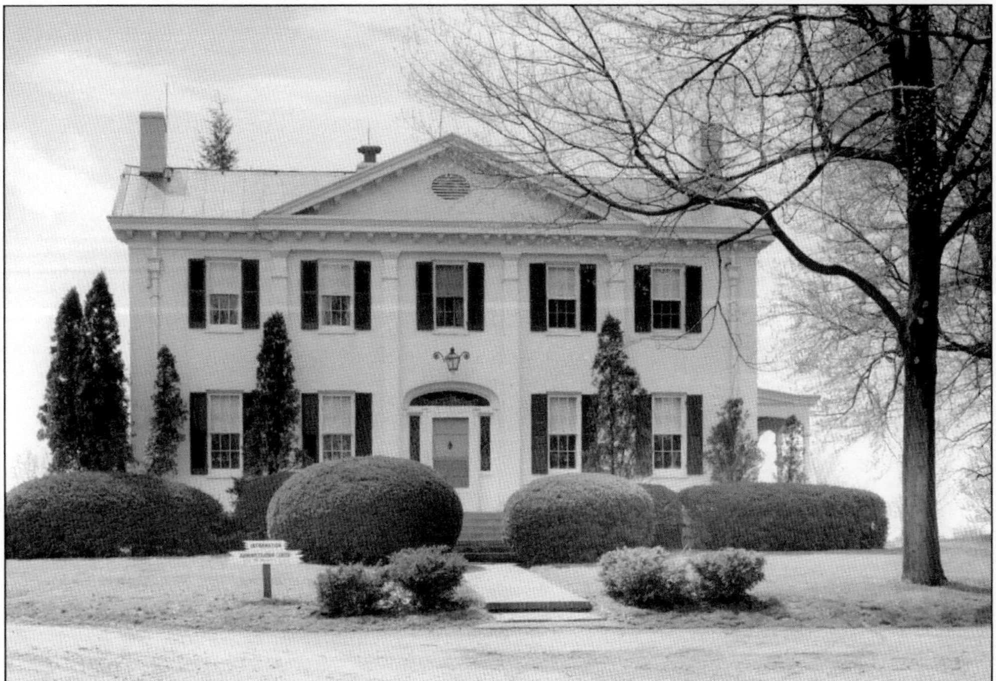

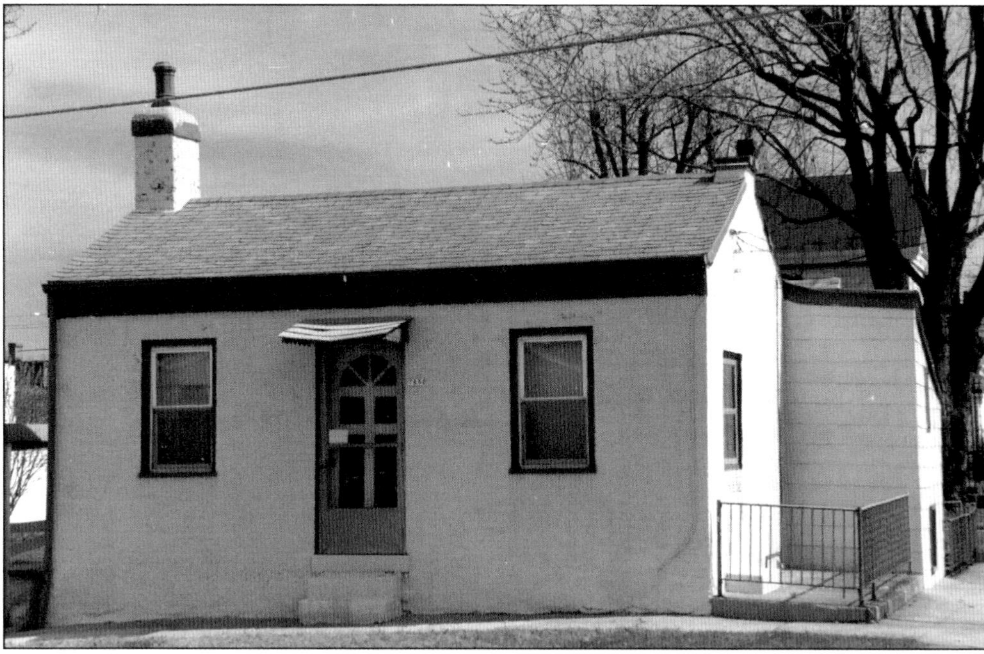

This home at the northeast corner of Hastings and Harrison Avenues is believed to be the earliest house in Mt. Healthy that is still standing. It is a Cape Cod–style home with a center entrance, a gable roof, and a rear addition that extended the roofline. End chimneys efficiently heated the house in the winter. It was common to place early houses at the edge of the property.

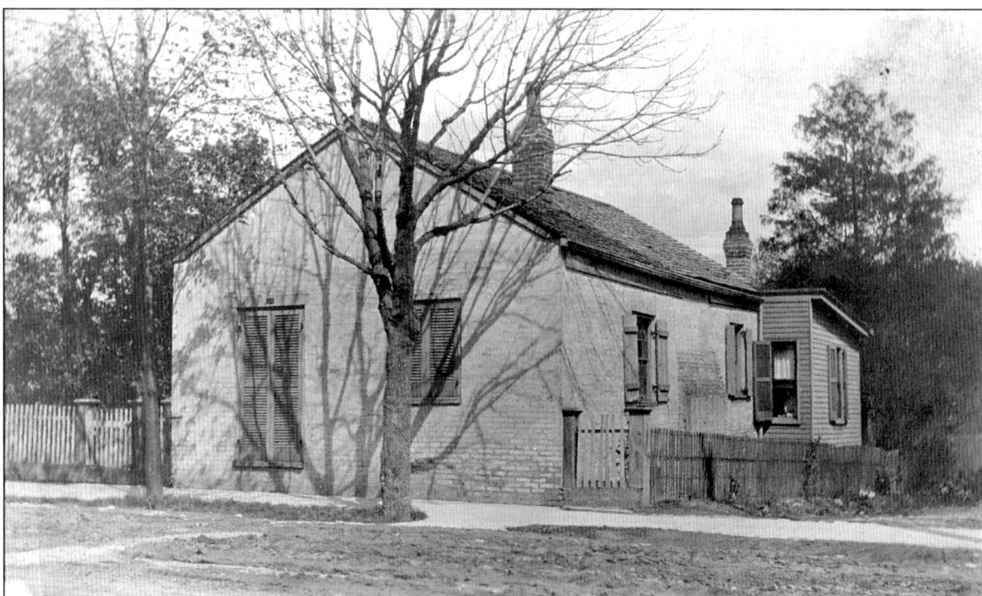

Elias Compton's home is believed to be the first brick house in Mount Pleasant. The bricks were probably formed and fired on site. The simple linear style of this home is reminiscent of folk houses built in the New England tradition. Sturdy and compact extensions were often added to the rear or side of a dwelling. Shown is a frame addition added at a later date.

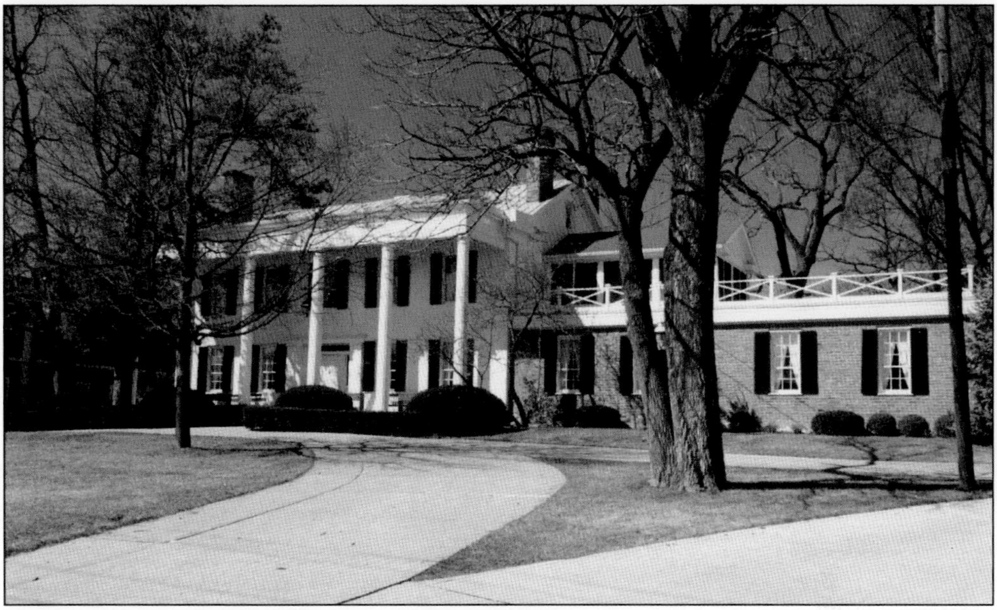

Built in 1833 by Ebenezer Stevens, a shoe merchant from Salem, Massachusetts, this Greek Revival house is considered one of the most interesting and grandest in Mt. Healthy. It is filled with antiques and has five wood-burning fireplaces, thick walls, and original, hand-planed woodwork. It is now the Paul Young Funeral Home. A full-length front porch and new parlors were added to the right to accommodate the business.

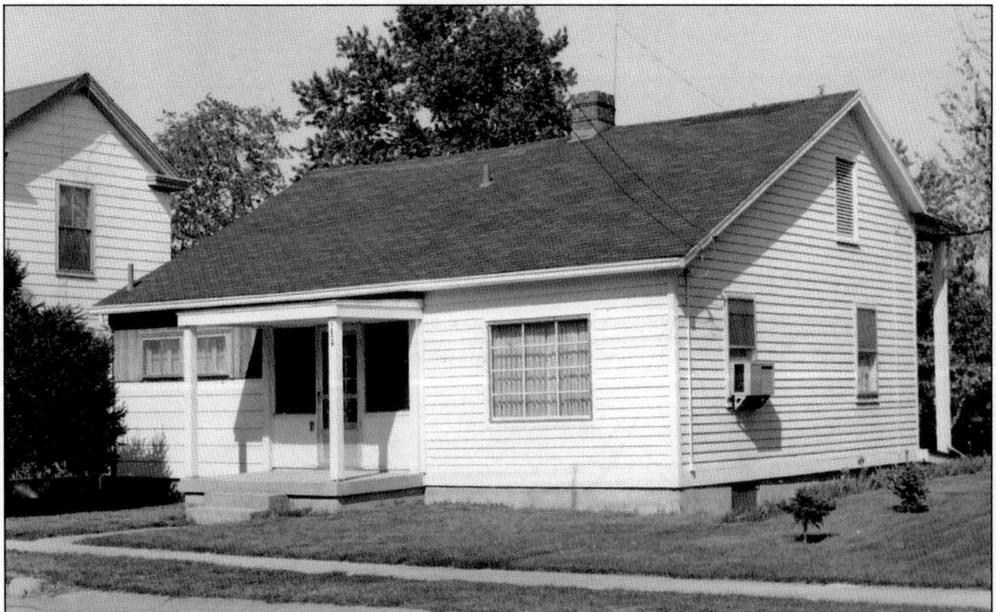

This simple three-room, one-and-a-half-story frame cottage was the birthplace of poets Alice and Phoebe Cary. Originally located on the Cary farm near Galbraith Road, it was moved near the corner of McMakin and Perry Streets in Mt. Healthy. In 1948, the cottage was moved again to 7804 Perry Street. The original style of the home is reminiscent of early farmhouses in the area.

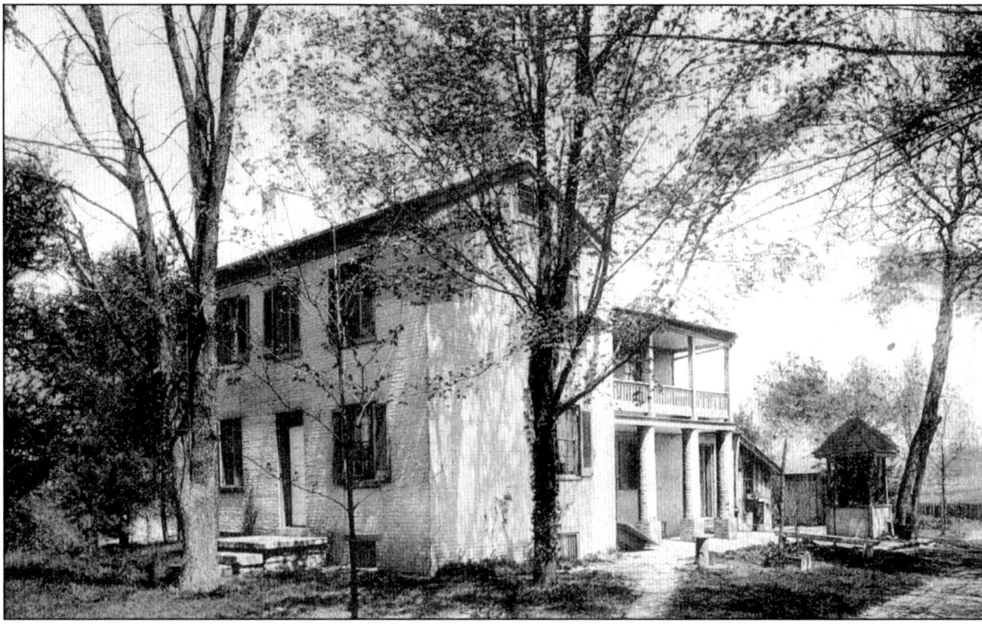

This beautiful 1837 farmhouse was built by Robert Cary on land purchased from his father and early settler, Christopher Cary. Robert was the father of poets Alice and Phoebe Cary. The home was built of bricks fired on site. The second-floor balcony overlooks the old sycamore trees and shades a terrace below. Located on Hamilton Avenue in North College Hill, it is now part of the Clovernook Home for the Blind.

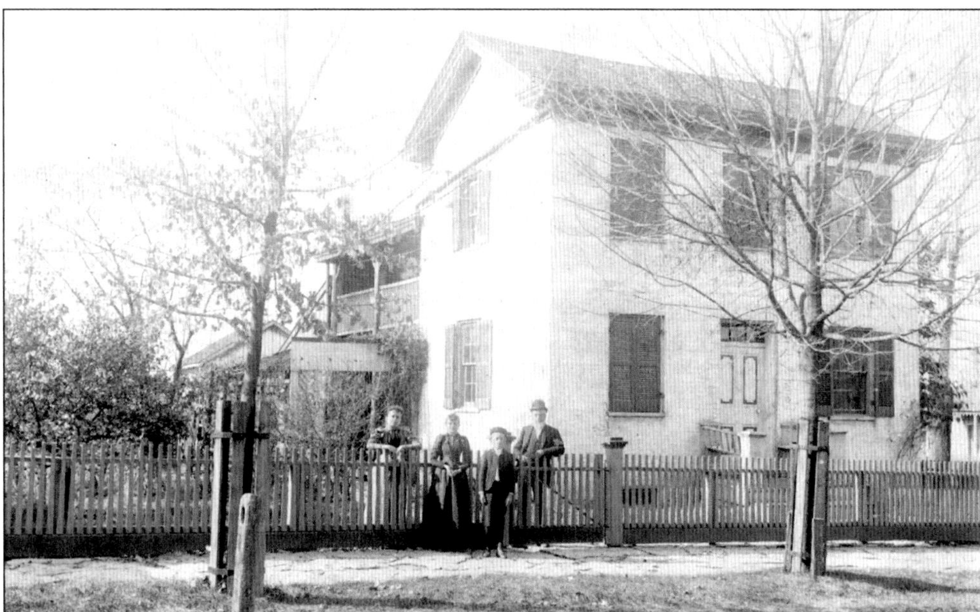

Located on the busy toll road in Mount Pleasant, this home is reminiscent of the no-nonsense spirit of the community. The two-story rectangular blockhouse is typical of the mid-Atlantic "I" style popular at the time. It was easy to build and provided good ventilation in the hot, sticky Ohio summers. The picket fence kept stray animals out of the garden while allowing neighbors to share gossip as they passed by.

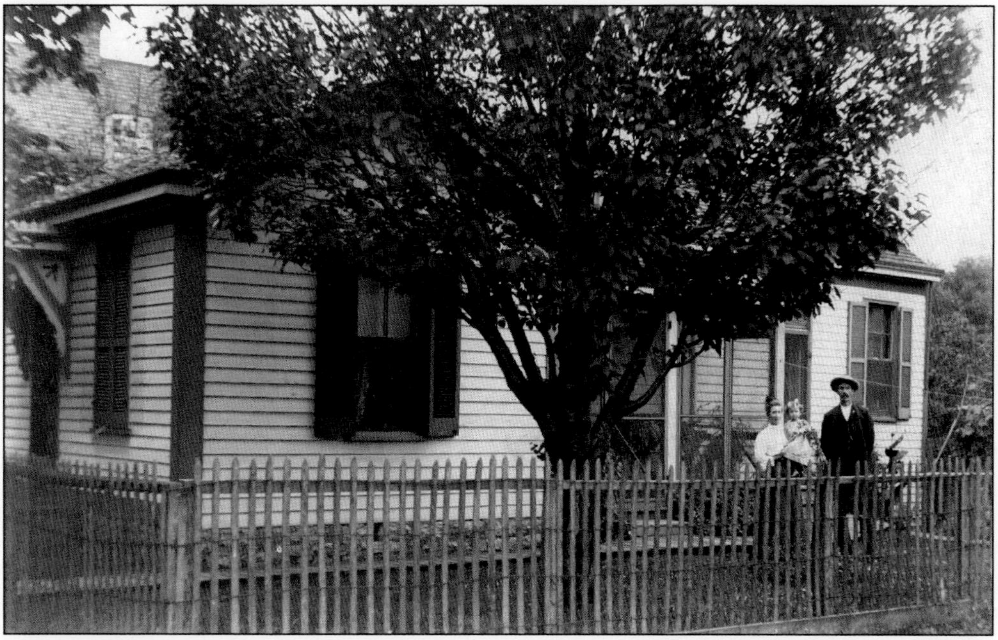

Robert Semmler and his family proudly pose in the side yard of their beautiful hall-and-parlor frame home. During the summer months, they enjoyed the added living space of their screened-in porch. One can also see the front entry, which shows a more decorative and formal entrance to the house. Located on Harrison Avenue, this home was part of the Hastings addition to Mount Pleasant.

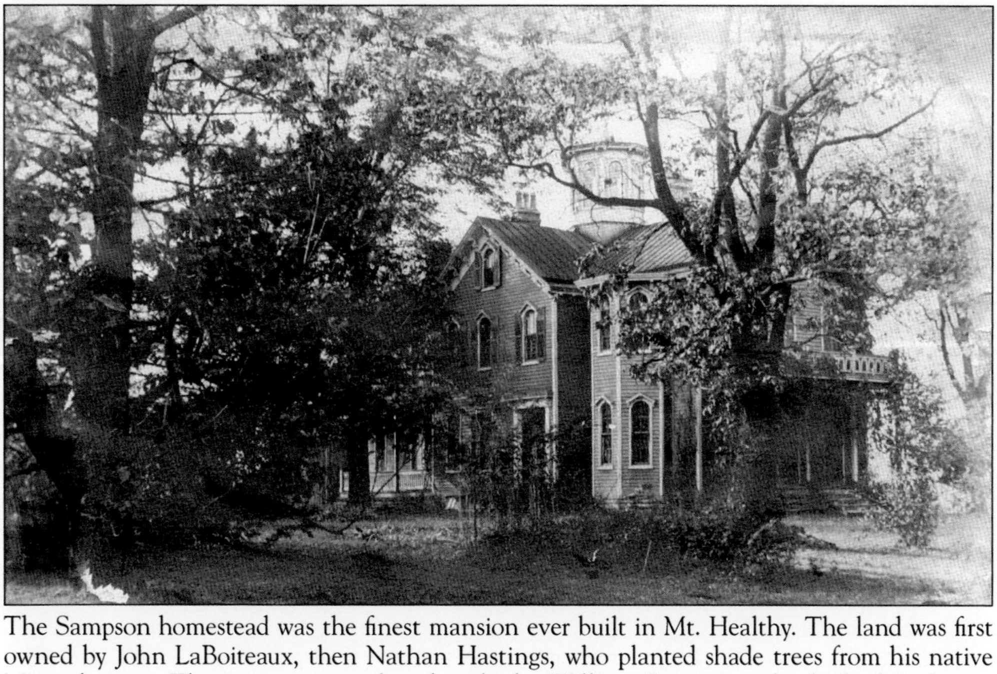

The Sampson homestead was the finest mansion ever built in Mt. Healthy. The land was first owned by John LaBoiteaux, then Nathan Hastings, who planted shade trees from his native Massachusetts. The property was then bought by William Sampson, who built this elegant frame mansion at a cost of $20,000 in 1967. The woodwork was made of Georgia pine. In 1909, the land was sold for construction of the high school.

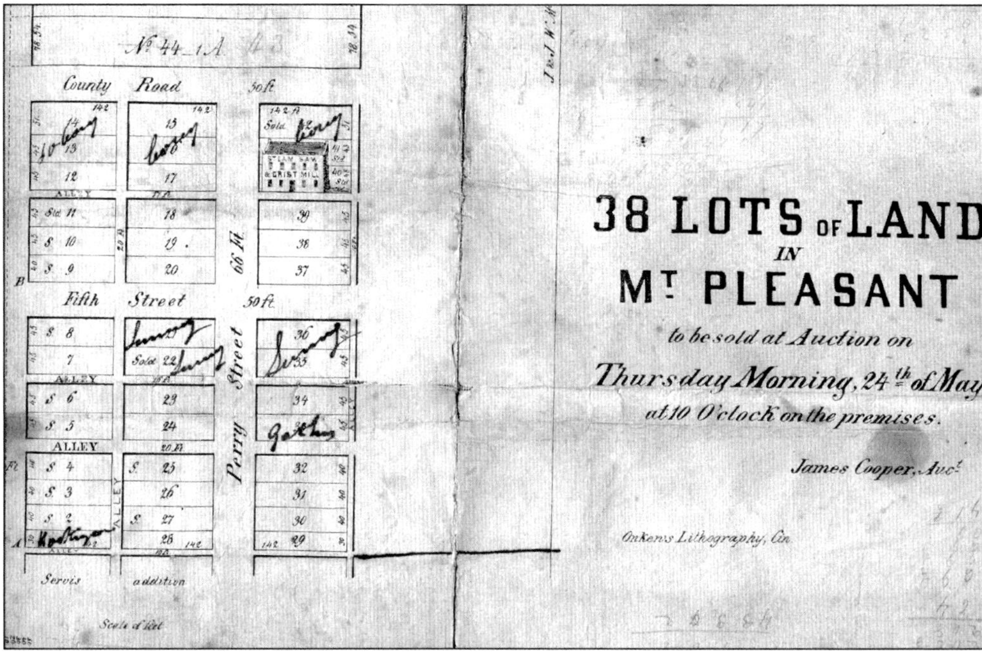

Early landowners created additions to Mount Pleasant as a way to disburse their land or to raise money. An addition contained planned streets and a series of numbered lots. Property was often sold at auction as advertised here, or the designated lots were distributed to heirs. There were a total of 18 additions to Mt. Healthy. New residents helped the community grow.

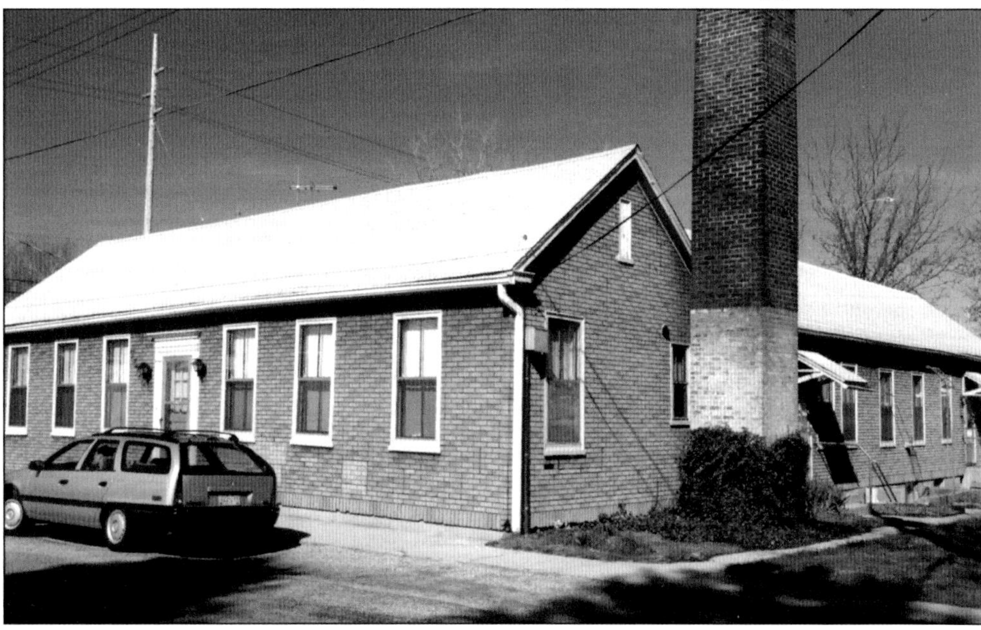

Mt. Healthy is reported to have had up to 30 tailoring shops at one time. They were sprinkled throughout the southeast part of town, mostly near Perry Street and Kinney Avenue. The family-run tailor shops were located in single houses or in small one-story additions. After the Hessler Tailoring Shop closed, the 1880s building was converted back to a residence. Today it stands facing Elizabeth Street near Compton Road.

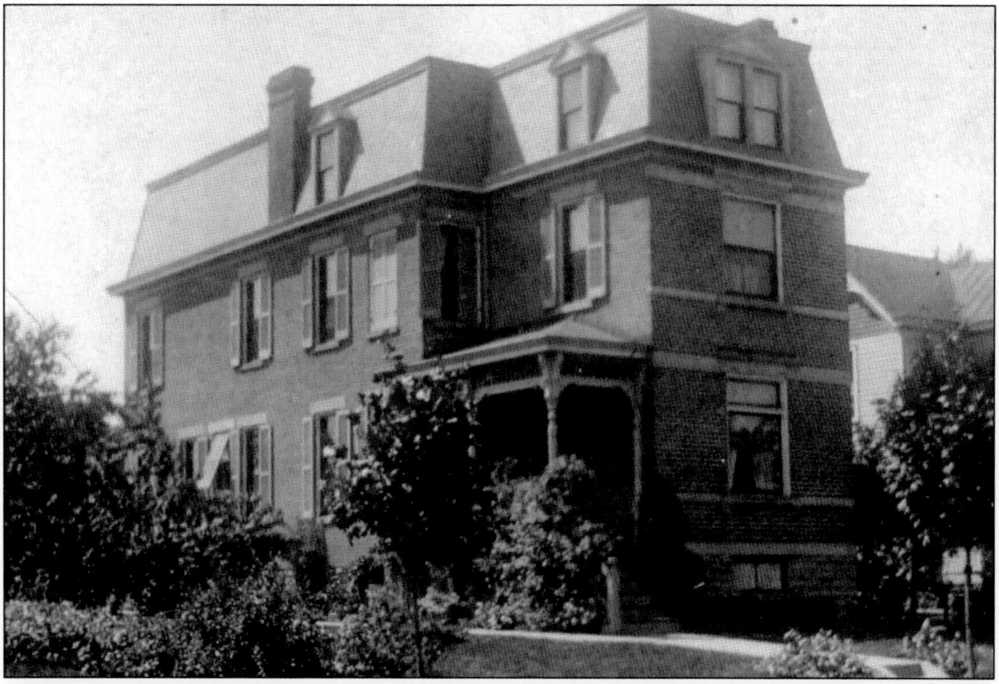

This Second Empire house with its mansard roof and pediment dormers is located on west Compton Road between Werner and Harrison Avenues. The three-story house has a porch with turned columns and a spindle frieze. The stone belt courses accent the window head and sill on the main facade. Elizabeth and Mary Hill lived in this house, which was part of the Gilbert LaBoiteaux addition of 1881.

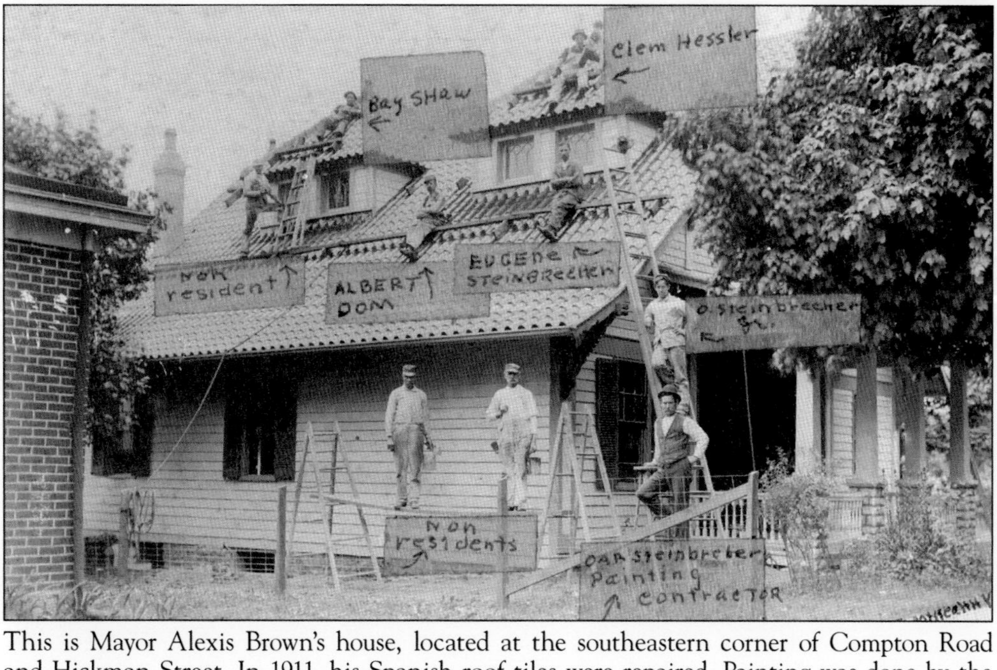

This is Mayor Alexis Brown's house, located at the southeastern corner of Compton Road and Hickman Street. In 1911, his Spanish roof tiles were repaired. Painting was done by the Steinbrechers. Workers are identified on the image.

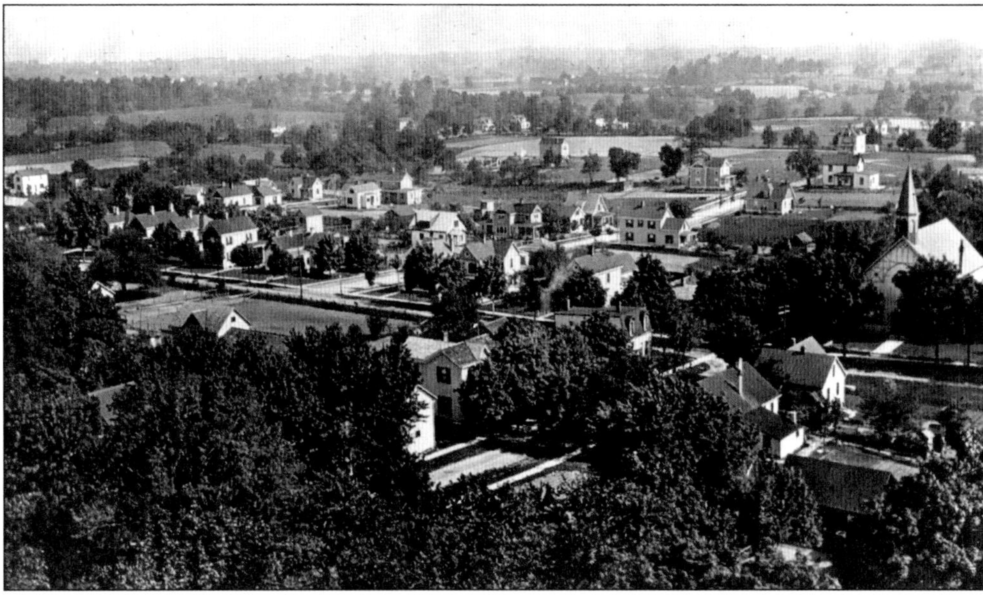

Taken between 1890 and 1928, this aerial view of Mt. Healthy reveals the growth of the community in that period. The majority of the buildings were Colonial in style with a smattering of Victorian. The streets followed the LaBoiteaux and Hill plat, running north-south and east-west. Mature trees, rolling hills, and a thriving business district attracted families to the community.

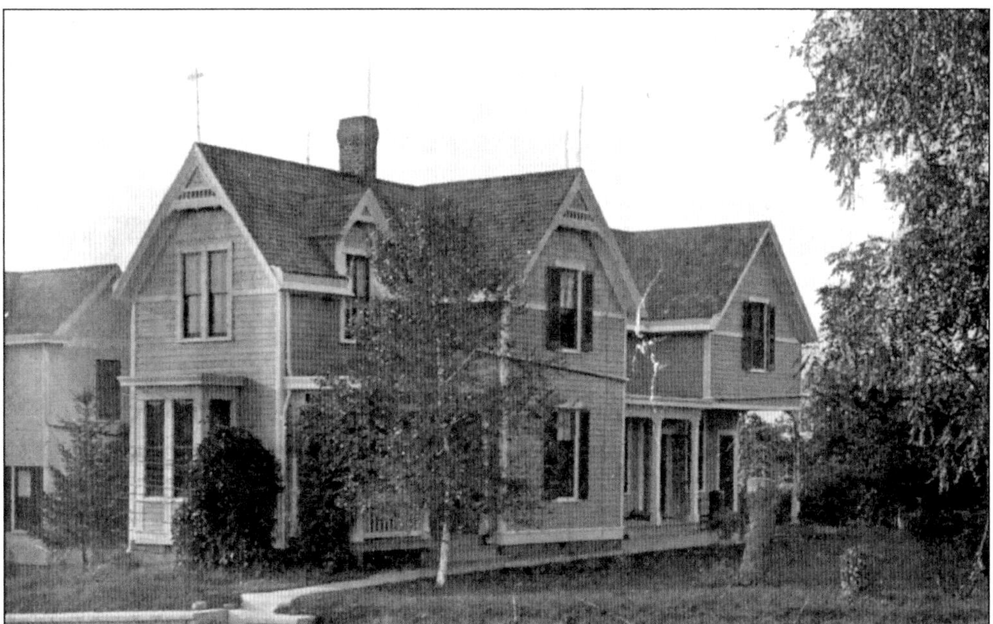

This beautiful Victorian stick–style home contained many eclectic elements common in its day. The steeply pitched roof with cross gables and the horizontal and diagonal boards are details that give the style its name and add visual interest to the facade. Set among mature trees and summer gardens, this picture gives a glimpse into life around 1900.

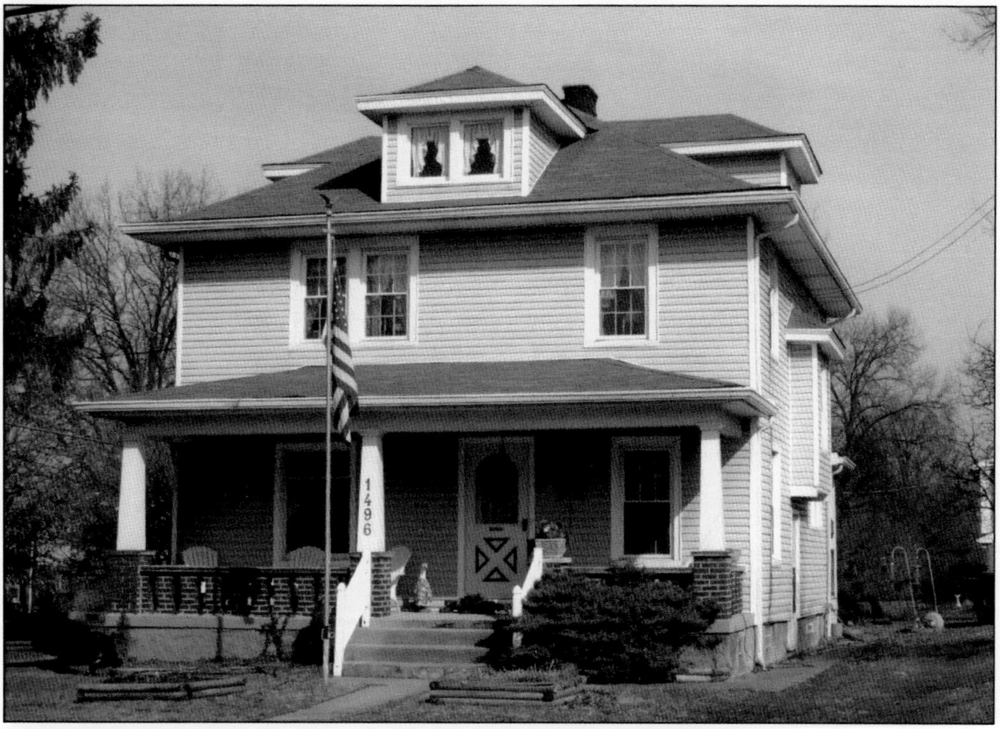

From 1908 until 1940, the Sears Roebuck and Company sold homes through its mail-order modern homes program. Customers could choose a style of house that fit their taste and budget from a catalog. Alterations could be made that customized the house and made it unique. This Sears house was built in 1921. (Author's collection.)

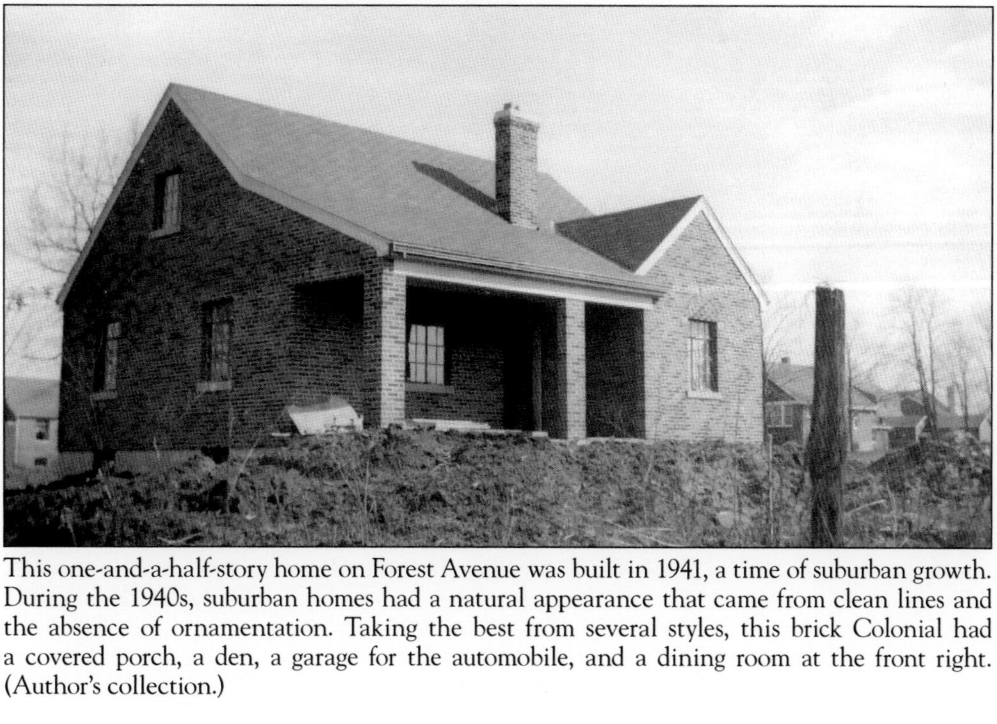

This one-and-a-half-story home on Forest Avenue was built in 1941, a time of suburban growth. During the 1940s, suburban homes had a natural appearance that came from clean lines and the absence of ornamentation. Taking the best from several styles, this brick Colonial had a covered porch, a den, a garage for the automobile, and a dining room at the front right. (Author's collection.)

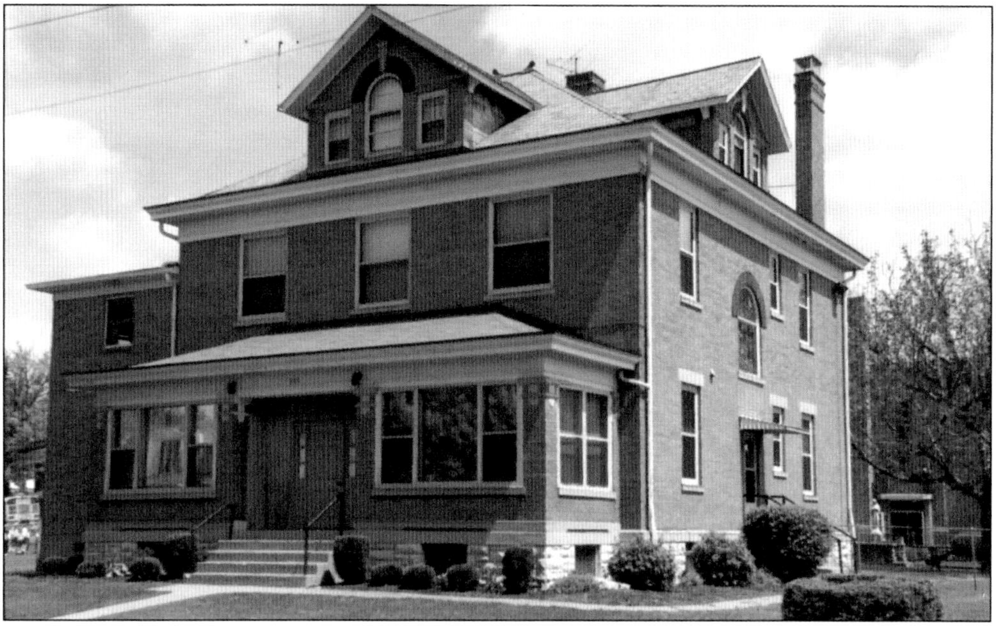

Built in 1917 as the rectory for the Church of the Assumption, this classical American foursquare house was the pride of the parish. The hipped roof contained two dormers that were adorned with classical elements. A large stained-glass window depicting the Assumption could be admired from the street. In 1994, the rectory was demolished to make way for the new parish center. (Courtesy of the Church of the Assumption.)

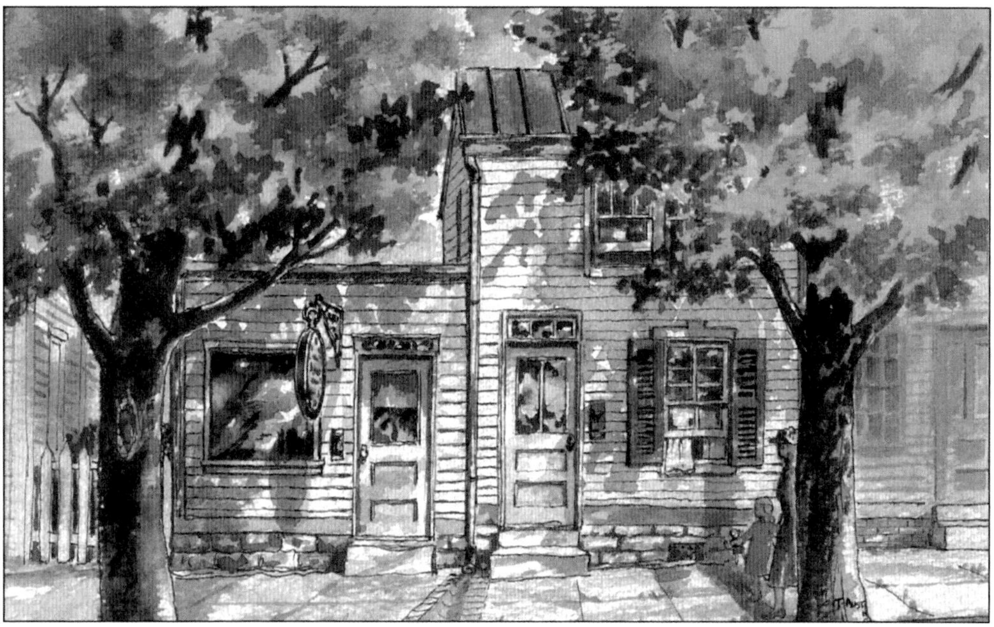

In 1920, Clara and William Effler found Mt. Healthy to be the perfect community to open their jewelry shop and raise a family. They purchased this lovely single-story storefront (left) and attached residence. Both buildings were simple frame structures with transom windows above the doors. The store was remodeled in 1927, and then the Efflers moved their family to a residential area of Mt. Healthy. (Courtesy of Bill Effler.)

This three-story building with its mansard roof and elaborately bracketed cornice was a beautiful example of High Victorian Italianate popular in the 1860s. Known as the Moser Building, it originally housed a grocery and general store. In 1876, the Independent Order of Odd Fellows moved into the second floor of the building and later purchased, remodeled, and renamed it the Odd Fellows temple.

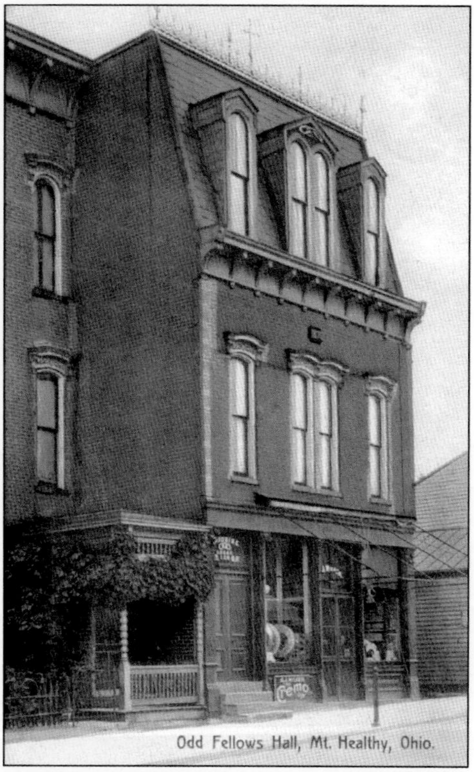

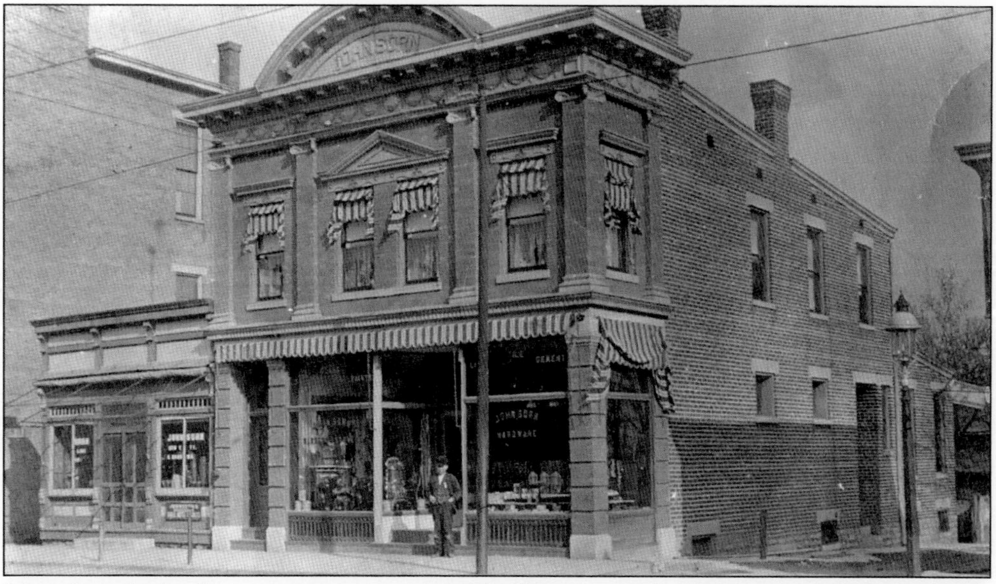

John Sorn built this two-story commercial building around 1900 using the classical-style architecture popular in its day. Mixtures of Gothic and Italian Renaissance Revival could be seen in the richly ornate roofline, the triangular arch above the second-story window, and the dome above containing the Sorn name. To modernize the building, many of its classical elements were removed. This building has been razed.

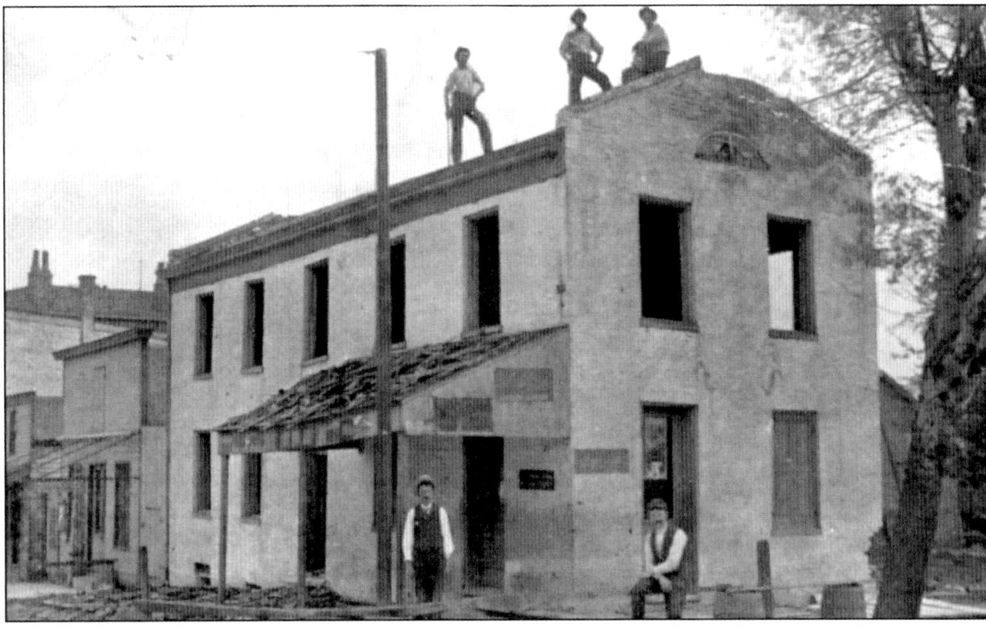

The desire to modernize led to the removal of an old landmark from the center of the business district. Standing on ground level is Martin Neese (left). Neese relocated his grocery store across the street. Contractor Red Bitter (standing, right) built the new building. Following shopkeeper's practice, the new Esses Building had stores and a second-floor residence. It is in service today. Workers on the roof are unidentified.

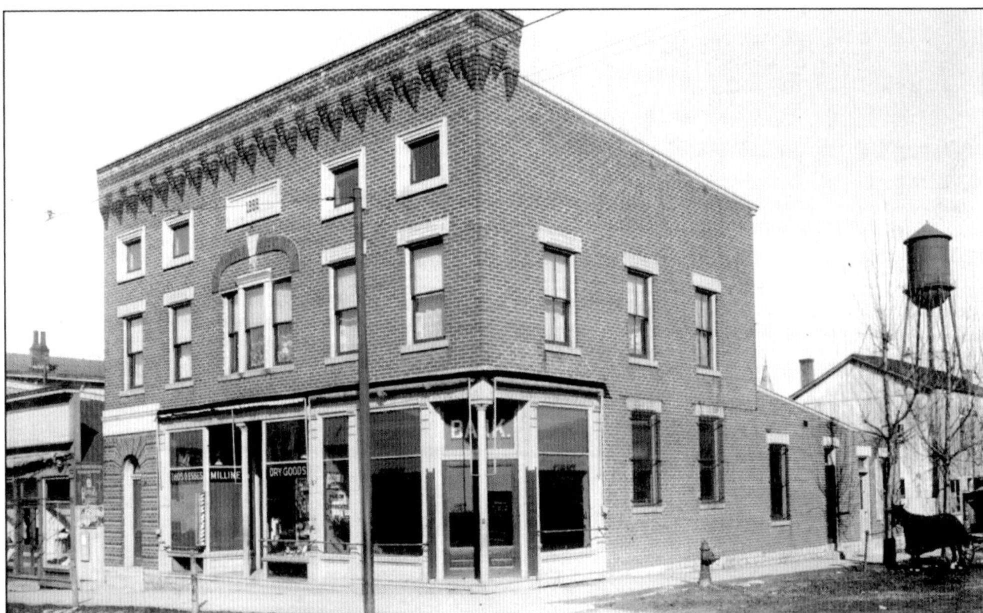

The Esses Building was built in 1899 at the northeast corner of Hamilton Pike and Compton Road. Below the large stone panel is a tripartite window that has a segmental arch and keystone. In 1912, the building was occupied by Thomas D. Esses Dry Goods and the First National Bank of Mt. Healthy. By 1940, Esses owned the building and used the entire first floor for his dry goods business.

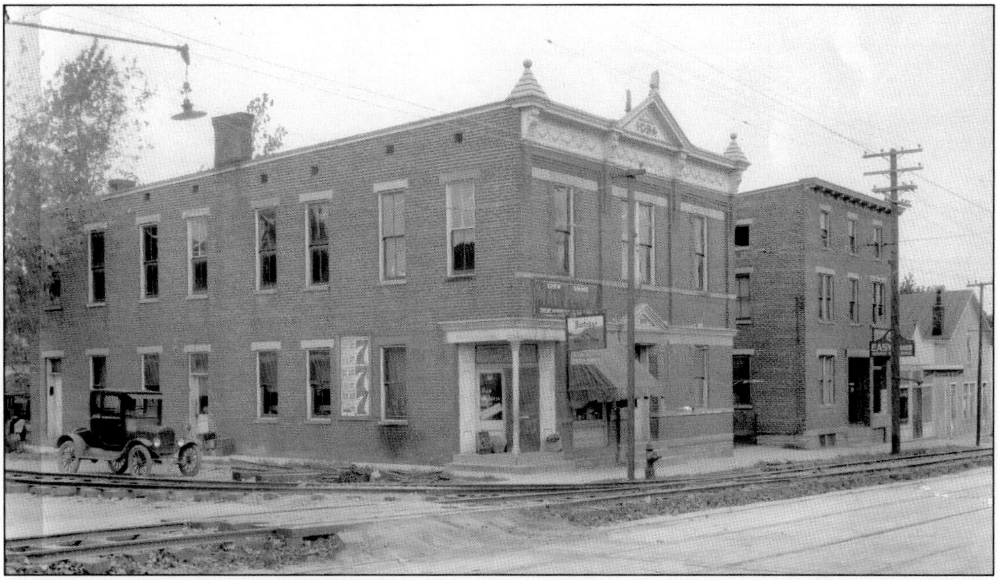

The Independent German Benevolent Association (IGBA) was organized for the mutual support of German immigrants and their relatives. Built in 1905, its two-story Second Renaissance Revival building was crowned with a pediment topped by a finial with "IGBA" on it. This building is one of the key buildings of Mt. Healthy's business district. The second floor housed silent movies and was the meeting place of many organizations.

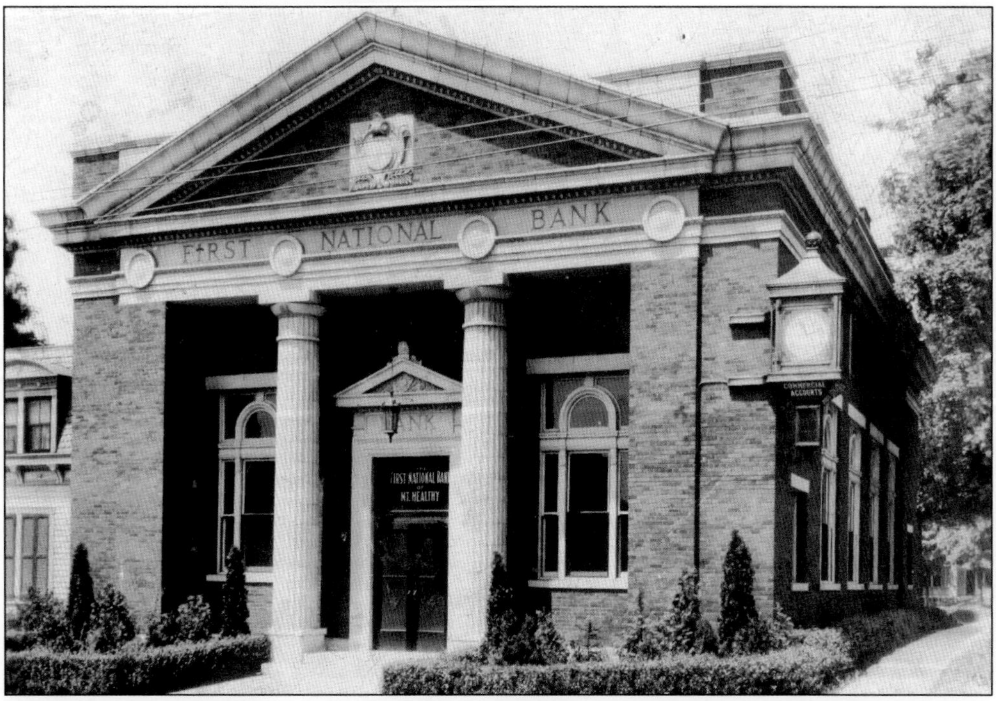

Neoclassical was the style of the day when this bank was built around 1925. The tall, fluted columns that rise up to the second floor, the low pitched triangular gable, and the solid brick facade give the impression of history and permanence. Today this building is the home of the US Bank, Mt. Healthy branch, and continues the tradition of serving the residents of the community.

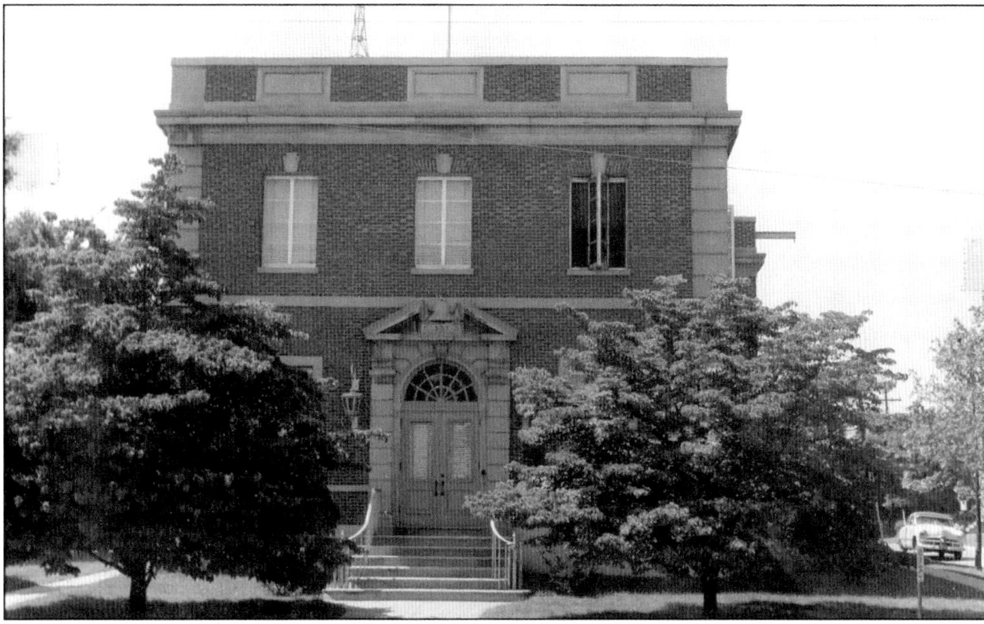

Constructed by the Cincinnati and Suburban Bell Telephone Company in 1929, this building housed the exchange operations for the area. It is a superb example of the classical revival style of architecture that became popular during this period. The central entrance, framed with broken pediments and heavy double doors, is crowned with an elliptical fanlight. Located just south of the main business district, it was a beautiful addition to the streetscape.

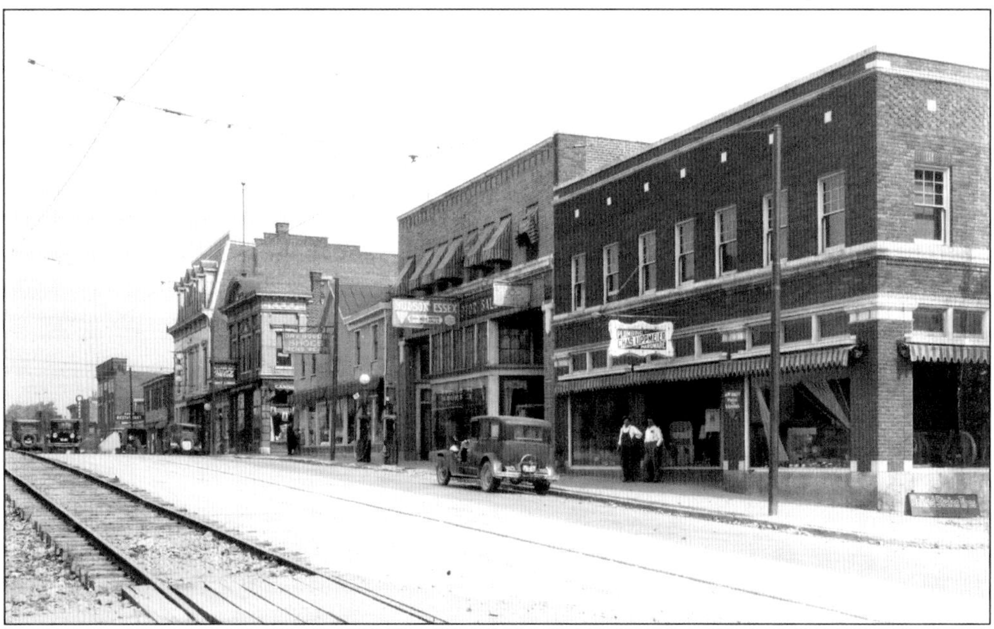

This streetscape shows the variety of architectural styles found in the business district at the beginning of the 20th century. Borrowing from classical architecture, Greek and Renaissance Revival was the style of choice. Built of brick with heavy detailing on cornices and doorways, the buildings continue to serve the community. Mt. Healthy has always been proud of its business district, with its diverse architecture and variety of shops.

Eight

Enjoying Time Together

The early pioneers of Mt. Healthy built their homes on farms far from the center of town. And although long hours were required to develop the land, the need to build a community was equally as important. In the beginning, religious gatherings occurred in homes and provided the opportunity to cement friendships and enjoy social discourse. As roads were built, networking improved, and families came together to support and enjoy each other's company.

Social organizations with a focus on service to the community began in the mid-1800s and continue to thrive today. The Masonic lodge was installed in March 1844, and the Independent Order of Odd Fellows was instituted in February 1849. As the village grew, the Mt. Healthy Garden Club, the Mt. Healthy Playground Mothers, and many other groups were formed. All worked to make Mt. Healthy a better place to live.

National holidays have traditionally provided an opportunity for the community to come together. Mt. Healthy Days have been celebrated with an ice-cream social and a display of antique cars that draws enthusiastic crowds. Best of all, the good cooks of Mt. Healthy have many opportunities to share their specialties.

Music in all its forms has intrigued and inspired Mt. Healthy families. Residents have gathered to enjoy events such as band music and concerts given by the Cincinnati Symphony Orchestra in Johnson's Grove. The Carmen Male Quartet and Mt. Healthy Music Club have provided opportunities for talented musicians to perform.

Sports were not ignored. Teams of amateur players were organized each season, and competition was rigorous. Baseball has a long history in the community, and cheering on the home team has brought together generations of kids and adults. From its very beginning, Mt. Healthy families have involved themselves in a variety of activities that have developed individual interests and community pride.

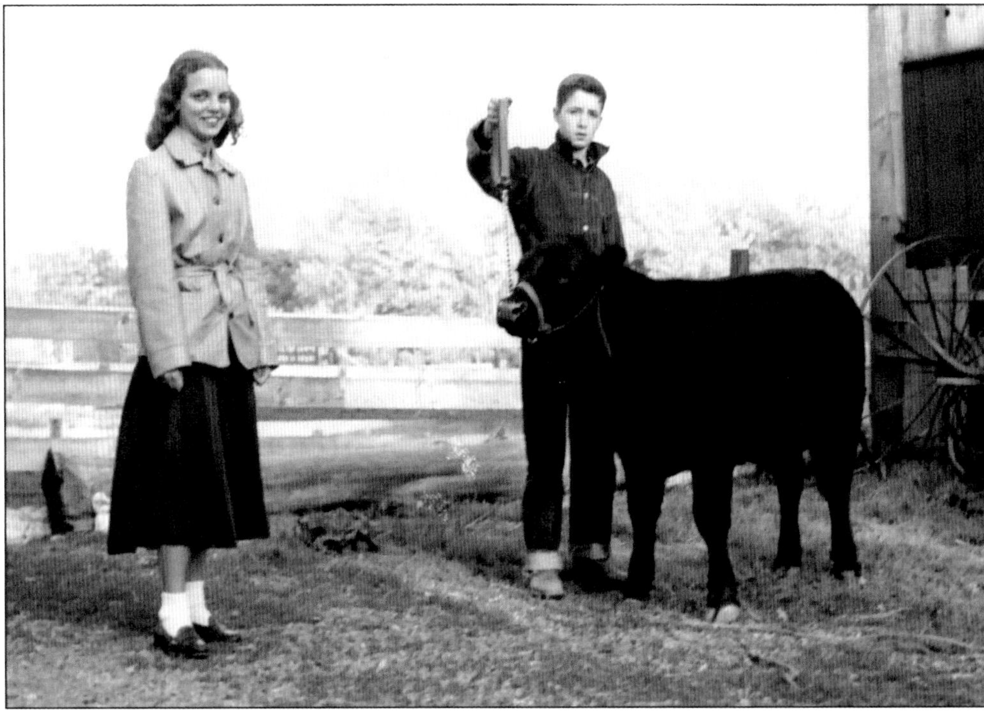

Members of 4-H learn by doing. Many Mt. Healthy youth participated in farm projects, including David Hinson (right), who used his prize money from the previous Hamilton County Fair to buy the Black Angus steer he raised for the next year. Charlen Ehrhardt (left) won an Ohio scholarship for her leadership work. During the 1950s, approximately 150 Mt. Healthy youth participated in 4-H activities each year.

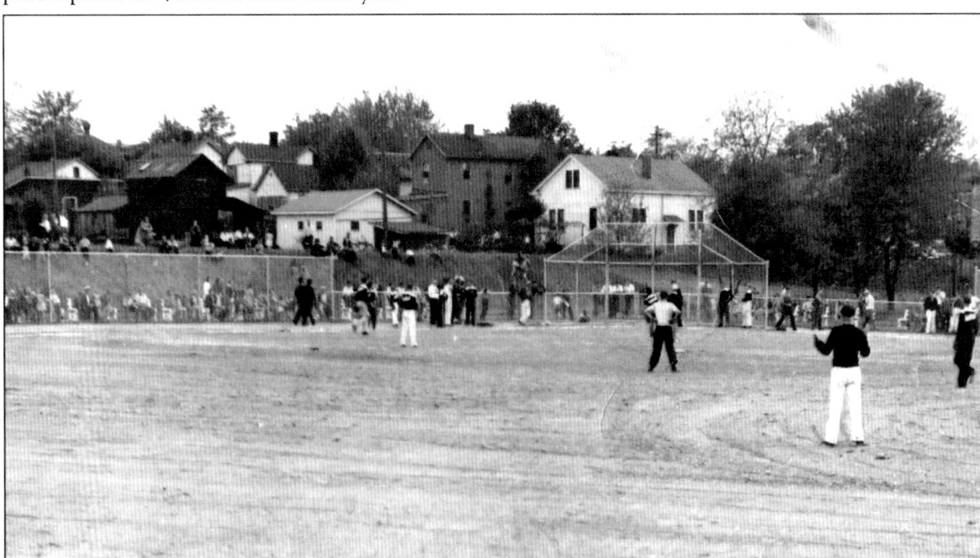

In November 1939, a bond was approved for the construction of the municipal park. Baseball was popular in Mt. Healthy, so it was natural to construct a baseball field. This is the first baseball game held at the park in 1940. Known for its efficient use of space and wide range of activities, the Mt. Healthy park was selected as the best park in southwestern Ohio in 1973.

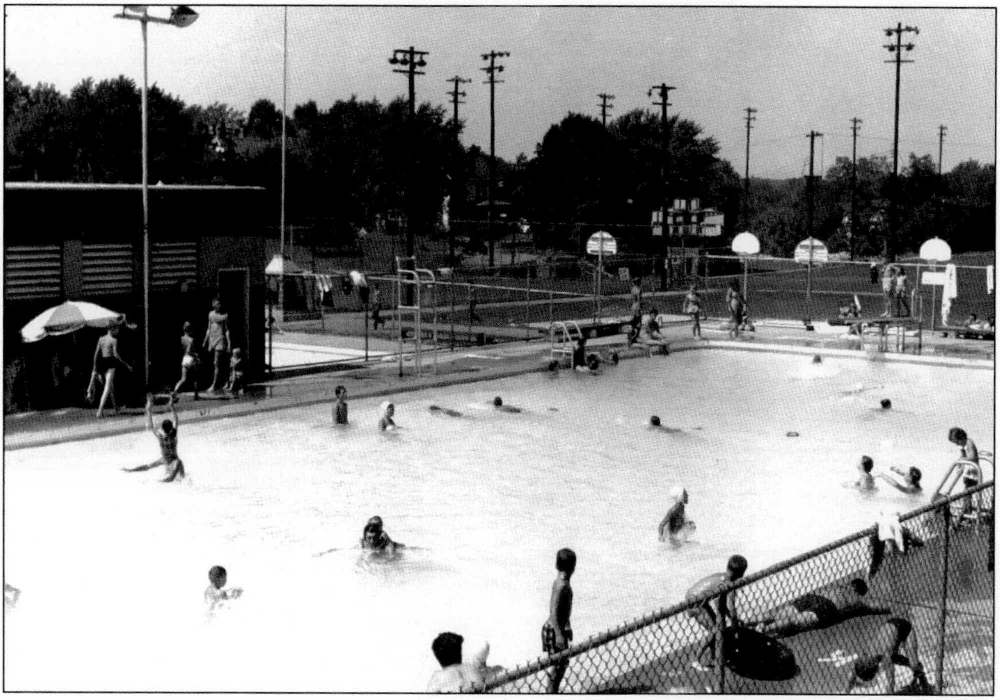

Beginning in the summer of 1941, children enjoyed swimming lessons and sunbathing. In 1943, the Mt. Healthy Playground Mothers club was organized with the goal of creating a place where parents could drop off their children and know they were safe to enjoy the day or evening. The club sponsored activities such as arts and crafts classes; weekly movie night; dances, including some with popular deejay Bob Braun; and the annual carnival.

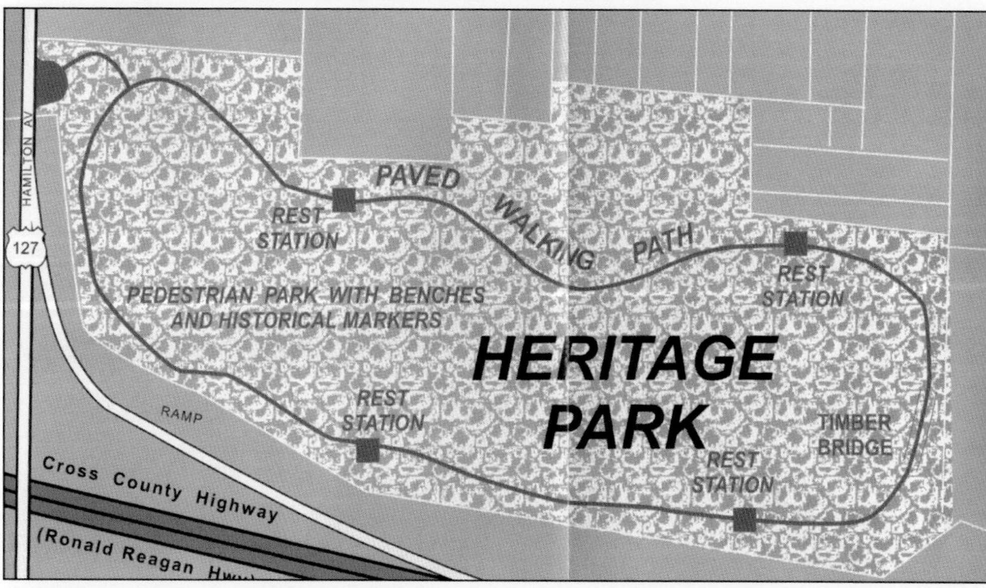

In addition to the municipal park, Mt. Healthy has two other recreational areas. The Nature Center, with picnic areas and a walking trail, is located near the old Brickyard Lake at the south end of Forest Avenue. The Heritage Park, a "walkers" park, is found near Hamilton Pike where Charles Chaney had his mulberry grove.

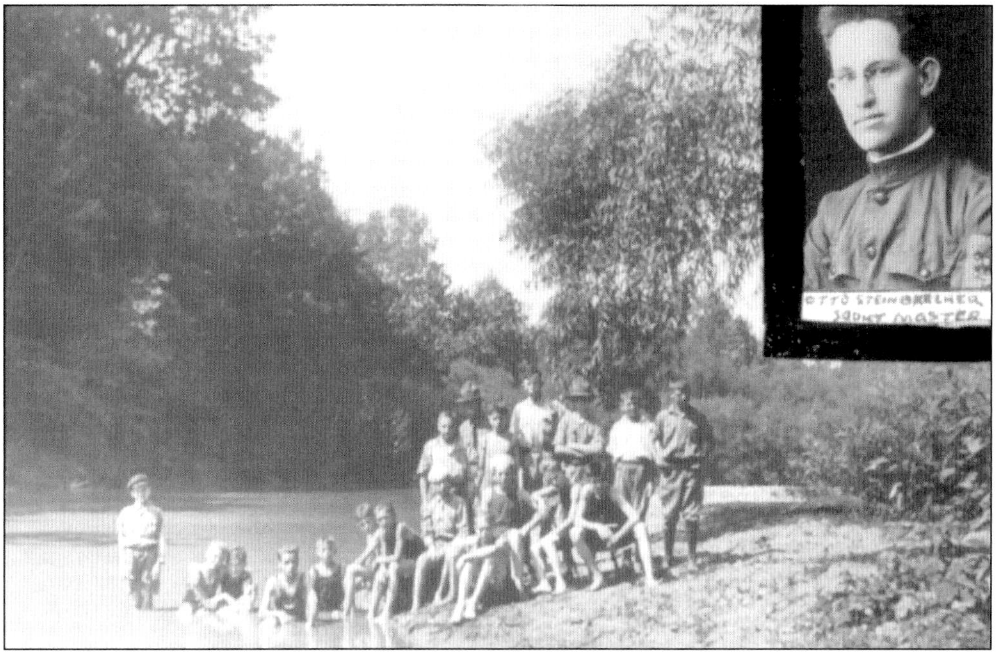

At the dawn of the 20th century, Scouting became very popular with American youth. The first troop of Boy Scouts in Mt. Healthy was organized at the Methodist church by Reverend Kelch. This photograph shows the Scouts in 1918 enjoying a swim at Camp Anderson in Indian Creek in Venice. Scout master Otto Steinbrecher is shown in the insert.

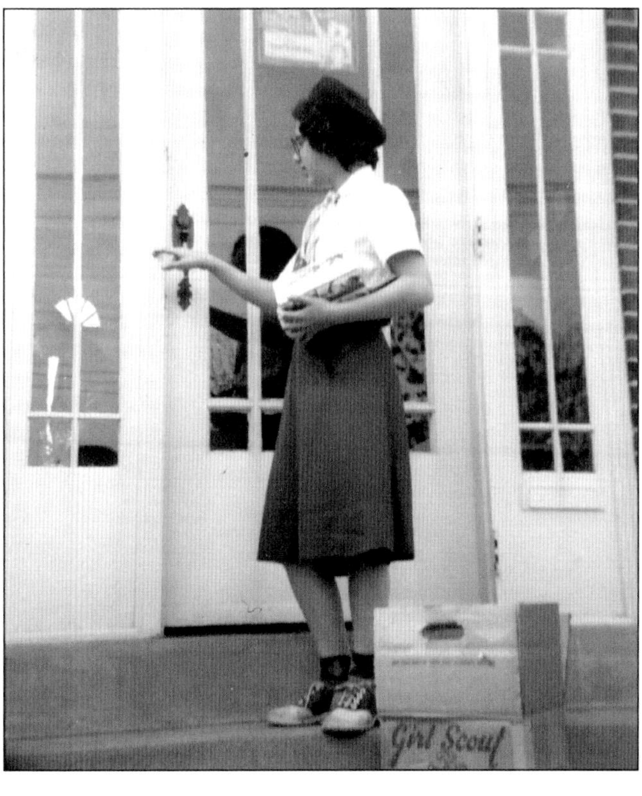

"Would you like to buy a box of Girl Scout cookies?" asked Carmen Ehrhardt. Senior Troop 2, under the leadership of Lucille Ehrhardt, was dedicated to service projects such as the Volunteer Ground Observers Corps, selling poppies for disabled veterans, and fund-raising for polio research. Scouts acquired camping skills and participated in annual international suppers. The popular Scouting program had many members continue involvement through their high school years. (Courtesy of the Charles and Lucille Ehrhardt family.)

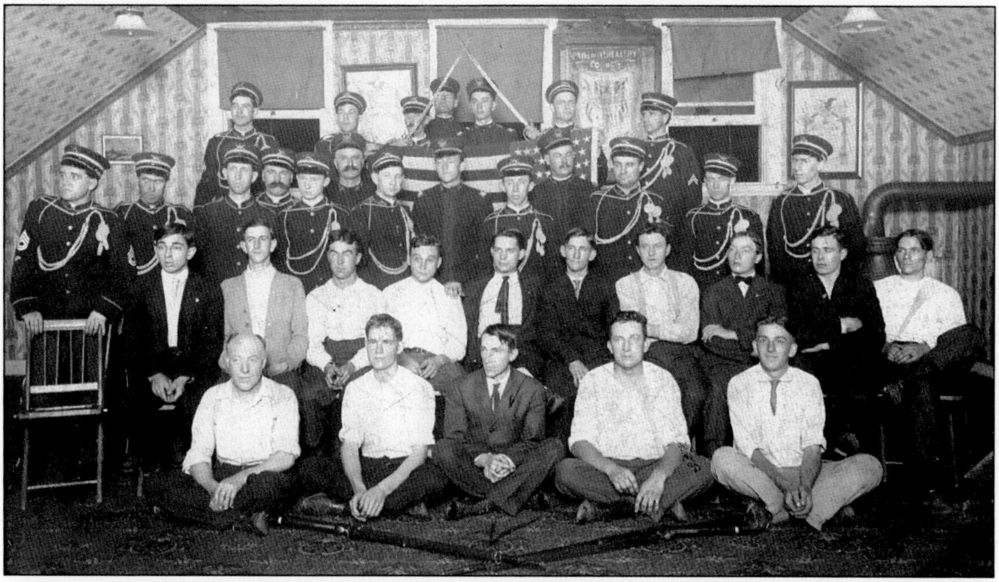

In the early 1900s, George Paris introduced the Junior Order of United American Mechanics to Mt. Healthy. The fraternal organization was open to males between the ages of 16 and 50. Membership was divided into two categories—social members and those enrolled in the insurance program, which provided a sick and funeral fund for its members.

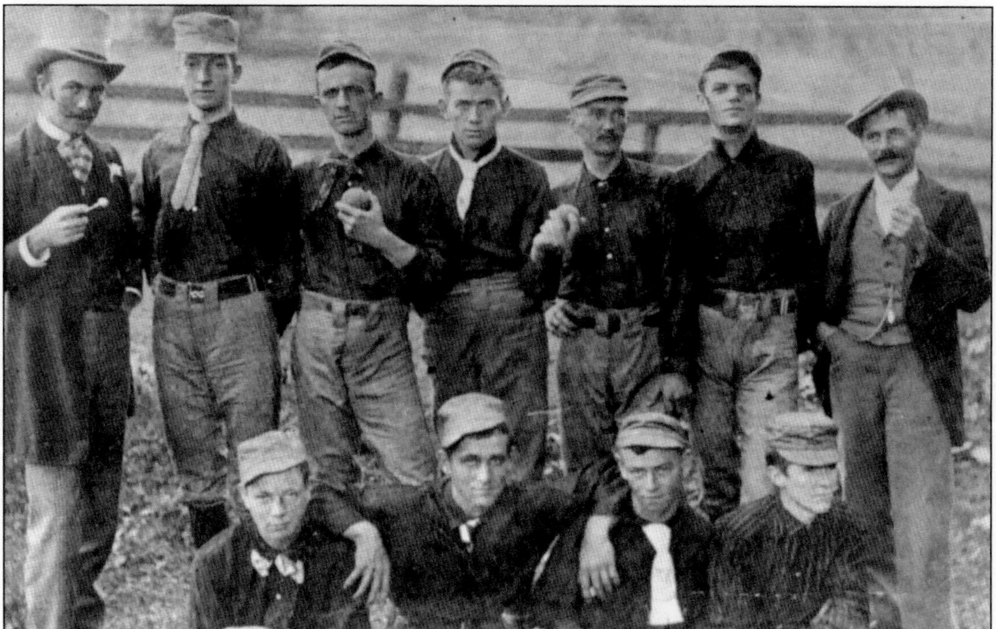

Mt. Healthy was known for its amateur baseball teams. The Ravens won most of their games in the 1890s, only suffering defeat to two semiprofessional teams. From left to right, the 1895 Ravens included (first row) Roy Jones, Charles Moser, Charles Wolf, and Dud Dom; (second row) manager George Deneke, Cliff Diserens, Harry Dom, Harry Hoffner, William "Sully" Noble, George Sweitzer, and manager Delph Jones. Missing were substitutes Edgar Hunt, Louis Prett, and Otto Knopp.

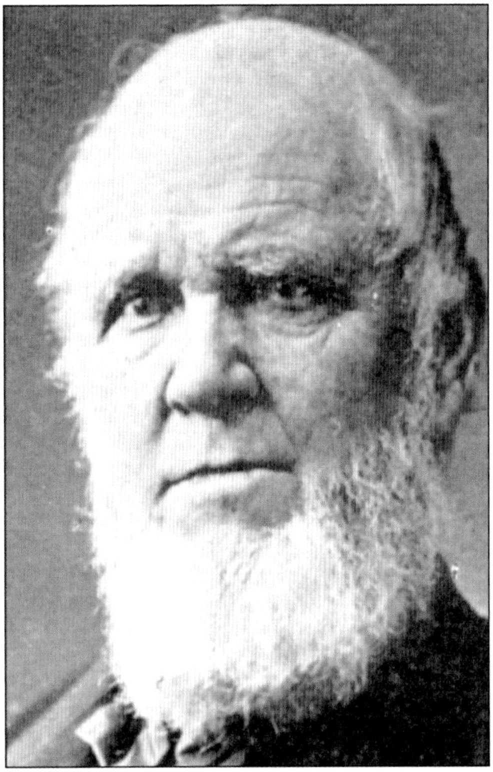

A Masonic lodge was organized in Mt. Healthy in 1844 and has supported community activities over the years. John McMakin was master for six years. He was highly regarded by the brethren, and in 1853, the lodge was renamed in his honor. He was a brigadier general of the Ohio militia during the Mexican War, a representative in the Ohio legislature from 1846 to 1848, and later a Hamilton County commissioner.

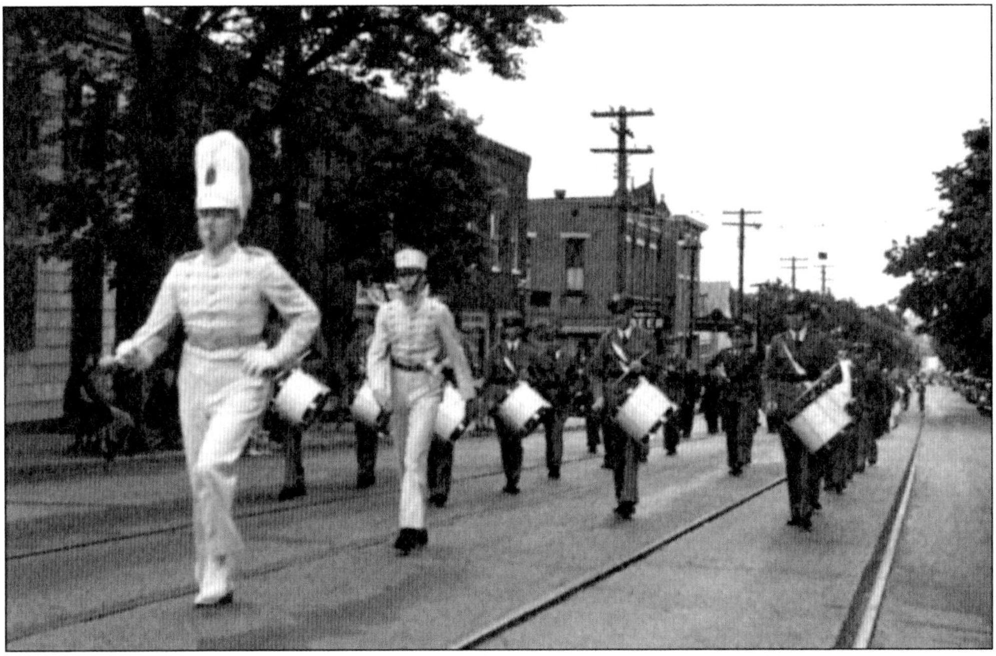

Mt. Healthy, founded by soldiers, has the tradition of honoring local veterans. The American Legion Wesley Werner Post No. 513, an organization of Mt. Healthy veterans, sponsors the annual Memorial Day parade. Here the legion's drum corps, under director Emil Thirion, marches on Hamilton Avenue in the 1938 Memorial Day parade.

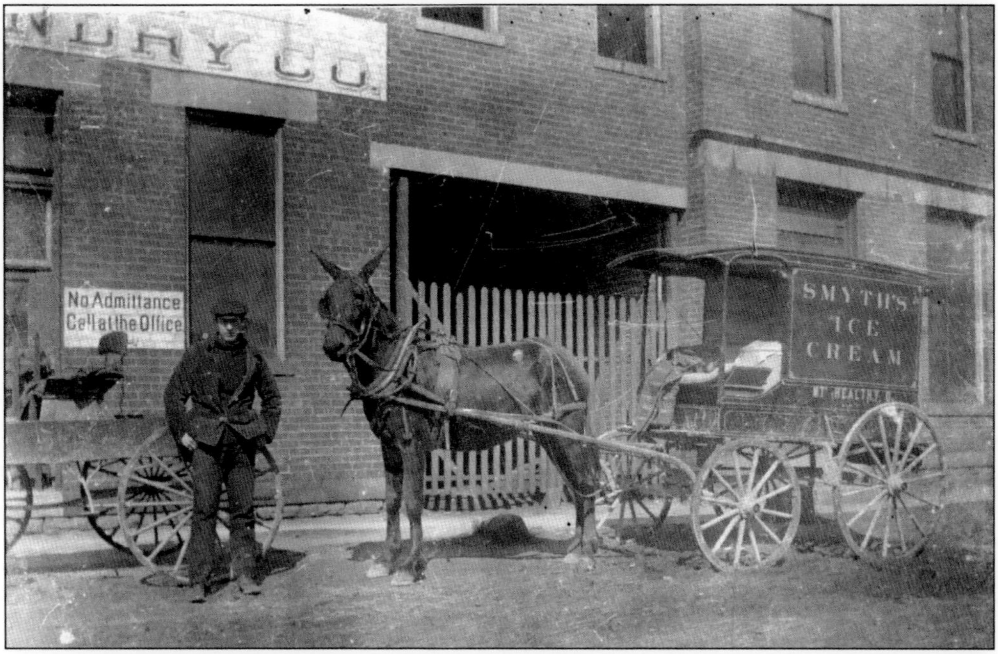

Coming together for an ice-cream social is a Mt. Healthy tradition. It goes back to the early days of Smyth's Ice Cream. H. C. "Doc" Smyth first operated a drugstore but soon developed a reputation for making the best ice cream around. He sold ice cream from this mule-drawn delivery wagon at many picnic groves all over Hamilton County.

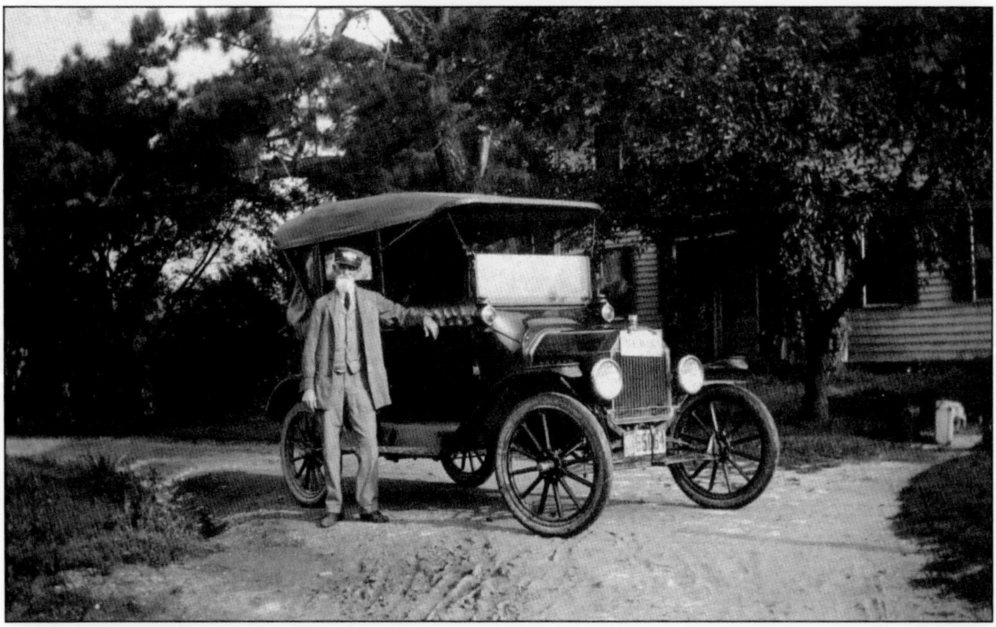

Since the early 1900s, Mt. Healthy residents have had a love affair with their antique cars. Car dealerships, automobile repair shops, and gasoline stations have been staples in the community. Each year during the Mt. Healthy Days celebration, antique cars are included. Here is Wilson Rogers, proudly showing off his 1910 tin lizzie, regarded as the first affordable automobile in America.

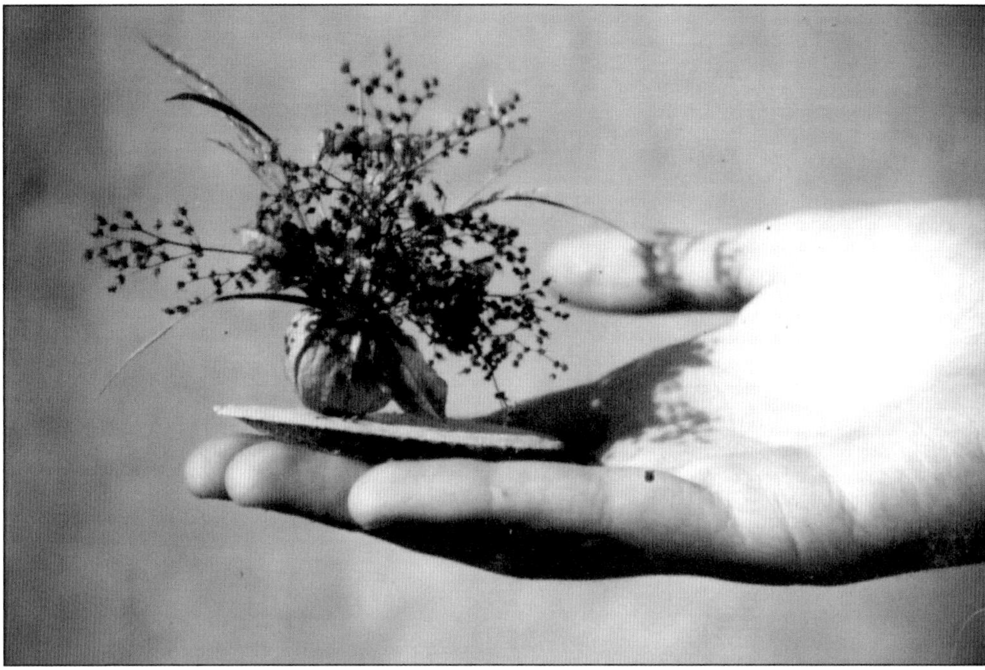

In 1930, Georgia Mohorter gathered flower lovers and organized the Mt. Healthy Garden Club. The club provided victory garden programs during World War II, flowers for events, and plantings at the veterans' memorial. Beautiful flower shows were held in the school gymnasium and in merchant store windows. Here is Henrietta Goosmann's 1950 prize-winning miniature arrangement, "All in a nut shell." (Courtesy of the Mt. Healthy Garden Club.)

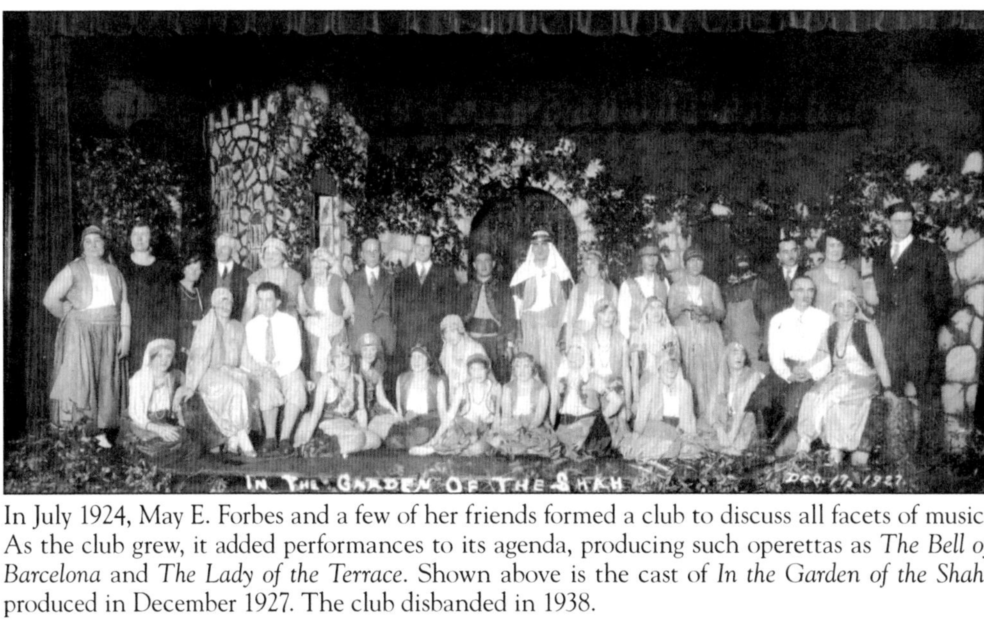

In July 1924, May E. Forbes and a few of her friends formed a club to discuss all facets of music. As the club grew, it added performances to its agenda, producing such operettas as *The Bell of Barcelona* and *The Lady of the Terrace*. Shown above is the cast of *In the Garden of the Shah*, produced in December 1927. The club disbanded in 1938.

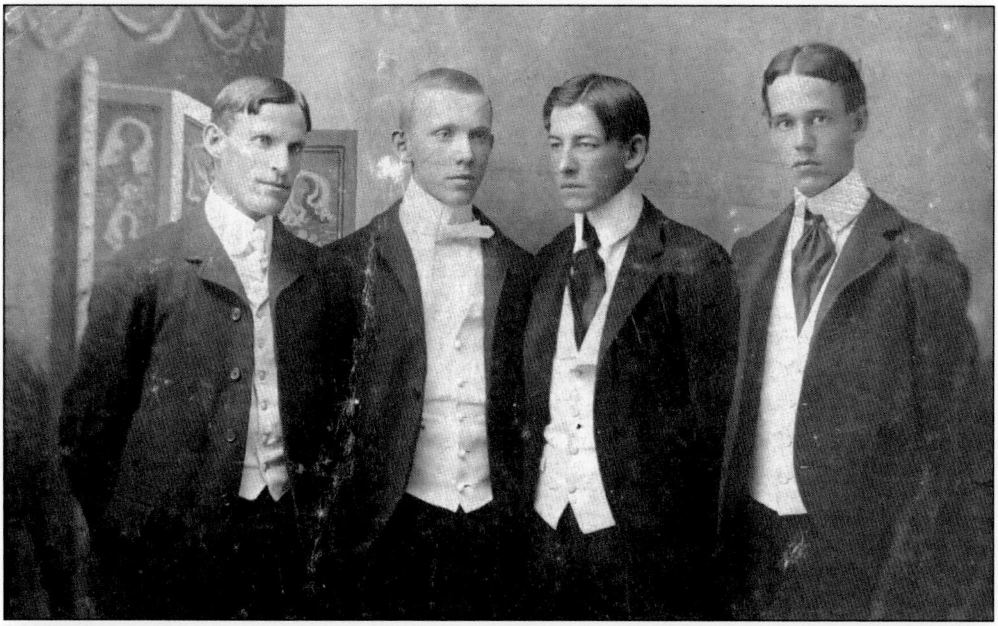

In the early 1900s, four young men formed a men's quartet called the Carmen Male Quartet. They became quite well known and were asked to give concerts throughout the Springfield Township area. Pictured from left to right, Stewart Moser sang second bass, Earl Hunt sang first bass, Fred Walker was the first tenor, and Louis Steinbrecher was the second tenor. From all accounts, their charm and good looks made them very popular with the young ladies.

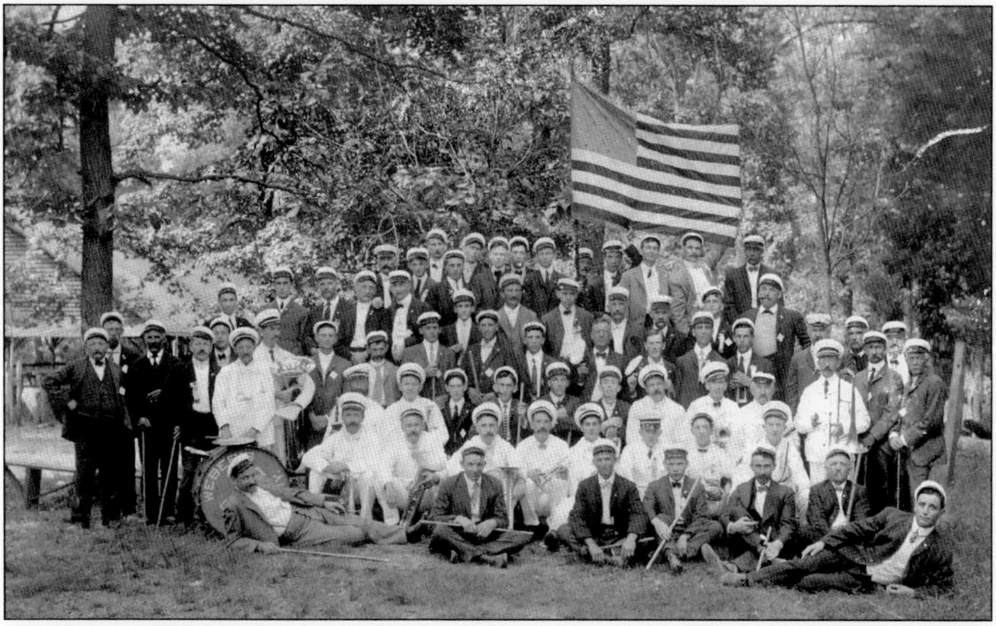

Organized in 1892, members of the Mt. Healthy Smokers' Casino met weekly to play cards and smoke pipes. At the end of the evening the "pipe inspector" ensured that all pipes were cleaned properly or the member was fined 5¢. Ill or disabled members received a weekly stipend from the organization until they were back on their feet. This 1905 photograph shows members of the Casino with the Weber Band at Johnson Grove.

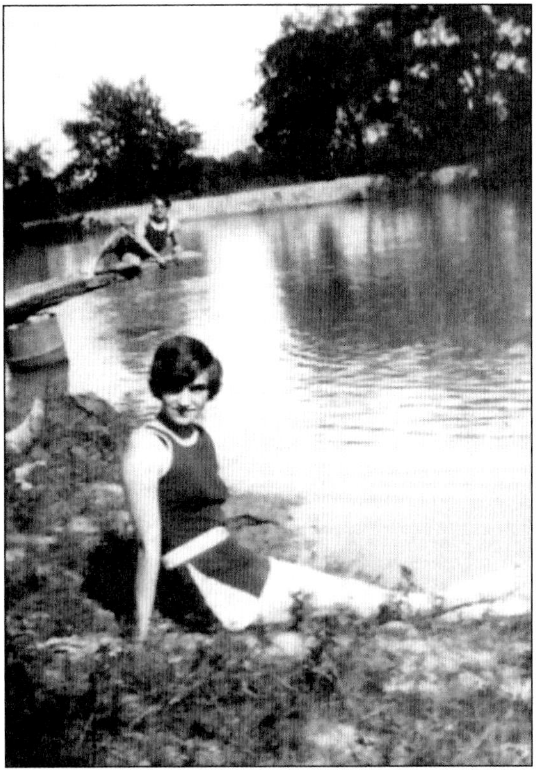

Ann Waldeck Wiehe (front) and Steve Guilner enjoyed the cool Muth Pond. H. C. Muth raised goldfish in 15 small ponds. Muth was the first user of a shipping method that took live fish over long distances. The motion of travel aerated the water, providing the necessary oxygen. In the summer one could swim for a 10¢ fee. Crawdads nipped toes if one did not move quickly.

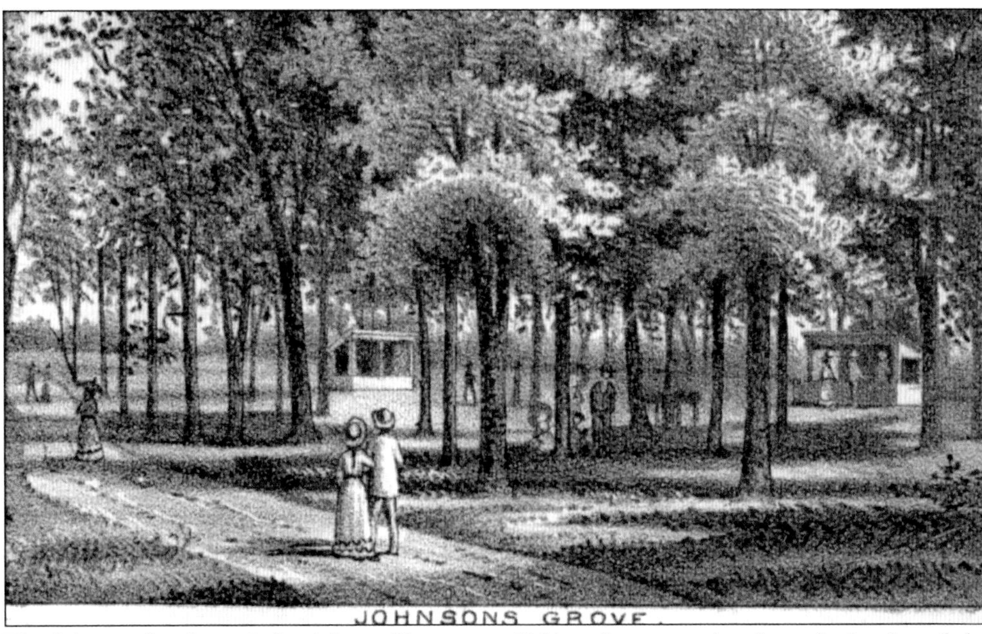

The Johnson family settled in Mount Pleasant in 1804 and continued to farm the land until the death of Benson Cary Johnson in the early 1900s. After his death, the property was developed into an amusement park called Johnson's Grove. It became the entertainment center of the town. A dance hall, ball fields, and horse paths were included. Sunny days were spent picnicking on the grounds; evenings were spent dancing under the stars.

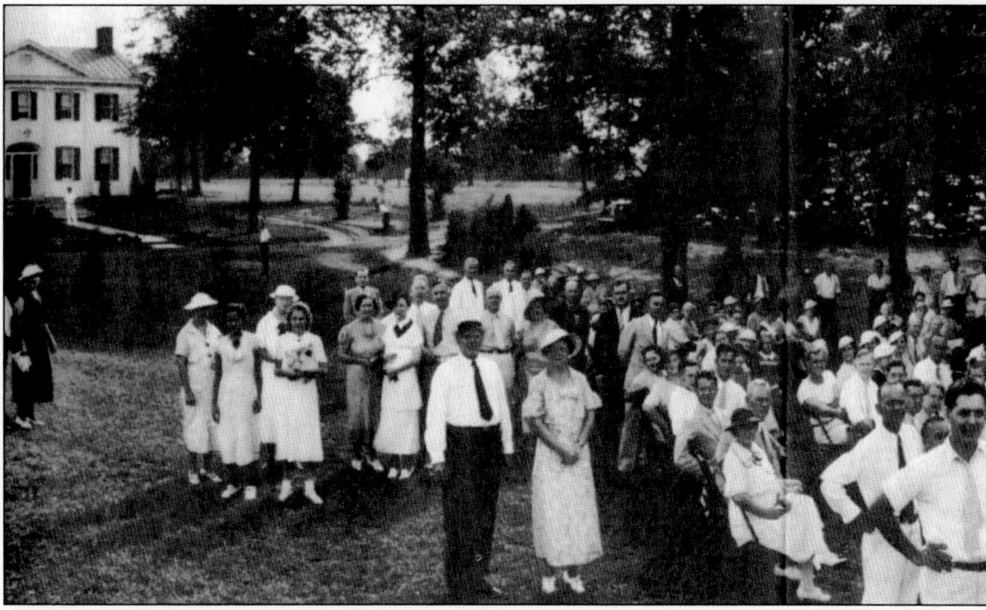

Concerts in the park were a tradition that began at Johnson's Grove and continue to this day. In 1932, the park site was developed into Arlington Memorial Gardens. The beautiful grounds provided the perfect setting for summer concerts. Shown here is the eighth concert of the summer, played by the Cincinnati Symphony Orchestra on September 13, 1938. (Courtesy of Arlington Memorial Gardens.)

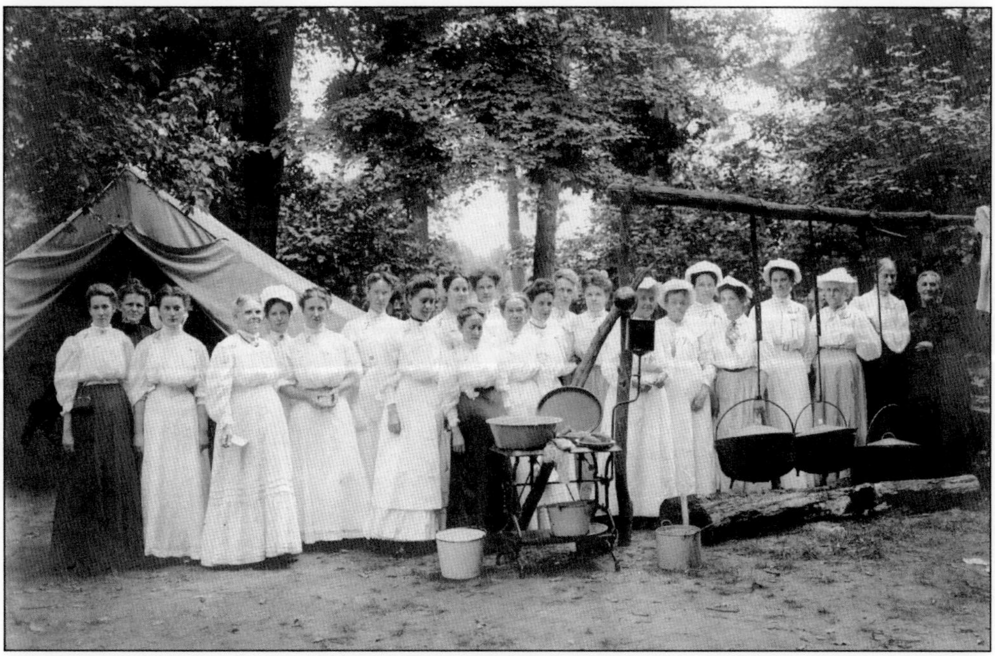

The women attending the Springfield Township Pioneer Association picnic at Johnson's Grove gathered to cook lunch. Mt. Healthy women have the reputation for being good cooks. They were known for delicious food at picnics and at church dinners, which often featured chicken potpies, and for specialties such as Methodist church candy.

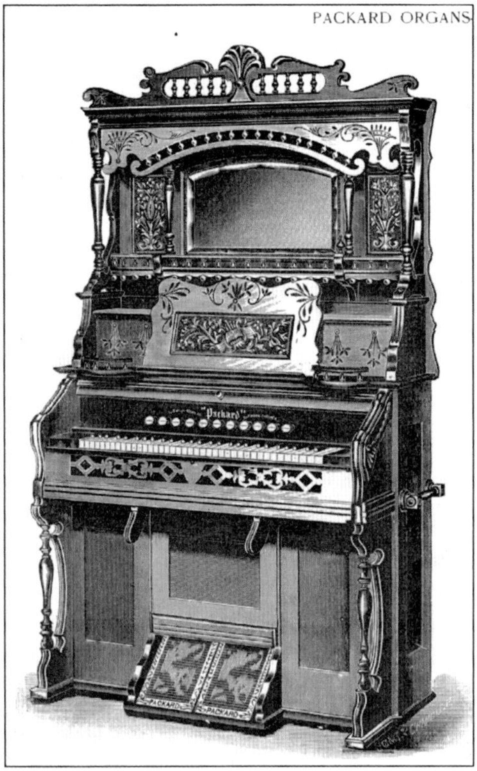

In 1907, many fashionable parlors had a reed organ. People gathered around and sang hymns and Christmas carols. This deluxe Packard organ belonged to Florence May (Hill) Johnson, who married and moved to Vinton County and Ross County and taught school. The style number 377.74 organ originally cost $117, when a typical organ cost $26. Johnson's great-niece Cynthia (Hill) Crabtree donated the organ to the Mt. Healthy Museum.

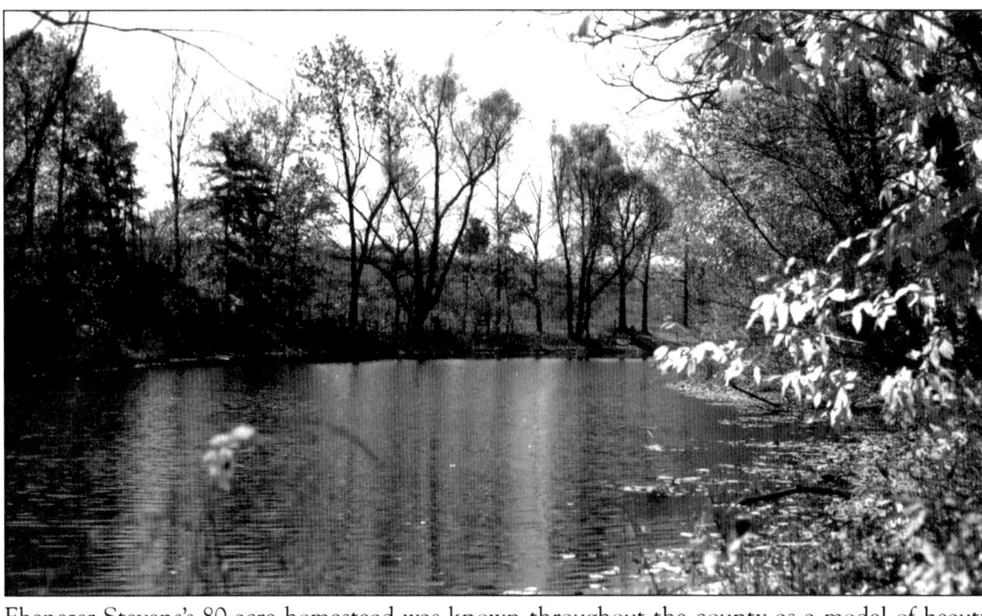

Ebenezer Stevens's 80-acre homestead was known throughout the county as a model of beauty and practicality. His home was surrounded by well-kept fields, magnificent gardens, and this lake. In 1844, the first Hamilton County Fair was held on Stevens's farm. Local residents participated in judging farm animals, cheese, honey, and farm implements. The judges included T. B. Weatherby, Charles Chaney, Nathaniel Smith, James Sampson, Will Cary, and Steward McGill.

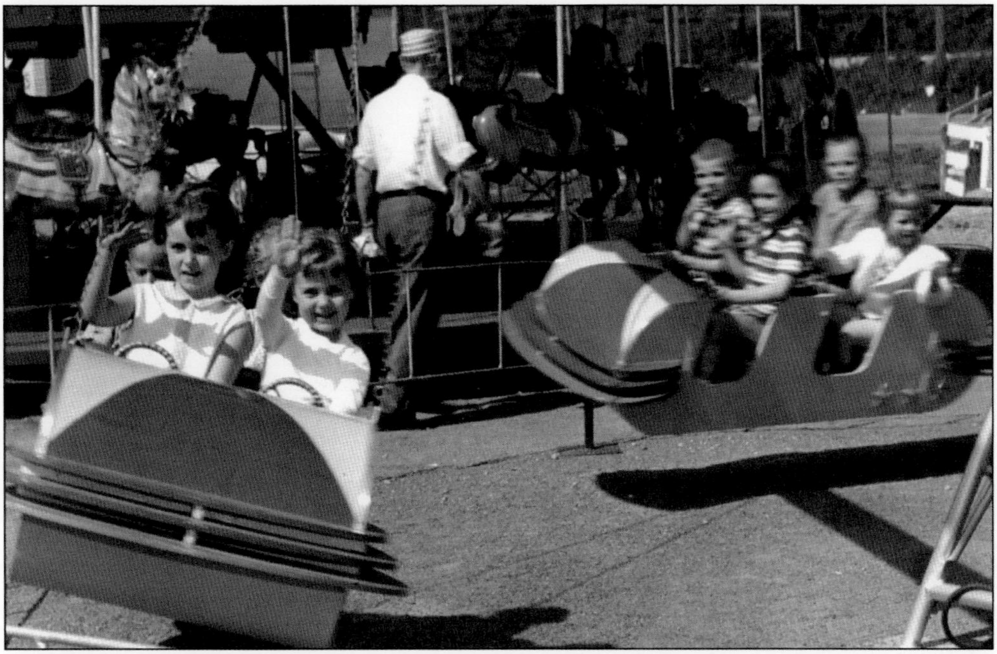

In 1924, Henry Stricker decided to develop a private park and picnic grove on 55 acres he owned in Mt. Healthy. Sticker's Grove was closed to the public except for a few days a year but could be rented for private functions, such as weddings or family reunions. A dance hall and pony and boat rides were added. In 1972, the park was relocated to Ross.

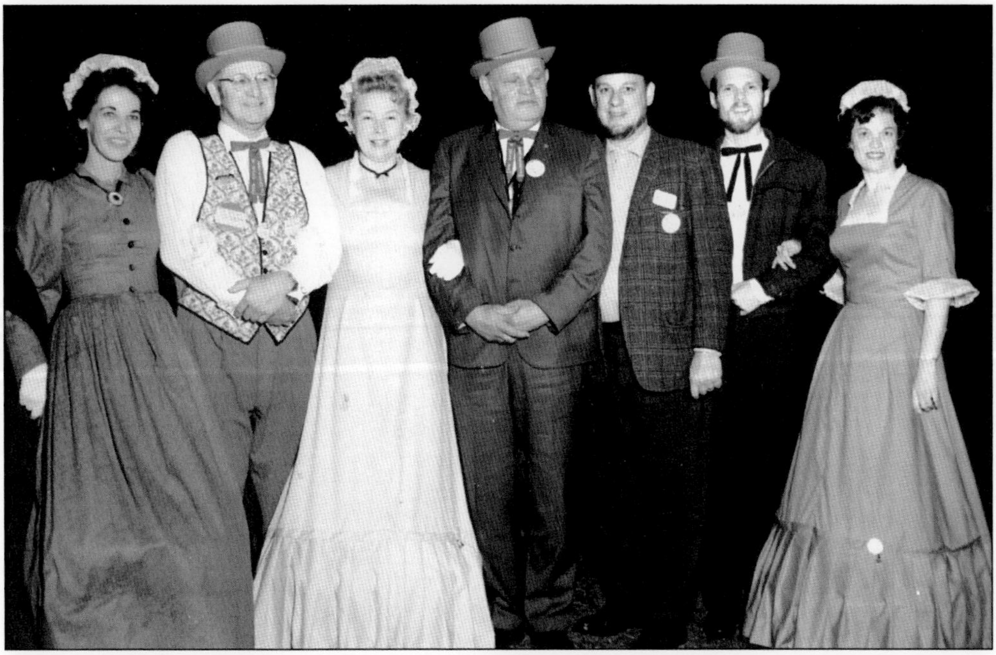

The year 1967 was packed with events celebrating the 150th birthday of Mt. Healthy, its sesquicentennial. Beard-growing contests, historic walking tours, vintage costumes, and heritage plays gave participants a glimpse into what life was like in the early days of the village. Pictured above are costumed friends enjoying one of the many events.

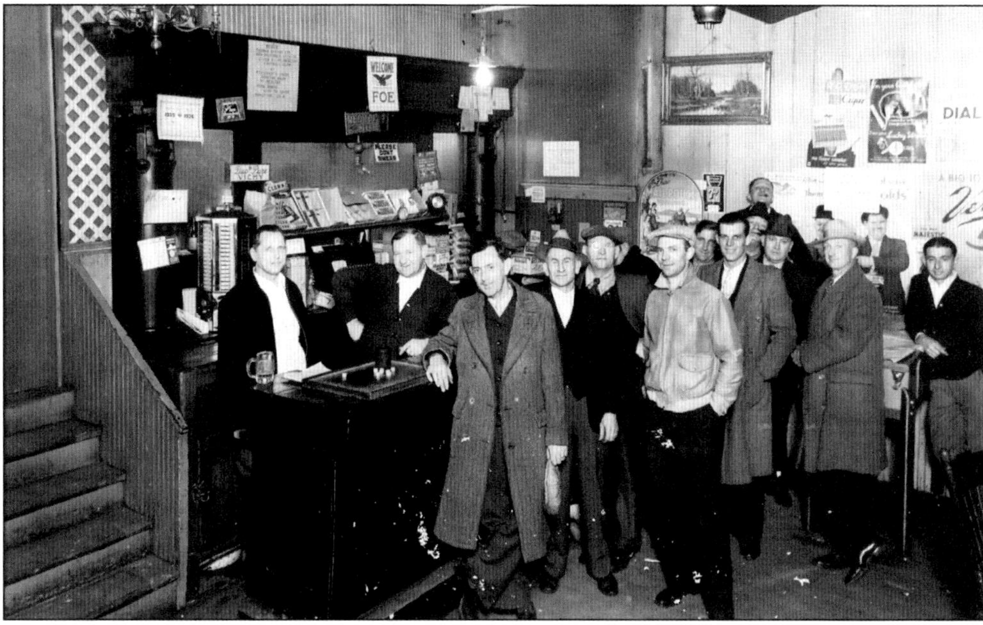

The building that originally housed Jacob Skillman's livery stable became the watering hole for Mt. Healthy men. Opened in the 1930s as an all-male bar, the Stag Café was the place to go for a few beers and a good game of euchre. The farewell tribute to the Stag came in February 1988, a week before it was to be torn down to make way for a bank parking lot. (Courtesy of Joy Cumbow Packer.)

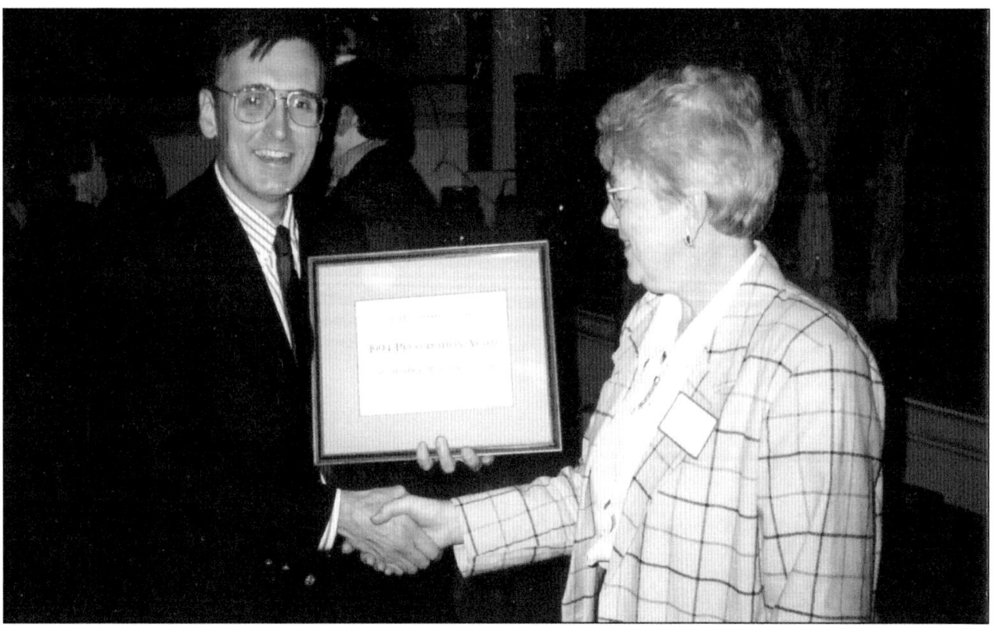

The Mt. Healthy Historical Society has promoted the preservation of community history since 1962. Its creative use of the original Mount Pleasant Union Meeting House and Mount Pleasant Toll House garnered it the 1994 award for preservation from the Cincinnati Preservation Association. Shown above is Marian Blum, Mt. Healthy Historical Society's curator, accepting the award from Jerry Leshner of the Cincinnati Preservation Association.

Nine

TAPPING THE TALENT

This chapter is about the famous people, the notable people of Mt. Healthy, those who achieved some degree of fame either in the community or in their profession. They follow in a chronological order by birth dates.

However, the real notable people of Mt. Healthy are all the pioneers, the early settlers who came with determination for a better life to build Mt. Healthy through their industry and thriftiness. They are an inspiration and a guide. They worked hard to build successful businesses and beautiful buildings. They loved and cared for their families, provided for their children, and gave them opportunities. They created a great tradition for all to follow.

The same spirit can be seen in each following decade and era. Mt. Healthy produced citizens who contributed to the community. It developed many successful businessmen and businesswomen, all leaders in their professions, and provided many educators who taught in local schools and colleges.

Mt. Healthy pioneers were religious and supported their churches and their ideals. They also had opinions on political issues and supported them based on a good understanding of the issues and accepted the consequences. Over the years, a concern for fellow man has appeared in environments including work, play, and home.

Mt. Healthy people are thrifty, which means more than saving money. Thrifty means choosing the best uses for money, such as investing in maintaining their houses or setting priorities in governmental services. For example, Mt. Healthy continued to use its wells for water until the early 1900s.

This chapter salutes the pioneers and all the noble traditions they set for others to follow.

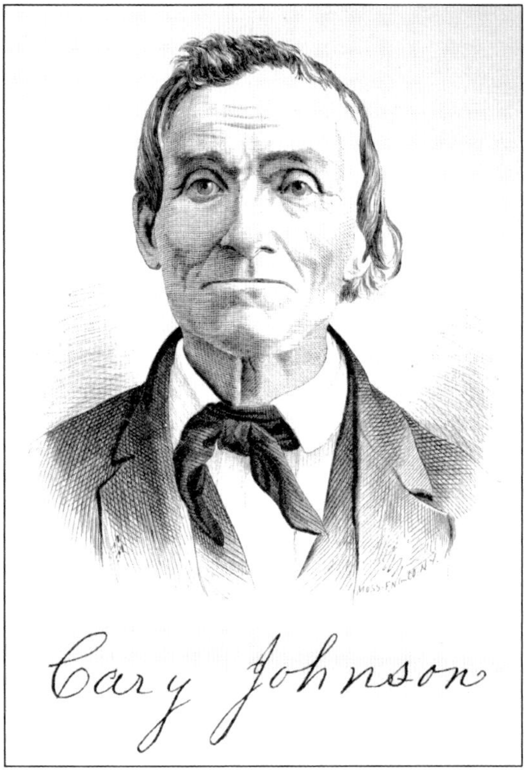

Abner Johnson of New Jersey purchased 320 acres from John Cleves Symmes, consisting of one half of section 32 of the Miami Purchase. Johnson then sent his 23-year-old son Cary to secure his land and clear the forest. The young carpenter built a log cabin, dug a well, and developed the farm. Then in 1807, Abner deeded the property over to Cary and his brothers, Andrew and Samuel.

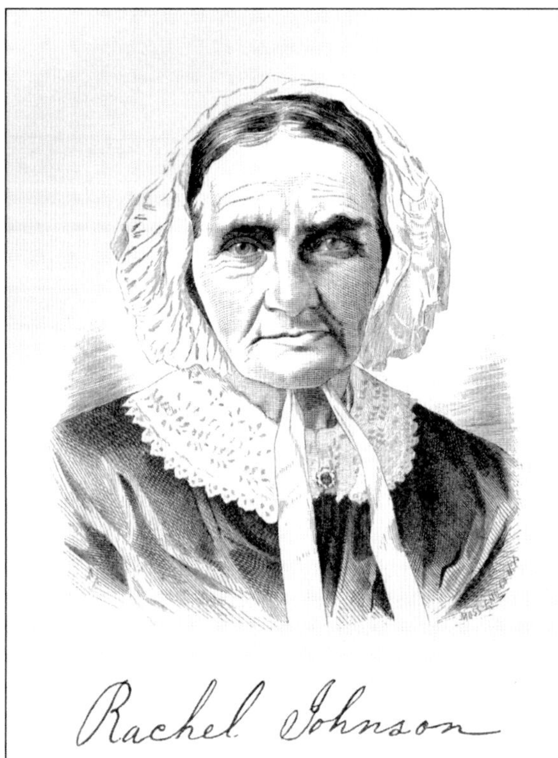

Rachel Jessup became the wife of Cary Johnson in September 1805. They began their marriage in a small log cabin on the land deeded to Cary by his father, Abner. Rachel bore nine children, two of whom died in early childhood. After 16 years of living in the log house, Cary hand built a beautiful brick home for his wife that stands today on its original site.

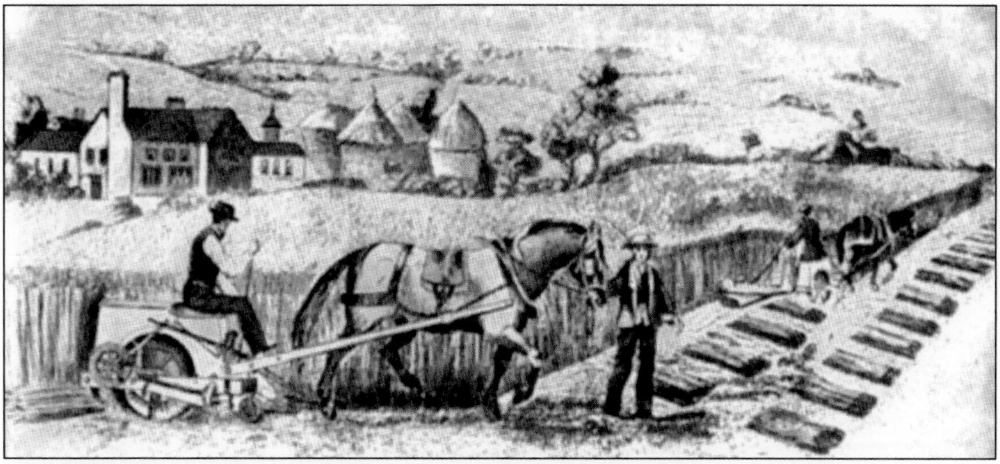

On December 31, 1833, Obed Hussey, a Quaker living in New Burlington, received patent No. 7928X for a major improvement in machines for reaping or cutting all kinds of small grain and grasses. His reaper was drawn by horses hitched in front and had a side cut and a platform on which the operator stood and raked off the grain. (Courtesy of Dave Huser.)

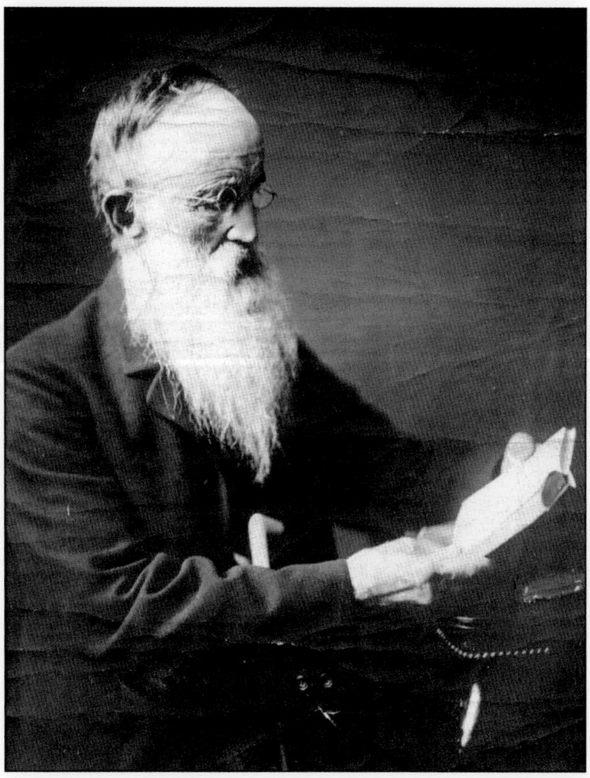

One of the colorful members of the LaBoiteaux family was Gilbert. At the age of 10, he carried mail on horseback from Mt. Healthy to Cincinnati. He followed the 1849 gold rush to California and joined the Union army during the Civil War. He wrote for the local papers under the pen name Homo and especially enjoyed writing poetry. An ardent abolitionist, he died at the age of 94.

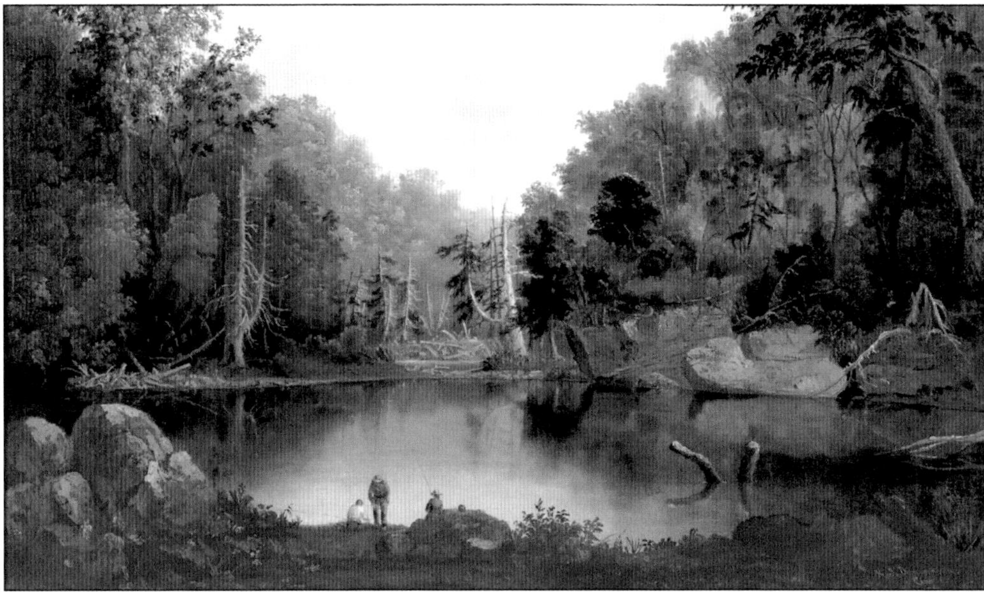

Robert Scott Duncanson moved to Mount Pleasant in 1841 to live with his mulatto mother. In Cincinnati, the self-taught artist received financial support from wealthy abolitionist patrons and quickly became known internationally as a great American landscape artist of the mid-19th century. His famous 1851 painting, *Blue Hole, Flood Waters of Little Miami River*, is found in the Cincinnati wing of the Cincinnati Art Museum. (Courtesy of the Cincinnati Art Museum.)

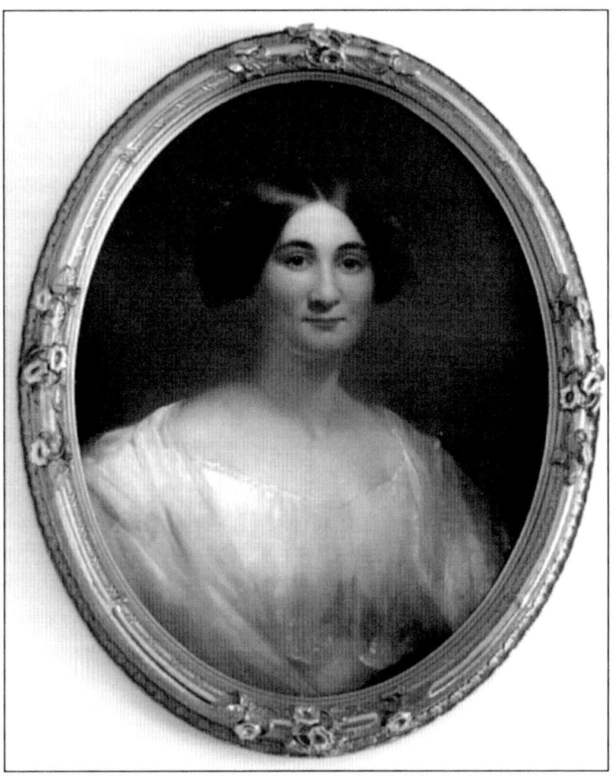

Born on April 26, 1820, Alice Cary became a noted poet of her day. She and her sister Phoebe spent their early years on the family farm near Mt. Healthy. Although formal education was limited, their parents encouraged the girls to pursue knowledge and think critically. Alice's first published piece was titled "The Child of Sorrow." After moving to New York City, her reputation grew.

Born on September 4, 1824, Phoebe Cary developed a love for literature and a talent for poetry. In 1851, she left her family to join her sister Alice in New York City. There she became known for her wit and the deep feelings of her poems. She strongly supported the women's rights movement and for a short time worked with Susan B. Anthony on the newspaper the *Revolution*.

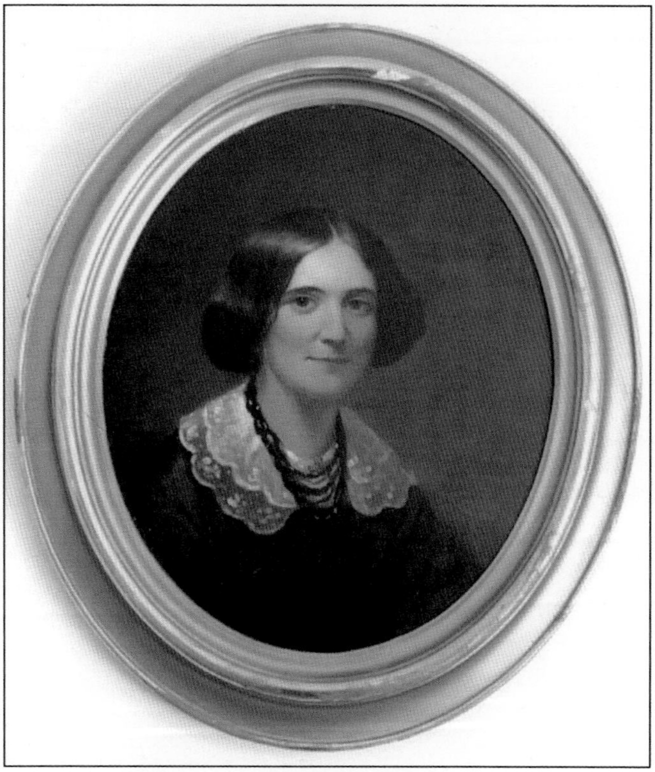

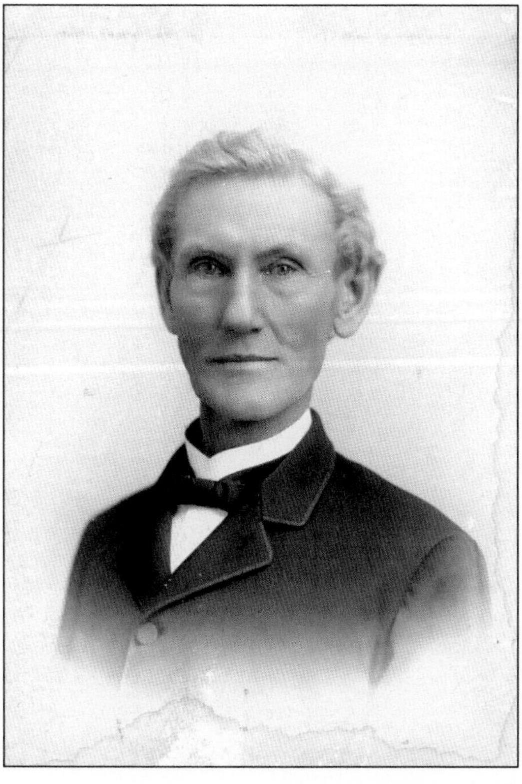

Clark Lane was born in New Burlington in 1823, with family roots in blacksmithing. His successful Hamilton-based company, Owens, Lane, Dyer and Company, manufactured agriculture machinery. Lane is known as Hamilton's first philanthropist. He built a library and offered it to the city. This began the Lane Public Library system of Butler County. Although he worked in Hamilton, he remained active in Mt. Healthy's Odd Fellow's lodge for over 60 years. (Courtesy of Suzanne Weickel Hull.)

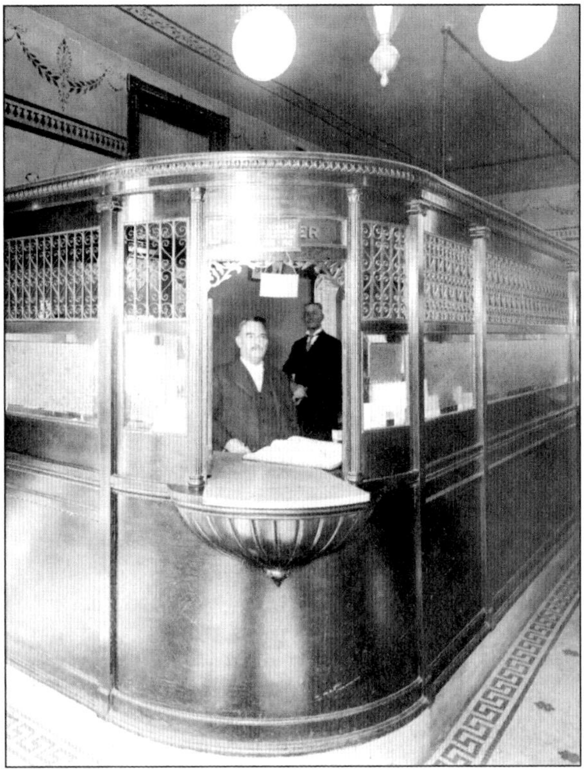

Alexis Brown (front), cashier, is shown on February 12, 1912, at the First National Bank. He was known as the "boy soldier" because he enlisted in the Civil War on July 13, 1861, at age 13 and served for four years. Brown served twice as Mt. Healthy's mayor. In 1887, he was also a founder of the Mt. Healthy Savings and Loan and was its secretary for 40 years.

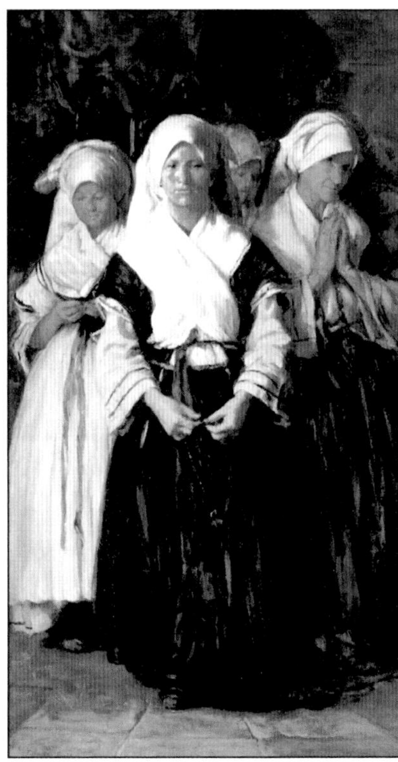

Elizabeth Nourse was born in Mt. Healthy in 1859. She was one of the first women to become internationally known for oil painting. Her subjects were hardworking women with their children and rural life. She received her art training in Cincinnati. In 1887, she moved to Paris. Nourse's famous 1891 painting, *Peasant Women of Borst*, is exhibited in the Cincinnati Art Museum. (Courtesy of the Cincinnati Art Museum.)

In 1931, the high school yearbook *Zem-Zem*, was dedicated to Dr. Lafayette Neufarth, who had served as president of the board of education for almost 25 years. Neufarth was one of the best-loved doctors in town; he delivered almost every child born between 1880 and 1930. He was civic minded and served as an 1893 councilman and as a director of the First National Bank.

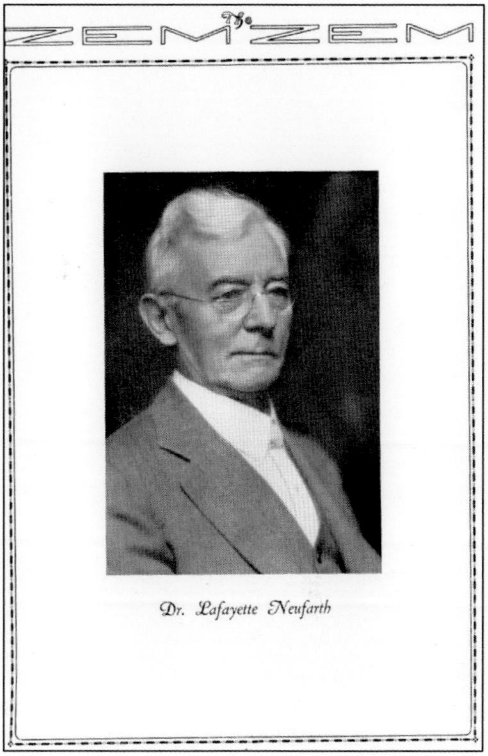

Dr. Lafayette Neufarth

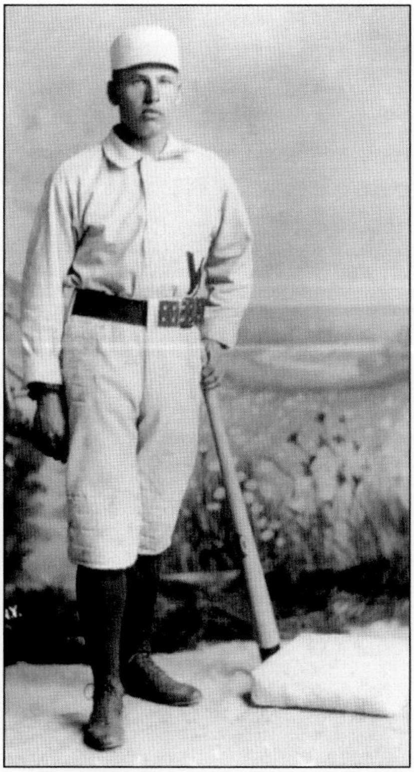

William Ellsworth "Dummy" Hoy retired from 14 seasons of professional baseball to a farm at the south edge of Mt. Healthy. Hoy was an outstanding defensive player who once threw out three runners at home plate in one inning. He was deaf and mute and received hand signals from his third-base coach, not, as rumored, from umpires who began using hand signals around 1905, several years after Hoy retired.

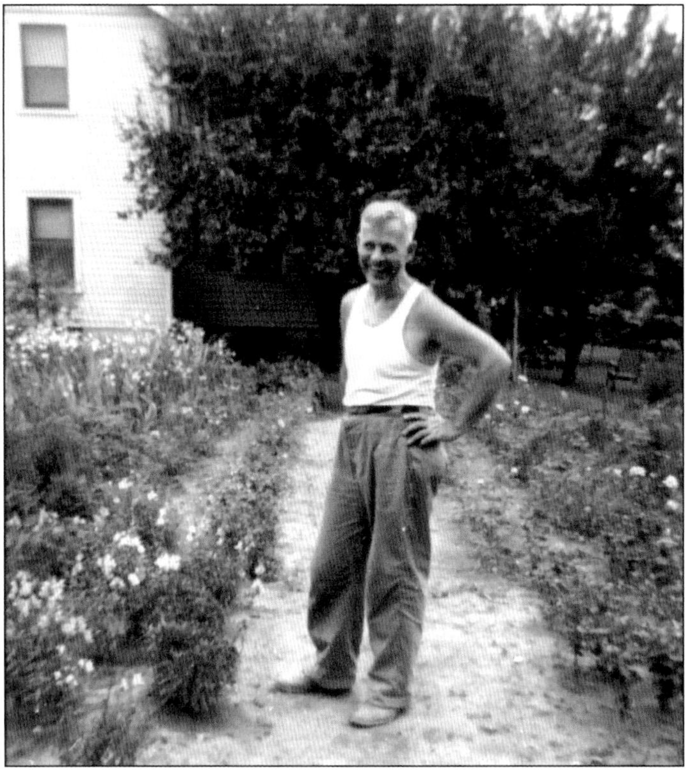

Paul H. Smyth, an executive with the Johnson and Foy Paint Company, was known for his community service as mayor and past master of McMakin lodge where he was a 50-year member and treasurer for 40 years. Smyth specialized in growing vegetables that he started in his small greenhouse attached to his garage. (Courtesy of the Mt. Healthy Garden Club.)

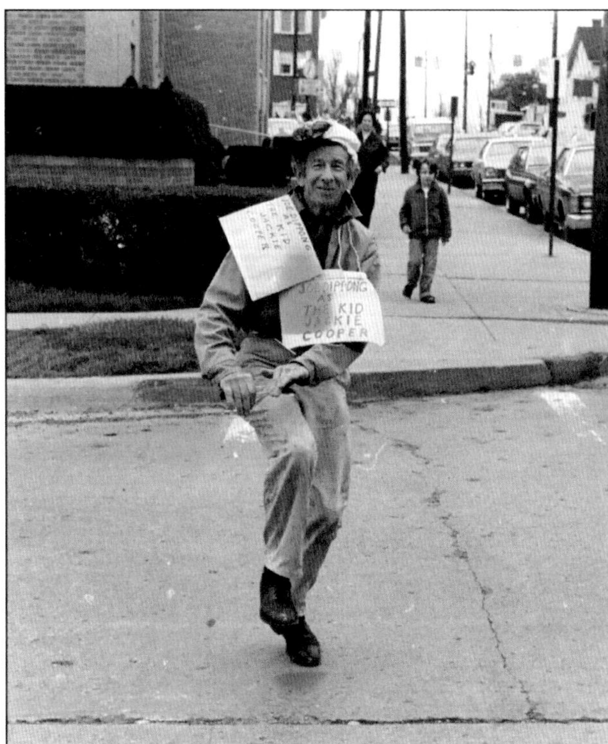

One of the dearly loved mid-20th-century citizens of Mt. Healthy was Joe Dippong. Known as "Mr. Spoons," Dippong sported any number of wild costumes and joined in parades throughout Hamilton County. His specialty was playing the spoons, and he was loved, especially by the children. Parade organizers sent him personal invitations to join their festivities.

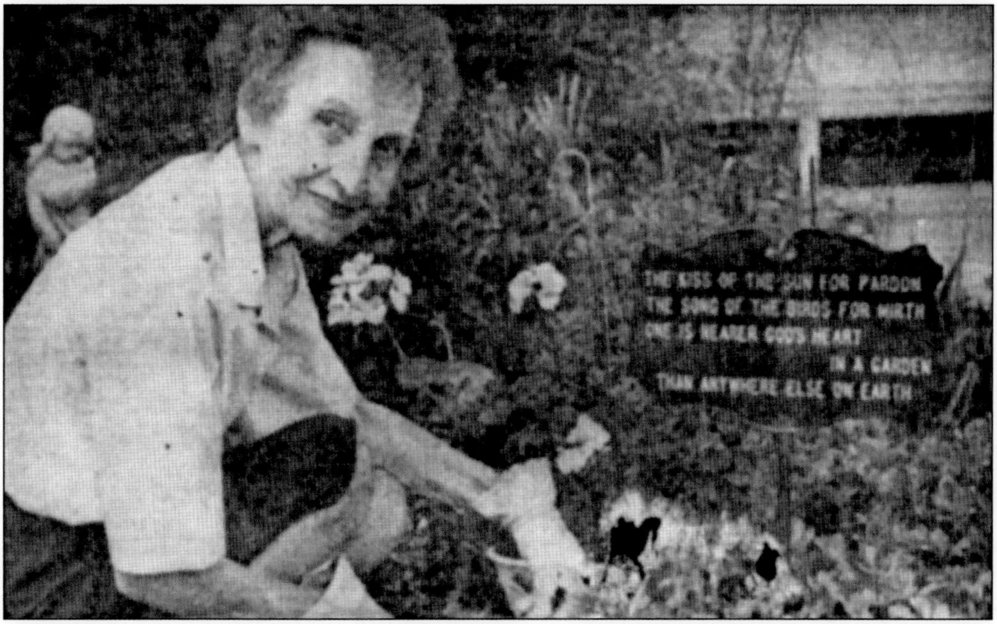

Daisy Jones, garden editor for the *Cincinnati Post and Times-Star*, wrote her popular column, "Down to Earth," for 30 years. Jones first became known for columns based on interviews with returning World War II soldiers. She was the recipient of a distinguished service award by the Federated Garden Clubs of Cincinnati. The Daisy Jones Tribute Garden flourishes in Mount Airy Forest Arboretum. (Courtesy of the Mt. Healthy Garden Club.)

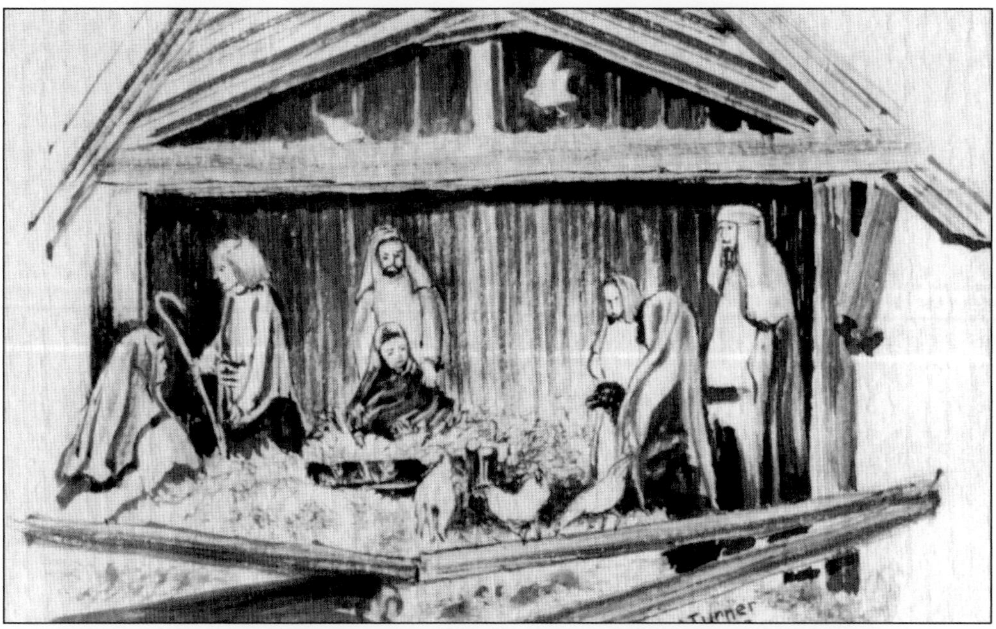

The Nativity scene at Paul R. Young Funeral Home is a 60-year Mt. Healthy holiday tradition. Each life-sized sculptured figure was molded in wax by Paul R. Young Sr., who studied at the London Madame Tussaud's Wax Museum. Young's Nativity is annually visited by about 5,000 people. This was Mayor Leroy Meier's Christmas card in 1983. The sketch was created by Jim Turner, a highly regarded local artist.

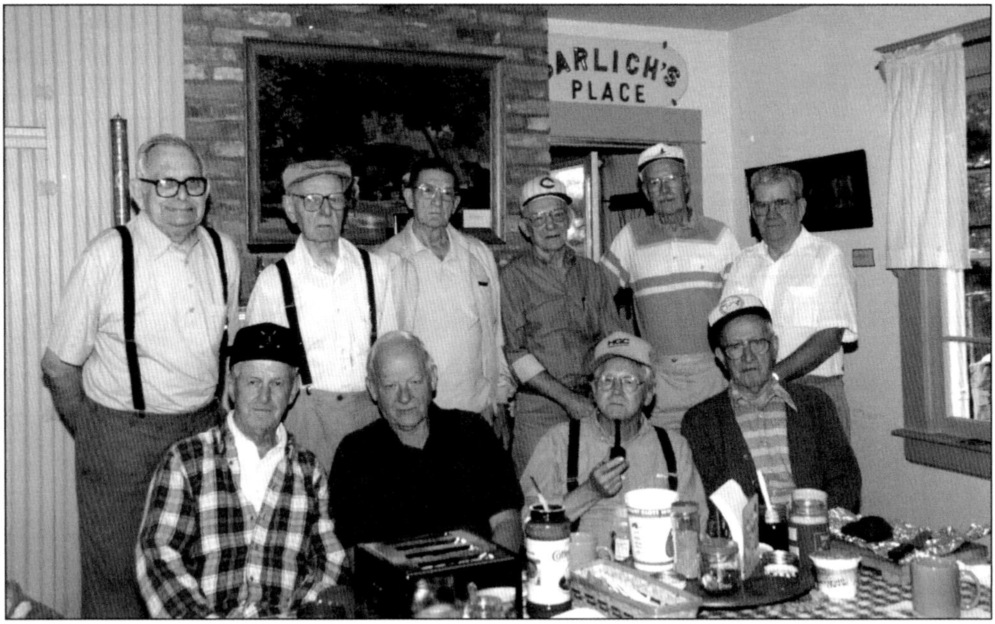

The "Toll House Gang" gathered around the table at the old tollhouse. They swapped stories, shared a cup of coffee, and kept Mt. Healthy's past alive. These longtime residents restored pieces of the community history. From left to right are (first row) Harry Waechter, Dick Garling, Jim Turner, and Kermit Schafer; (second row) Norb Fischvogt, Frank Stout, Ben Benson, Pete Morris, Vierling Blum, and Dave Campbell.

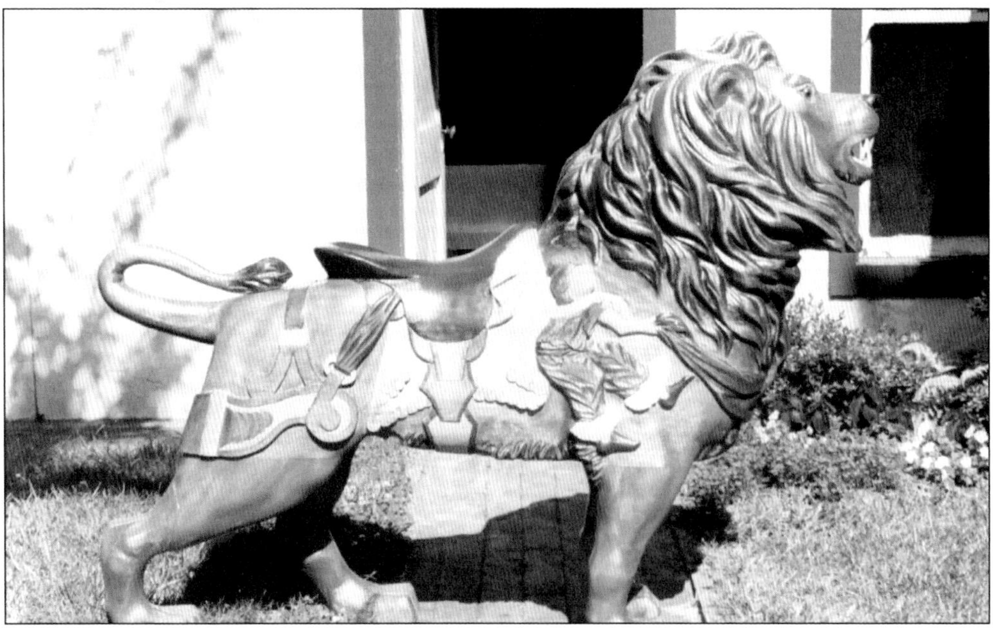

Woodcarver Robert Curley grew tired of barbering and turned to carving wooden carousel animals, especially horses, rabbits, and lions. Between 1860 and 1930, most large American cities had amusement parks with a carousel. During the 1980s, the rare carousel animals regained popularity. Curley created about 100 reproductions of the most famous animal styles. Shown here is a copy of the Dentzel Lion as carved by Curley. (Courtesy of Robert Curley.)

At the age of 15, Suzanne Farrell left Mt. Healthy to pursue her dream of becoming a great ballerina. After studying at the School of American Ballet, she joined the New York City Ballet and shortly after became principal dancer and muse to the great George Balanchine. Born Roberta Sue Ficker in 1945, Farrell has been honored as a legend in the ballet world.

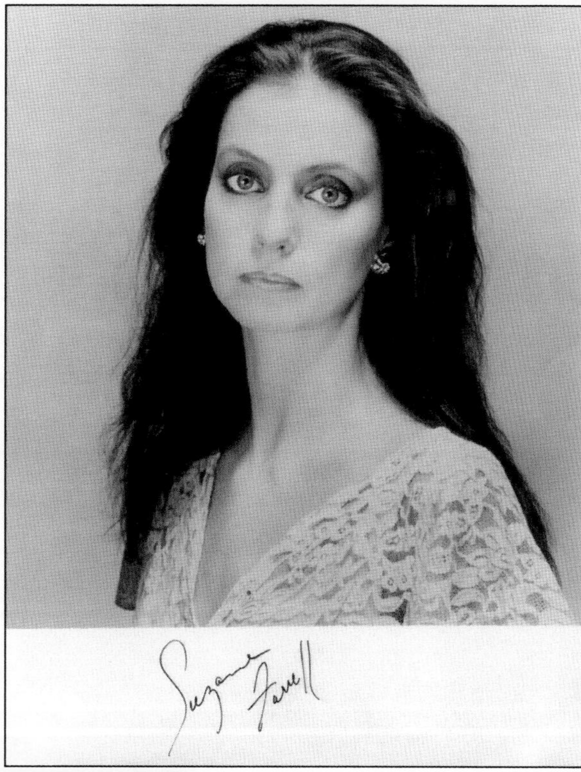

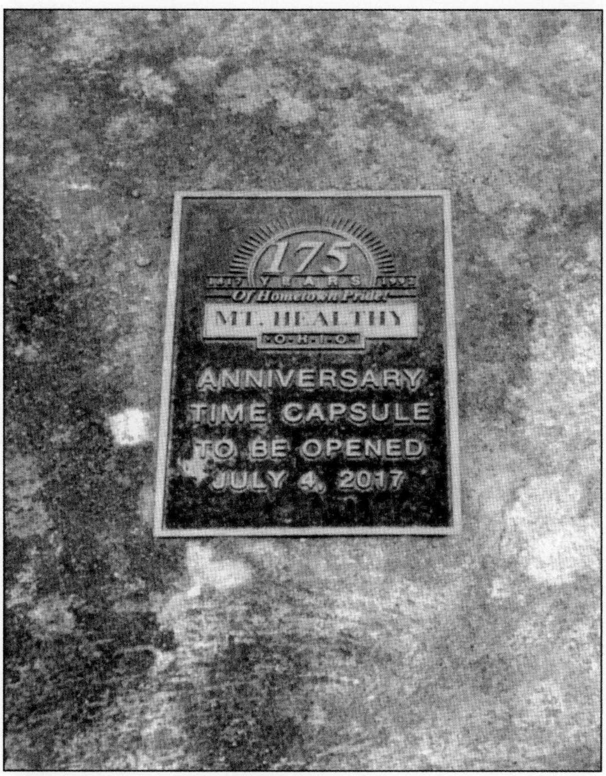

The community of Mt. Healthy is always looking forward with a positive attitude. This anniversary time capsule was planted in 1992 near the old meetinghouse and will be opened on Mt. Healthy's 200th birthday. The marker reads, "175 years (1817–1992) of hometown pride. Anniversary time capsule to be opened July 4, 2017." (Courtesy of the Mt. Healthy Garden Club.)

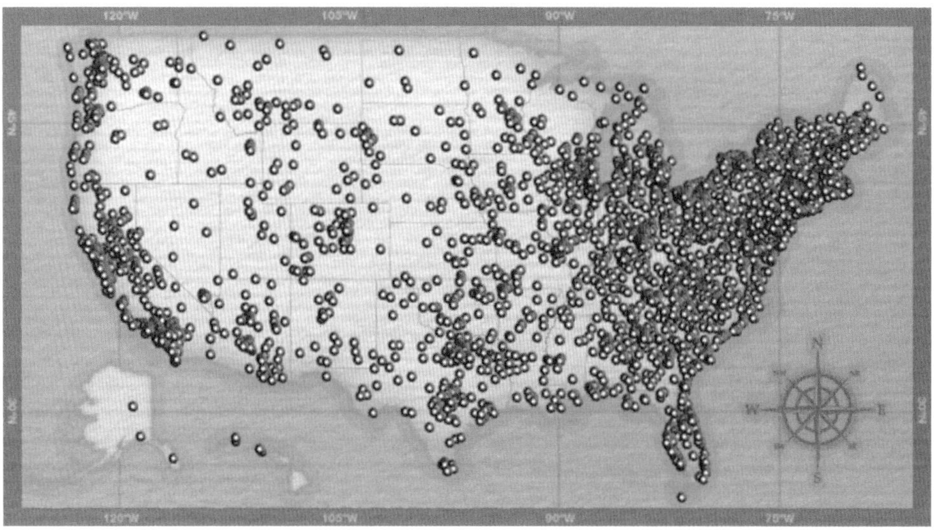